COLOSSUS: The True Story of
William Foulke

COLOSSUS: The True Story of William Foulke

Graham Phythian

TEMPUS

First published 2005

Tempus Publishing Limited
The Mill, Brimscombe Port,
Stroud, Gloucestershire, GL5 2QC
www.tempus-publishing.com

British Library Cataloguing in Publication Data.
A catalogue record for this book is available from the British Library.

ISBN 0 7524 3274 5

Typesetting and origination by Tempus Publishing Limited
Printed in Great Britain

Contents

Goodness me, look at this huge goalie!
Dan Cruickshank presenting the BBC documentary
The Lost World of Mitchell and Kenyon (2005)

A football wonder is Willie. Perhaps the most talked-of player in the world. A leviathan with the agility of a bantam. The cheeriest of companions; brims over with good humour; and in repartee as difficult to 'score' against as when between the posts…
…Made his name with 'The Blades'.
…Has played cricket for Derbyshire. At Chelsea has amused the crowd by punching the ball from his goal to well over the halfway line…
…Offered his services to the 'All Blacks'!
Association Football and the Men Who Made It (1906)

The real great man is the man who makes every man feel great.
G.K. Chesterton (1874–1936)

Introduction

Now, boys, now, boys, now for a jolly spree,
Ran, san, tiddly-ann, come and have a round with me;
Come and have a round or two, I don't care what you do,
But I say, clear the way, for the rowdy dowdy boys.

Sheffield United supporters' song *c.*1900

Goalkeepers are crazy.

Well no, they're not, not necessarily. But it's interesting – and entertaining – to explore how such a widely accepted belief comes about. We can all recall enough arresting incidents on the football field to help support the view of the last line of defence having a suspect collection of marbles. Who can forget the scorpion save of Colombia's René Higuita? Or the gallop of Schmeichel the 'mad Dane' (Sir Alex's words, not mine) up into the Bayern penalty area in those final emotion-charged minutes in the Champions' League final of 1999? Or Grobbelaar's shambling antics during the penalty shoot-out in another European final?

I'm sure the reader can add to this list. Perhaps it's to be expected that the person upon whom the fortunes of the entire team ultimately depend should develop at least some sort of neurosis. If an outfield player drops a clanger, it's not necessarily a big deal: there are safety nets, as it were. A 'keeper's mistake, though, is usually terminal. Add to this the fact that the goalie's job is to leap *into* the way of missiles hurtling at him sometimes faster than speeding motorway traffic, and perhaps the wonder is how sane the guys are.

Whatever. Come with me now to a time of more than a century ago, to make the acquaintance of a goalkeeper whom many consider to have double-handedly launched the semi-mythical tradition of the wacky custodian. This is the biography of the decidedly larger-than-life William Henry Foulke (1874-1916).

Over the years 'Little Willie' has gathered around him his own collection of tales. For example, the received wisdom about his twilight years is that he spent them in poverty as a sad sideshow on Blackpool beach, saving penalties from holidaymakers at a penny a go, from which activity he caught pneumonia and died. It's a grand tale, a poignant coda to the career of the leviathan, a salutary parable of the once mighty brought to a sober reckoning. Yes – except that there's not a word of truth in it. Foulke died after a short illness in a Sheffield nursing home, having spent his retirement years in that town as a pub landlord, shopkeeper and sports and music hall fan.

And what about the other oft-repeated stories? We have heard about the naked twenty-two-stone juggernaut, still dripping from the post-match bath, raging through the corridors of Crystal Palace in search of the referee who had just allowed a dubious equalising goal against him in an FA Cup final. The match official, so it's said, wisely chose discretion over valour and hid in a boot cupboard until his pursuer was persuaded to abandon his efforts to rip the door off its hinges. The gospel truth, a diverting fable, or a mixture of the two? Did Bill Foulke once really swing on the crossbar and bring the goal crashing down? Did he pick up George Allan, the Liverpool centre forward, by the ankles and repeatedly dab his head in the goalmouth mud? Is it true that he once polished off all eleven of his teammates' breakfasts while they were out on a training walk? Was one of his après-away game party pieces to gather up a railway porter under each arm and walk along the station platform with them? And what did he really have to say to Tory Prime Minister-elect A.J. Balfour after an FA Cup final victory?

The tales go on and on. How many of them really happened? It's tempting to dismiss closer examination with the thought: 'If they're not true, then they ought to be.' Anecdotes, after all, often contain an impressionistic truth. And why be a killjoy? The Rabelaisian always raises a laugh, usually victimless. Why not leave well enough alone? Let me answer this in a roundabout way.

If you want to see Foulke in action, you'll have to track down the scant footage of the 1901 FA Cup final replay at Bolton. (Since I wrote this in early 2004 some more film footage of Willie Foulke has been discovered, in the storeroom of a chemist/photographer's shop in Blackburn. It shows him in action in the League game v. Bury in September 1902, and is to be televised in a BBC documentary.) Less than three minutes are left to posterity, but it's enough for several strong impressions to emerge. There are two sections: the players entering the field, and some goalmouth incidents. In both segments Foulke is an unmistakeable figure in his Sheffield United stripes and black full-length goalie's trousers. As the teams jog onto the field – Needham leading out his troops – Foulke's boyish face is set and serious. Despite his bulk (at the time he was well over twenty stone) there is an impression of athleticism in his movement, and no sense of the cumbersome. What also strikes you is his agility and springiness in the action sequences, one of which was filmed from a spot directly behind his goal. There's no trace of ponderousness in his style: jaunty, mobile, on his toes and ever following the ebb and flow of play with an alert eye. We see him get up easily to a high shot, and clear the lines with a left-footed daisycutter.

Our view of him now perhaps calls for modification: within the giant figure of fun a keen brain is ticking away. 'Fatty' Foulke shows himself to be a surprisingly athletic practitioner of the goalkeeping art. There is a sense of a resolution of powerful opposites that we feel would repay closer scrutiny. Just as we owe it to our language to liberate it from the lazy cliché, so we owe it to our heroes to paint them in their truest colours. Otherwise, if we accept the facile and the inexact, isn't their heroic quality, the very reason for which they're revered in the first place, devalued? And from those distant seasons there emerge heroes aplenty.

As we follow Bill Foulke's unique and eventful career, we will come across prolific striker Steve Bloomer, the complete midfielder Ernest Needham, the original wizard of dribble Billy Meredith, and the ultimate all-round athlete C.B. Fry. We will marvel at the Corinthians club in their invincible heyday. We will witness the great days of Sunderland – 'the team of all the talents' – the double-winning Aston Villa, the first great Spurs side, the early toddling steps of Manchester United, the birth of Chelsea, and the tooth-and-nail battle for national supremacy between the two Sheffield clubs.

There were giants in those days.

G.P.P.

1: Early Years

Object lessons for Dec. 1883 – Jan. 1884:

Hay-making

The Railway Station

The Rainbow

Ice

Gold

From the *Blackwell Colliery School Log Book, 1883*

The feature of the game was the goalkeeping of W. Fowkes
(sic) of Blackwell, who certainly has the making of a first-
class custodian.

Derby Daily Telegraph (20/12/93)

William Henry Foulke was born in Dawley, Shropshire, on Sunday 12 April 1874.

That much is certain: then controversy seems to follow our man virtually from birth. The first bone of contention is the spelling of his name. At least six versions have seen the light of day:

(a)   Foulk

(b)   Faulks

(c)   Fowkes

(d)   Foulke

(e)   Foulkes

(f)   Ffoulk

(a) is on his birth certificate, (b) – almost certainly a transcription error – is on the 1881 census. (c) is an early reporter's error. (d) is the one he preferred, and the one usually – after repeated reminders from the man himself – employed in football matters. (e) is the version his wife preferred, and the one on his grave-stone inscription in Burngreave Cemetery, Sheffield. (f) was used occasionally in later years by the *Manchester Guardian*, although its unwarranted double-barrelled initial was possibly a leaden Edwardian joke.

His birth certificate seems to supply more questions than answers. The address of the newborn is given as Old Park, Dawley. The column for 'father' is blank. His mother's name is Mary Ann. Her 'signature' is just an 'X' – 'The mark of Mary Ann Foulk, Mother.' Since William had a younger brother, born in 1881 (see chapter 10), the apparent absence of the father here is a puzzle.

Dawley in those days was a fair-sized coal-mining town, a satellite of Telford. Its most famous son before Bill Foulke hit the headlines was one Captain Matthew Webb, who gained lasting fame by being the first person to swim the Channel, in August 1875.

Some fifteen months before that, William (just four weeks old) and his elder brother Thomas (aged four) had been taken to Blackwell in Derbyshire, to live with their grandparents James and Jane. The village of Blackwell, a few hundred yards from the Nottinghamshire border, traditionally renowned for its cheese, was now being exploited for its rich coal seams. During the first decade or so of William's life it was to grow from an isolated hamlet to a bustling mining community, quadrupling its population in those ten years.

Blackwell lies close to the railway line which joins those two mighty centres of early football: Sheffield and Nottingham, with a third, Derby, about fifteen miles to the south-west. In retrospect, the mining village seems ideally, almost centrally, situated for a player of immense talent and potential to come to the notice of the scouts of the area's big clubs. As it was, three First Division outfits were headhunting our William before he'd turned twenty.

Foulke was fortunate, too, in the timing of his entry into the football world. In the year of his birth it was still the amateur gentlemen of leisure who ruled the roost. Four weeks before William was born Oxford University had defeated the Royal Engineers 2-0 in the third ever FA Cup final, held at The Oval. But that same year there were the first murmurings of change.

Sheffield FC took part in the trophy for the first time that year, losing narrowly to Clapham Rovers in the third round. The *Illustrated Sporting and Dramatic News* stated: 'Football nowhere thrives more rapidly or is cultivated with more enthusiasm than in the town of keen blades.' The Sheffield story is rejoined later.

Thirteen years later, by the time William left school, the changes had been huge, and irreversible. Blackburn Olympic had led the provincial working-class charge on the FA Cup, beating the Old Etonians in the 1883 final. Professionalism, for so long taboo, had been legalised. And within a few weeks William McGregor would be writing to major clubs of the North and Midlands suggesting the launch of the Football League.

If Foulke had been born a quarter of a century earlier, his football, had it existed at all, would have been restricted to a peripheral oddity, a winter supplement to his village cricket. He would certainly never have become a professional, and never have reached the exalted levels he did with Sheffield United. And without this platform, he would probably never have been given his chance at County cricket.

Transport Bill Foulke twenty-five years or so into the future, and he would have struggled in the faster post-war game, beset by livelier, fitter forwards and subtler tactics. The change in the offside law in 1925 would probably have sounded his death knell as a player. In the foxy and circumspect build-ups towards goal under the old rule, there was more time for a 'keeper to assess the situation, and for William to get away with his risky habit of running out to kick clear. With the reduction of the number of defenders in the offside equation from three to two, speed became the essence of attack. The shots from afar and the one-on-one situations that Foulke was to become so adept at reacting to would have been replaced by fast through balls, shifting the pivot of attack with unsettling rapidity. We can but speculate how well William would have dealt with the challenge of a Dixie Dean – now there's a combat to stir the imagination.

No: as we shall see, William Henry Foulke was a man of his age *par excellence*. The 1881 census shows nine people living at 122 Primrose Hill, Blackwell:

Name	Position	Occupation	Age	Place of birth
James Faulks *(sic)*	Head	coalminer	60	Dawley, Shropshire
Jane Faulks	Wife	-	55	Dawley, Shropshire
James Faulks	Son	coalminer	31	Wolverhampton, Staffs.
Noah Faulks	Son	coalminer	25	Dawley, Shropshire
Alfred Faulks	Son	coalminer	18	Dawley, Shropshire
Thomas Henry Faulks	Grandson	scholar	11	Dawley, Shropshire
William Henry Faulks	**Grandson**	**scholar**	**7**	**Dawley, Shropshire**
Thomas Cadman	Boarder	coalminer	22	Wombridge, Shropshire
John Perrey	Boarder	coalminer	36	Wellington, Shropshire

So it was no doubt a crowded home life at no. 122, but with six wage packets coming in at that time, we can assume the occupants were comfortably above the poverty line. We can imagine too, with eight males of varying ages in the house, the interest in sport, and the impact this would have had on the two youngest. Immediately opposite the line of terraced houses that made up the Primrose Hill development was the wall surrounding the cricket pitch, and football had at least three designated terrains within the village.

William and Thomas attended the Colliery School, built in 1876 by the Hucknall and Blackwell Co. Ltd for its workers' children. The school logbook rarely mentions a scholar by name unless there were problems with learning or attendance (or the occasional outstanding achievement) from which it may be surmised that both brothers were academically sound. An inspector's report praises the 'accuracy and spirit' of the childrens' singing.

In William's class was one Beatrice Duff, who had been born in Sheffield. She was to return there, a move dictated by her father Robert's job on the railways. The Duffs' Sheffield address would be Marcus Street, a quarter of a mile from where William was to have his first digs in that city.

In November 1887 it was recorded: 'A large number of children from the upper standards have left the school for work.' November was the leaving month in those days, it being the end of the school administrative year. At age thirteen, William had completed his formal education, and would be following his brother into working at the pit.

Blackwell has maintained a proud sporting tradition since the nineteenth century. Local lad Jimmy Simmons – a relative of the Foulkes – was to play for Sheffield United in the 1915 cup final. The cricket ground was used for many county matches, and has a place in the record books, as the venue of the world-record ninth-wicket stand (283 in June 1910). That same year William was no doubt delighted to see the progress of his old village football club through the earlier rounds of the FA Cup. Ashbourne, Long Eaton, South Normanton and Clay Cross were disposed of in qualifying rounds, then the colliery team travelled to Mansfield to play the powerful Town side. Surely the end of the road? Not so: Blackwell pulled off a minor giant-slaying sensation by winning 1-0. They met their match in the following round, losing 1-6 to Darlington, who went on to show their mettle in the first round proper by defeating Sheffield United!

Other sons of Blackwell who have made a name for themselves in professional football are Harold Hill (Notts County and The Wednesday), Terry Adlington (Derby County), Harry Jones (Forest), and Don Harper and Ryan Williams (both Chesterfield). Elijah Carrington played County cricket for Derbyshire. It's an impressive list for such a small community.

Today the pits themselves are long gone, of course, and the ravaged landscape of black sheds, winding gear and spoil heaps that William would have seen has healed and settled into softly rolling greensward. But the village football team – Blackwell Miners' Welfare FC – lives on, playing with a fair measure of success in the Central Midlands League. The sturdy and forbidding dark brick wall surrounding the main cricket pitch at Primrose Hill is still there. The row of terraced houses where Bill Foulke and family lived, just across the road from the cricket ground, was demolished in 1947.

It used to be said that if a football manager was short of a player, all he had to do was to go to the nearest colliery pithead and shout down the shaft. This is no doubt another of those 'goalkeepers are crazy' adages that football culture has spawned, but as usual there is a rich vein of truth in it. Colliery teams traditionally struck fear into their opponents and it's not that hard to work out why. The tough physical graft at the coalface ensured fitness, and working in difficult and often dangerous conditions forged a team spirit that transferred itself brilliantly into the sporting arena.

Sport, especially football, was openly encouraged and sponsored by the pit bosses. Other philanthropic gestures had gone a long way towards forming the village community: the mining company would have built a hospital and a library, as well as the school and housing, during the 1870s. Now the social values of team games and competitions became apparent. A commentator of the early twentieth century was to state: 'Generally the best sportsman was the best workman and the most useful citizen in the end.' And, we may slyly add, he was more likely to allow his mind to be distracted from the issues of pay and work conditions. Those years saw an ongoing battle between the bosses and the newly unionised miners, and out of all Derbyshire, it was the Blackwell pits that gained the reputation of being the most militant. The disputes occurred almost annually. The working man was finding a political voice, and it's noteworthy that a teenaged William was there to hear the early cross-class dialogues and pinpointing of injustices. I'm sure we can trace his keen sense of right and wrong, his great-hearted generosity, as well as his impatience with privilege he felt was undeserved, to that time.

The census of early 1891 shows William, aged sixteen, 'coal miner', still living at 122 Primrose Hill. The ten years have brought sweeping changes in the list of other occupants, though, reflecting the bustling, lively era of the mining village. Grandmother Jane has remarried, to a man twenty or so years her junior (and she has been a little economical with the truth as regards her age!) and a fresh crop of pit workers in their twenties have come to rent lodgings. Tommy has gone, presumably married, but has continued to live and work locally. (The electoral roll of 1910 will show him living at 155 Primrose Hill.)

It's round about now that Blackwell cricket and football teams, playing ad hoc matches against neighbouring collieries, first begin to make their appearance. For William and Tommy's development as cricketers, the reader is referred to chapter 7. As for the football team, whose home ground was the colliery pitch at Scanderlands, it was strong enough to graduate to the Derbyshire League a couple of years later. And word travelled about their goalkeeper: destined for great things they said; a tall slim lad (as he still was!), strong, agile enough to get down for the low shots and ever willing to leave his line to perform as an extra back.

It was in the 1892/93 Derbyshire League that Blackwell carried all before them. William, who turned nineteen that year, was omnipresent. The attack contained brother Tommy and a remarkably strong and aggressive centre forward known as Cockayne. In a match against local rivals Clay Cross Town this striker charged into a goalmouth melee and (the rules being what they were) scored by steamrollering goalie, two full-backs and the ball into the net!

Keeping goal in this sort of league proved a useful apprenticeship for William, not least because of the roughhouse context. Fist-fights and send-ings-off were fairly common.

The Colliery attack ran riot that year. Typical results were: 10-3 *v.* Alfreton (away), 4-0 *v.* Riddings, 9-0 *v.* Wirksworth, 7-0 *v.* Ilkeston Town, 7-1 *v.* Tibshelf ('three goals downhill, and uphill four'), 10-1 *v.* Ripley Town, and the campaign was rounded off with a 9-1 rout of Alfreton. This brought the season's tally to 114 goals for, 29 against.

Easily winning that league ensured their promotion to the more senior Derbyshire Challenge Cup League. Here among their opponents were such substantial outfits as Heanor Town and Matlock – of which more in the next chapter. The Blackwell club was deemed strong enough to take on an XI from Derby County. The big fish, clearly nervous, decided to include the great John Goodall, an ex-Preston England international, in their side as centre forward. He would have good reason to remember his first encounter with our Willie.

2: To Sheffield for £20

We must have him.
    Sheffield United director Joseph Tomlinson, speaking of Foulke, spring 1894.

William Foulke, United's new, tall, cool goalkeeper, the Alfreton man (sic).
                                                    Sheffield Independent (3/9/94)

According to Foulke's obituary in the *Athletic News* of 8 May 1916, there took place a 'friendly' some time in 1893 between Blackwell Colliery and a Derby County XI. The County forwards were given a hard time by the lanky teenage colliery goalkeeper. At one point John Goodall himself joined the attack, and rose to meet a cross with his head. Like a flash the 'keeper was off his line, and cleared with a mighty punch. Unfortunately he made contact with Mr Goodall *en passant* and dislodged a couple of the great man's teeth. The result of the game seems to have been lost in the mists of time, but the tale of this tall and powerful young goalie who so discomfited an England international spread like wildfire.

The Blackwell side, newly promoted to the Derbyshire Challenge Trophy League, acquitted themselves well that year. And unusually, it was the 'keeper who was mentioned in dispatches more than any forward:

23/9/93   Heanor Town 2, Blackwell Colliery 1
Foulke, who was admired for his goalkeeping, prevented Heanor scoring several additional goals. (*Sheffield Independent*) Tommy Foulke took the corner which led to Blackwell's equalising goal.

7/10/93   Blackwell Colliery 7, Derby Junction 1
… a rasping shot… cleverly saved by Foulke, was loudly applauded. (*Sheffield Independent*)

16/12/93   Derby Junction 3, Blackwell Colliery 3
Junction were doing nearly all the pressing, and they were only prevented from scoring by the exceptionally fine goalkeeping of W. Foulke. (*Derby Daily Telegraph*)

13/1/94   North Wingfield 1, Blackwell Colliery 1
A stinger was sent in to Foulke, who saved. (*Sheffield Independent*)

27/1/94   Blackwell Colliery 4, Staveley Wanderers 0
Tommy Foulke scored in this one…

3/2/94   Blackwell Colliery 4, Heanor Town 2
… and twice in this one! This was Heanor's first defeat of the season.

24/3/94   Derby Town 3, Blackwell Colliery 0
But for the excellent form shown by the Blackwell custodian more points would
have been registered. (*Sheffield Independent*)

28/4/94   Derby Town 3, Blackwell Colliery 0 (Final of the Derbyshire
Charity Cup – see below)
The Blackwell goalkeeper, a really clever lad named Foulke, kept goal in fine style.
(*Derby Daily Telegraph*)

The team finished fifth in the Derbyshire Challenge Trophy League.

Elder brother Tommy, despite his scoring ability, was to progress to play goal
for Wellington Town (Shropshire), the club that would be renamed Telford
United in 1969.

By now three First Division clubs were preparing to move in to snap up
the younger Foulke. It was Sheffield United who were marginally quickest off
the mark.

Then, as now, money talked. Professionalism (legalised in England in 1885) – dou-
ble-edged though it was seen to be – suited William. It was the lubrication of lucre
that oiled the wheels of his move from relative obscurity to an ambitious top-flight
club. Once he was there, it was the relatively high wage packet, with a generous
(and negotiable) bonus system, that was a major factor in inducing him to stay.

Of course there was a dark side to professionalism. The doom–mongers had
plenty of evidence to support their view of money being the root of all ills, in
sport as elsewhere. The stories of Machiavellian ploys to capture or protect professionals' signatures are legion. We recall the secretary of the short-lived (but
successful) Blackburn Olympic hiding top striker Dewhurst down a coalmine
when they were being besieged by the well-off clubs. It was seen to be perfectly
in order to dangle inducements such as a job or a pub to run in order to sway
players' decisions. Blades fans will cite the case of Foulke's teammate Tommy
Morren, waylaid by trainer George Waller at Sheffield railway station as the
half-back was supposedly on his way to sign for Reading!

The caricaturists of the day depict a 'never the twain shall meet' situation reflecting rigid class divisions. On the one hand was the gentleman amateur: the natural all-round athlete in his state of grace playing for the love of the game. On the other was the professional: man after the fall, tempted and corrupt, specialising in the one sport that paid, susceptible to all the wiles and grotesqueries of mammon. Professionals had at least the potential to be 'cads of the most unscrupulous kidney' (Corinthian C.B. Fry's memorable, if not immediately completely accessible, phrase). It's a good point at which to continue this digression, and look at the formation and ethos of the Corinthians, who will feature in our story.

Illegal backhanders over and above permitted expenses had been whispered knowledge in football circles since as long ago as 1879. The Lancashire mill town of Darwen had progressed to the FA Cup quarter-finals that year, and had had the temerity to take the elite amateurs of the Old Etonians to three hard-fought matches. On their team were two Scotsmen, Fergie Suter and Jimmy Love, and, to borrow Bryon Butler's observation, they hadn't come south for a change of climate. As Suter was later to confess, you went and had a chat with the club treasurer as and when circumstances demanded, and were suitably looked after. Lancashire clubs became notorious for under-the-table payments, whereas Sheffield, at the time kowtowing to London, kept up at least an appearance of amateur purity for some more years. And professionalism wasn't legalised in Scotland until 1893 – which accounts for the mass migration of Scottish players into the Football and Southern Leagues during the decade or so before.

A look at the results of the England-Scotland matches during those years of 'shamateurism' makes interesting reading:

1878	Glasgow	Scotland 7	England 2
1879	London	England 5	Scotland 4
1880	Glasgow	Scotland 5	England 4
1881	London	England 1	Scotland 6
1882	Glasgow	Scotland 5	England 1

To the old school, the reasons for England's poor displays were rooted in the weakening of the national game by the influx of Scots, which in turn was down to the illegal factor of pay for play. They also saw the competitive nature of the FA Cup as a divisive force: clubs were actually refusing to allow players to appear in internationals if they were needed for a cup tie!

To N.L. ('Pa') Jackson, one of the England team selectors, the perceived ills cried out for one solution: the recreation of the Eden days of the all-conquering amateurs. And so the Corinthians, the spiritual descendants of the Wanderers, came into being. The best of the public school and university old boys would be brought together, and the team would be run on strictly amateur lines. The players would adhere to the highest standards of sportsmanship. Clause seven of their constitution forbade them from competing for any little tin idol; their games would be restricted to friendlies, exhibitions, and charity matches.

For a time the new side enjoyed almost mythical status. They beat Blackburn Rovers' FA Cup-winning team 8-1 in 1884; soon the England team would sometimes be composed almost exclusively of Corinthians.

If anything, the class divisions of the time were celebrated whenever the Corinthians took the field. Printed team lists are telling: the gentlemen would be granted the privilege of their initials, whereas the professionals are designated by the stark surname alone. The amateur side would turn up sporting top hats and canes, puffing the odd cigar. On the pitch they would assume an apparently nonchalant, superior manner as they sidled into position in their white shirts, hands in the pockets of their knee-length black shorts. (We are reminded of the motto of Balliol College, Oxford: Effortless Superiority. A nice trick if you can manage it.)

And where will Bill Foulke, the working-class icon, fit into all this? The crucial months will be March and April 1898, when Sheffield United, League Champions-elect, will twice take on the sublime might of Corinth. Foulke's performances, the results, as well as the attendant tales, are of interest. The story is continued in chapter 4.

To return to the Blackwell-Sheffield connection: Joseph Tomlinson, Blades director, had been a fine footballer in his day, a speedy forward for the powerful Heeley club. He was comparatively short and bearded, and some were to say in later years, a ringer for the future George V. One of his claims to fame is that he was a player – and scorer – in the first ever game under floodlights, which had taken place at Bramall Lane back in October 1878. He had been founder committee member of the United.

The referee for the Blackwell-Matlock cup tie in April 1894, a Mr Swaine, a good friend of Joseph Tomlinson, was so impressed by Foulke's goalkeeping display that he went straight to Bramall Lane to sing the youngster's praises. Tomlinson insisted to the committee: 'We must have him.'

Sheffield knew they had to act fast and to put together an attractive package for both team and man. Nottingham Forest and Derby County were rumoured to be eyeing William as well. Obviously John Goodall was prepared to forgive and forget Willie's ad lib radical dentistry if they were both to be on the same side.

Tommy's advice to his kid brother was to exercise caution, and to weigh up all possibilities before committing himself. The offer from the Blades, however, came within the week, and was too good to refuse: Blackwell Colliery would receive £20 for the transfer, plus a £1 a day retainer until the end of the season, a fortnight or so away. William himself would receive £5. In those days, this was big money for a relatively unknown twenty-year-old, and a golden passport away from working 'down t'pit'. Tomlinson secured William's signature after the Derbyshire Charity Cup final at Ilkeston on 28 April 1894. The story goes that the Blades director left the changing rooms with the completed papers in his pocket, and a second or two after he had closed the door, a Derby committee member entered, aiming to persuade William to sign for them.

Then, according to one version of events, there was a typical touch of mischievousness from the man: although the transaction was all done and dusted, he was summoned to Nottingham the following Monday to discuss matters with the Forest. After a tour of the ground and listening to some flattering overtures, he revealed that he'd already joined Sheffield United!

And so the young man barely out of his teens made the short train journey up the main London line to make his debut at Bramall Lane. There was much talk and speculation about the newcomer. The directors, his teammates and the fans were expecting great things. They were not to be disappointed.

3: The Rise of the Blades

In Foulke, Sheffield United have a goalkeeper who will take a deal of beating. He is one of those lengthy individuals who can take a seat on the crossbar whenever he chooses, and shows little of the awkwardness usually characteristic of big men.

Scottish Sport (2/1/95)

There is a curious common factor shared by the three professional clubs whose defence Foulke anchored: they were all relatively young, and in one case, Chelsea, newly born. There the parallels appear to end, unless we note the fact that, in one way or another, it was Willie who contributed generously to the forces that set all three clubs on their road to success. Quite apart from the number of games he played a major role in winning or rescuing, there's no getting away from the fact that he had a phenomenal crowd-pulling power. Since then, as now, a football club's finances were largely energised by the clicking of the turnstiles, all three clubs owed, and perhaps still owe, an immense debt to the man.

But there's another thing Sheffield United, Chelsea, and Bradford City had in common. Initially they were ideas inspired by a sports stadium that had already been in existence for some time. The latter two will figure in our story a decade or so in the future. For the moment a brief look at the traditionally fertile ground of Sheffield football, in which the seed of the United was to grow and prosper, will set the scene for the arrival of Mr Foulke.

In the beginning was the Sheffield club. Even before then, in the days of the pig's bladder, a cast of thousands (well, a few hundred a side) and simulated warfare in the streets, sides from Sheffield would take on sides from over the border in Derbyshire. Pitched battles of three consecutive days were not unknown, often resulting in mass injuries and lasting bad blood. Enter the Victorian public school old boys, with their civilising influence and affinity for codification. Local worthies took up the baton, and by 1857 the first version of the 'Sheffield Rules' saw the light of day. These were modified over the years, so that by 1871 the definitive set of laws appeared. There was a rudimentary offside rule, handling the ball was completely taboo for outfield players (it had been permitted under certain circumstances in the earlier version), and the corner kick was introduced.

For the next few years two sets of rules existed in England: 'Sheffield' and 'London'. Synthesis would not occur until 1877, brought about by the rampant popularity of the FA Cup. By then The Wednesday had worked their way to the forefront of the local clubs. They won the inaugural Sheffield Association Challenge Cup that year, beating the fancied Heeley side in extra time. Five years later they reached the semi-final of the FA Cup, albeit losing heavily to the wonder team of the eighties, Blackburn Rovers. In an earlier round they had beaten Heeley once more, playing at the cricket ground at Bramall Lane.

It was the passion and noise of an FA Cup semi-final at the same venue (Preston *v.* WBA, March 1889, attendance 22,688 – Preston were en route to their famous double) that inspired the idea of a new Sheffield club. It would be based at Bramall Lane, and the net would be cast far and wide in a search for players. The founding fathers – who included local dignitary Sir Charles Clegg – wanted only the best available professionals to grace the fine stadium. The name of this new club? Sheffield United.

For the first few years, perhaps unsurprisingly, United were playing catch-up with the long-established Wednesday. Then the gap began to close. Both teams were elected to the Football League when it was extended in 1892: Wednesday to an enlarged First Division, and United to the new Second Division, from which they were promptly promoted. So, with just one season

'Foulke's gentle kicks.' (Athletic News)

to go before Foulke's arrival at Bramall Lane, top-flight Sheffield football had polarised into what were to become, over the next decade, two of the strongest teams in the land.

Foulke's debut contained some happy omens. Playing against West Bromwich Albion on 1 September 1894, in front of a crowd of 10,000 at Bramall Lane, on the face of it the newcomer showed nary a trace of nerves. Alert and safe, and demonstrating an eye for the constructive clearance, he was a major factor in United's comfortable 2-0 half-time lead. When the Albion came out fighting in the second half, their pressure led to a goal. William, never a 'stay at home' custodian, ran out to make a courageous save, but couldn't hold the ball. Before he could get back to his station, Albion had the ball in the net. The last half hour saw a rejuvenated Albion almost steal an equaliser, but McLeod put a penalty wide of a post, 'Foulke just touching it'. After that, the United 'keeper, increasingly confident in his domain, didn't make any more mistakes.

The Blades team that day was: Foulke; Thickett, Cain; Howell, Hendry, Needham; Peden, Jones, Hall, Morris, Yates.

Three of them would still be there ten years later, at the end of the most successful run in the history of the club: Foulke himself, of course; the solid yet speedy back Harry Thickett; and the original Captain Marvel, the diminutive but richly skilled and tactically brilliant half-back Ernest Needham.

Needham's mentor, the talented Scot Bill Hendry, was captain on that day, but an injury the following New Year's Day during the friendly with Leith brought an end to his career. Bob Cain would leave after four more seasons, seduced by the Eldorado of the Southern League. Right half Rab Howell would have a rocky tale all his own, culminating in a murky climax in the spring of 1898, as the Blades raced Sunderland for the League Championship.

Back to William's debut season: recent cup-winners Wolves were next, dismissed 3-0 at Molineux. Already the hallmarks of Foulke's style of keeping goal were plain to see. He was a mobile, dominant presence, reading a game well and positioning himself perfectly to deal with the long shots; loose balls within twenty yards or so of his line were cleared with a thundering kick, and optimistic crosses were either disdainfully held or punched an impressive distance to safety.

Clearance punches and kicks were much more in vogue for custodians of those days, basically because the rules of the time were more generously in favour of the attacker who charged the goalie. It was perfectly in order for the forward to use brute force and bundle both man and ball into the net. Until 1892 it had been permissible to charge the custodian even when the ball was elsewhere. As the years progressed and Willie's bulk increased, attempting to push him around became a progressively more ludicrous tactic, as we shall see. He was to retain the clearance-kick habit, however, even though back then it was possible for the 'keeper to handle the ball as far as the halfway line. The immediate kick out to a well-positioned teammate (or into the blue yonder) was quicker and less risky than the gathering-up and pausing to assess which became the norm in later years.

Victories over Stoke, Nottingham Forest, Blackburn Rovers and Aston Villa followed for the Blades. There was a draw at Liverpool, where the 12,000 crowd took an immediate shine to the lanky newcomer. There was a glorious away win over The Wednesday, which put the Blades in second place in the League by the end of October. The only defeats in the first eight weeks of that season were two narrow squeaks, both against Preston North End, not quite 'The Invincibles' of a few years before, but still good enough to finish fourth that season. All seemed to bode well.

But William's halcyon days were to be rocked four times before Christmas. Once by a day of appalling weather (along with a referee's pig-headedness), and three times by a bogey team.

In mid-November 1894 English weather took a turn for the perverse. After a weekend of torrential rain the pitch at Perry Bar (the earlier home of Aston Villa) was transformed into a water park. A huge puddle stretched across the lower end of the gently sloping terrain, and the rest was little more than a quagmire. Referee Mr. Thomas, of Burnley, insisted the match take place. It got worse. Hardly had the game got underway when it started to bucket down again, and on a bitterly cold day the rain shifted into unrelenting sleet. The game grew increasingly farcical, but still the referee refused to call it a day. At one point Villa's Devey played in his overcoat. United were losing 0-1 at half-time, but in the second half their challenge collapsed. Villa had been able to change into dry kit during the interval, but in those days such a privilege wasn't always available for away teams. Needham was first to succumb in the dreadful conditions. He was carried off the pitch 'unconscious with exposure'. Without him the Blades disintegrated, losing four more goals (and three more players) as the half trudged and splashed on. Even the robust Foulke, who had adapted better than most to the cold and wet, was overcome by cramp in the last minute, and had to be carried from the field.

Mr Thomas was later censured by the Football League. The press had a field day: perhaps the most memorable imprecation flung in the official's direction was the 'something lingering, with boiling oil in it', wished by the *Birmingham Saturday Night* correspondent.

Two days earlier, United had again conceded five goals, in the United Counties League match with Derby County. Led by John Goodall, Derby County were one of the few teams who habitually nullified the Blades' natural strength, their half-back line, and countered with able strikers. In three games with them in the space of seven weeks United gave away thirteen goals. Ominously, somewhere in the right attack of the Rams would be the prodigy Steve Bloomer, aka 'Paleface', or 'the Destroying Angel'.

Bloomer was the same age as Foulke, but there the resemblance ends. The Derby man (born in the Black Country and taken on at the Baseball Ground as a teenager) wasn't especially tall (5ft 8ins) and had a deceptively frail (11st 3lb) washed-out look about him. But opponents underestimated him at their peril. He was capable of an electrifying burst of speed over a short distance, and his speciality was the lightning low-level shot, struck with the minimum of back-lift and therefore hard to see coming. He was to score nearly 400 League and cup goals, and hit the net 23 times for England, in a career that would last almost until the First World War.

He could dribble, too, steering the ball at speed through the most resolute of defences. How many times in those years did a Blades-Rams game resolve itself into a gladiatorial Foulke-Bloomer contest, with mind games having as much a part to play as footballing skills? Their climactic meeting would be in four years' time, in a pulsating FA Cup final. With John Goodall at the height of his inspirational powers, Derby had yet to lose to the Blades since both teams had made it to the top flight. Two 1-4 defeats — the second on a gloomy Christmas Day at Bramall Lane — brought an end to 1894. Bloomer scored in both games.

Otherwise, William had settled in quickly. An instant hit with the fans, he soon reached iconic status. Very tall — 6ft 2ins and still only 12st 10lb — in an age when a good average height would have been around 5ft 8in, he was meat and drink to the sports writers: 'the lengthy one', 'the octopus', 'he of the eagle eye and the long reach' were a few of the awestruck epithets printed in those early months. One of his party pieces was to pick up the ball with just one hand — some forty years before the great Frank Swift was to adopt the same trademark mannerism.

His mobile, confident exterior nonetheless masked a surprising access of stage fright before a game. Much later he confessed to taking a nip of whisky before big games to quell the butterflies. It was Tom Bott, in his pastoral role, who would slip William the hooch, as the club was renowned for being repressively teetotal.

The odd barney with a reporter gained him an early reputation of the enfant terrible. The dependable, great-hearted sportsman had a nervy irascibility crackling around the edges, as it were. A *Sheffield Daily Telegraph* reporter wrote something with which the big man disagreed, so the pressman was publicly subjected to the rough edge of Foulke's tongue as well as the lower reaches of his vocabulary. It was the same reporter who discussed 'the lengthy one's' merits with the Scottish half-back Willie Maley, during the United-Celtic friendly in October 1895:

> 'Now Foulke there,' he added, as the Blackwell giant saved a scorcher from the centre, 'he is a magnificent goalkeeper. And yet so is the Queen's Park man [Haddow], and still one knock in a match makes him so excited that many a time he loses games through that and nothing else. Is Foulke excitable?' 'He has been known to be,' I replied, diplomatically.
> *Sheffield Daily Telegraph* (15/10/95)

Note that he is still referred to as 'the Blackwell giant'. He was to commute from his Derbyshire village until 1899, using the rail pass paid for by the club. Needham and Thickett did the same, from Chesterfield and Doncaster respectively. Although during his weeks in training he lived in digs at 37 Marcus Street, just to the north of Sheffield centre in the suburb of Burngreave, his home village was still his spiritual centre. He would return there when not in training, and in summer would play cricket for the colliery side. But, typical of the young man drawn to a higher destiny, within a year or two he would probably have felt himself growing away from the familiar – 'that he should leave his house'. It was a kinetic process no doubt accelerated by a devastating event the following November.

He was certainly earning more as a professional footballer than he had down the pit. Within a year, as the committee grew to a realisation of his defensive indispensability, his wage packet increased to £3 a week, which included a 'retainer' wage over the summer. There were bonuses too: after listening to a players' deputation led by Needham, the committee agreed to the following: a ten-shilling (50p) bonus for an away win, and five shillings for a home win or away draw. These seem paltry sums at first glance, but this was when a fair weekly take-home pay for a working man was still around £1. A top wage for a railway worker at the time would have been about eight shillings (40p) a day. One thing hasn't changed over the years: each player was on a £1 bonus to beat The Wednesday, home or away! For the Christmas 1898 game, this was increased to a generous incentive of £5 for a win.

On the pitch, battle lines were drawn that first winter. As well as Bloomer, William had already encountered the nineteen-year-old Billy Meredith. It was in a friendly against Welsh club Chirk (where Meredith had started his career), with the Wizard scoring to make it 1-1. United were eventually winners 5-1.

Other recurring themes made their first appearance around this time, notably in the FA Cup. There would be a hammer-and-tongs struggle with a top club (or three); Foulke would give outstanding performances; the weather would play its part in the drama; and there would be a hotly disputed goal.

After disposing of Southern League leaders Millwall in the snow, the Blades faced West Bromwich Albion in the second round. Despite their lowly League placing, the Albion were a tough proposition in the cup, having won the 'Little Tin Idol' a couple of years before. At Bramall Lane the Throstles were held 1-1, largely thanks to two memorable saves from Foulke. In the first half he dived full length to tip a 'goal all the way' shot round the post. In the second Albion's Richardson broke through on his own. Showing an early relish for such one-on-one situations, the 'keeper dived bravely at the forward's feet and snatched the ball.

The replay was the following Wednesday. In between Willie had turned out for an England Select XI v. Scotland. After conceding an unlucky goal from a free-kick, United slowly fought their way back into contention. The equaliser arrived, eventually, deep into the second half. Then, with a few minutes left, an Albion forward unleashed a stinger from way out. Foulke was close enough to it to beat it down with his hands 'at least a foot this side of the line', as he was later to say. The referee consulted with his linesman – a cosmetic gesture, surely, as they were both some distance downfield – and awarded a goal! The stunned Blades at least retained enough fight to throw people forward in the last seconds, and Thickett thumped the bar with a powerful shot. But that was it – WBA were through, to progress to the final.

In the League United finished sixth, two places ahead of The Wednesday. Sunderland were Champions by a margin of five points.

William had played in every game bar one. The exception – he was rested after his stint of three games in five days the week of the FA Cup second round – afforded a first-team chance to reserve goalie Arthur Wharton. The slim and athletic Wharton, who was to return to Rotherham at the end of the season, is notable for having been the first black footballer to play professionally in Britain.

Villa won the Cup; but then in an eventful autumn they lost it, stolen from a shop window in Newton Row, Birmingham on the night of 11 September 1895.

Exactly two months later, on 11 November 1895, the Blackwell Colliery disaster occurred. An underground explosion during the night shift killed seven, two of them neighbours of the Foulkes on Primrose Hill. The incident was a shattering blow to the mining community, especially as the two main

'Winning' pits in the village had gained a reputation as being among the safest in the country. We can imagine the effect it would have had on the twenty-one-year-old William as he took his leave on the Sheffield train, while the pithead wheel, as a mark of respect to the dead, turned endlessly and silently over the mourning village. Perhaps he thought, naturally, as part of such a close-knit community: 'It might easily have been me.' Let's not forget that just over a year before, he had been working down the pit full time. In those painful days, William stared death in the face. It was the first time the young man had been exposed to it in such immediacy.

We may recall the thoughts of Olympic gold medallist Chris Brasher, writing in a more analytical age some seventy years later:

> I have a theory that it is essential for all truly great athletes… to have gone through… an experience when 'A man thinks that he is going to die.'
> *A Diary of the XVIIIth Olympiad*

In any case, afforded a respite from the present black reality of home life, he threw himself into training and matches, relishing the fresh challenges and new camaraderie of football. A permanent move to Sheffield was only a matter of time. And by then, of course, he had met up with Beatrice again.

In the football domain, for a while William himself seemed accident-prone. Early in the New Year he hurt the second finger of his right hand in punching clear during the 1-1 draw with Sunderland. The following Monday it was examined by club surgeon Dr Stokes, who discovered that the finger was broken. The enforced rest of nearly four weeks nearly drove Foulke frantic. He demanded to be allowed to play in the FA Cup match at Burton, but Dr Stokes (with whom, as we shall see, William didn't enjoy the rosiest of relationships) quite correctly forbade it. Reserve goalie Bradshaw, an ex-Staveley man, held the fort in his absence. Both League games without Foulke were lost, and the Blades could only draw their cup match with Second Division Burton Wanderers. Although Bradshaw had been named for the replay the following Thursday at Bramall Lane, a thunderous cheer greeted Foulke as he trotted out to play. Result: 1-0 to the home side.

Two days after that, the Blades travelled to Walsall for the quarter-final of the Mayor of Birmingham Cup. The train carrying the team ground to a halt outside Lichfield. The United goalie was the hero of the day as his height came in very handy in the helping-down of women and children passengers from the carriages onto the track.

They say that these things happen in threes. When Walsall was eventually reached, William sustained another injury, this time before he'd even left the hotel where the team had had lunch. There is a traditional Staffordshire pub game called 'Devil Amongst The Tailors', which consists of nine skittles set up in a diamond shape in the middle of the floor, and a wooden ball hanging from the ceiling on a rope. The object of the game is to swing the ball and try and knock down the pins with as few tries as possible. A hundred years or so ago the popular version of the game would have taken up most of the room, with a football-sized ball and two-foot high skittles. William was walking past while a game was in progress, and a lustily flung ball struck him a glancing blow on the brow. The wound bled copiously, but the flow was stemmed and the cut bandaged in time for the match (no question, of course, of Foulke sitting this one out).

The match was won comfortably, 5-2. It's worth following the Birmingham Cup-trail now. In the semi United met old rivals Derby County, and reversed the usual trend by actually beating John Goodall's team 2-0. Excuses were forthcoming: the match was at Olive Grove, almost at home for United, and Bloomer was recovering from the previous day's rough sea crossing after the international with Ireland. But the win was talismanic: five days later the Blades went to Derby to play a League game, and won by the same score. It was the Rams' first home defeat that season, and the first ever League win over them by Sheffield United. The *Sheffield Telegraph* captured the turning of the tide:

> Bloomer gave Foulke a rare handful, which he manipulated cleverly.
> (16/3/96)

On the right wing was young Walter Bennett, newly acquired from Mexborough, already a tricky dribbler and expert crosser of the ball. He became firm friends with Bill Foulke, and, like the goalkeeper, was to play a major role in the ensuing United bonanza.

In the final of the Birmingham Cup the Blades were pitted against the all-conquering Aston Villa side, League Champions that year and the next, when they would also win the FA Cup. The one-sided, uninspiring match took place at Villa's own Perry Bar, and the home side cruised to a 3-0 win. As the Villa captain John Devey held the trophy aloft, Willie couldn't resist the wickedly topical jibe: 'Be careful no one nicks this one.'

United's League performance for 1895/96 had been erratic, while showing glimpses of real potential. The only player to have received consistently good press reports (with the possible exception of Needham) had been Foulke. And there was the strident wake-up call: The Wednesday won the FA Cup, beating the Wolves 2-1 with a couple of Spikesley goals. Once more United had some catching up to do.

4: 'Where is There a Better Goalkeeper?'

Where is there a better goalkeeper than William Foulke? Sheffielders... hope to see him selected to play for England against Scotland. He is good enough.

Athletic News (8/3/97)

Foulke covered himself with glory — splinters and network, by swinging on the crossbar and bringing it down with a crash.

Sheffield Independent (15/2/97)

One of the recurring conundrums of those years was why Foulke received just the one England cap.

In the ten seasons during which William was playing well at a consistently high League and cup level, the England team took part in thirty full international matches. All of them were against Scotland, Wales and Ireland. The list of goalkeepers selected for those games makes interesting reading:

Player	Years	Club(s)	No. of Caps
Jack Robinson	1897–1901	Derby County/Southampton	11
Tom Baddeley	1903–04	Wolverhampton Wanderers	5
John Sutcliffe	1895–1903	Bolton Wanderers	4
George Raikes	1895–96	Corinthians	4
Billy George	1902	Aston Villa	3
William Foulke	1897	Sheffield United	1
Jack Hillman	1899	Burnley	1
Matt Kingsley	1901	Newcastle United	1

Ernest Needham, writing a series of articles in the sports publication the 'Green 'Un' in 1913, named the three best goalkeepers he had ever seen as Foulke, Robinson and Sutcliffe. When pressed, he declared that at his best, Willie Foulke had the edge over the other two. Unfortunately the selectors didn't fully share his enthusiasm.

Foulke's one cap was against Wales, at Bramall Lane, in March 1897. England won 4–0, in a very one-sided game. Needham scored one, Bloomer another and Everton's burly winger Alf Milward notched a brace. But William had too easy a time of it, with scant opportunity to impress with his usual range of goalkeeping skills. For the next international, against Scotland five days later, Jack Robinson, then of Derby County (and soon to be in Southampton's star-studded line-up), was preferred. England lost 1-2.

This is not to deny Robinson's undoubted prowess. He was a nippy and agile 'keeper, popular with the crowds because of his courageous, flamboyant style. Strangely, writing late in his career about the skills involved in keeping goal, he stated: 'It is in extravagance that the danger lies.' Another piece of advice: 'Never on any account use your feet if it is possible to use your hands.' We immediately think of Foulke and his eccentricities: his fast and foolhardy excursions from goal, his booting of loose balls clear beyond the halfway line when he had a mind to.

Perhaps there is a clue here as to why Robinson was selected more often when William was at his best, anchoring what was arguably the strongest club in England. Perhaps it was to do with personalities, and whether the face fit? A comment in a local newspaper, six weeks before the Wales game, seems to strike the chord:

> It is a pity that Foulke cannot curb the habit of pulling down the crossbar, which on Saturday ended in his breaking it in two. On form, he is well in the running for international honours, but the Selection Committee are sure to prefer a man who plays the game to one who unnecessarily violates the spirit of the rules.
> *Sheffield Daily Telegraph* (15/2/97)

The *Athletic News* had made much the same point, but with notably less finger-wagging:

> The Sheffield custodian is a good'un for his inches – and he measures quite a few – but his eccentricities at times are, I should imagine, scarcely appreciated by his backs. He can bring off what to all appearances is an impossible save, and at other times, when discovered in the proprietorship of two minds, uses the wrong one. However, his goal average speaks for itself, and they tell me he has been a very important man with the team so far this season.
> (2/11/96)

In any case, running out of the penalty area to kick clear – acting as an extra back, in other words – was good enough for the great Gyula Grosics, last line of defence of that all-conquering Hungarian side of the fifties. And not even Foulke would have been guilty of rugby-tackling an opponent in the other half of the field, like the oddball Peruvian goalie Quiroga in the 1978 World Cup. What were we saying about goalkeepers and their marbles?

To return: Robinson was four years older than William, with the necessary experience. Maturity was chosen over enormous promise. Incidentally, the phrase 'before you could say Jack Robinson' didn't originate with this fellow, but so famous was his speed off the mark that the saying was granted a new lease of life during his career. But as the *Athletic News* pointed out, there's no arguing with hard figures. In two seasons (1896-8) Foulke let in just 60 League goals. In comparison, in the same two seasons 1897 double-winners Villa conceded 89 and Derby County, Jack Robinson and all, leaked 111.

On the home front, William had met and wooed former classmate Beatrice Duff, who lived at the far end of the Sheffield street on which he lodged during the week. Marcus Street used to stretch for over a quarter of a mile from east to west in an elongated 'Z' shape between Brunswick Road and Rock Street. William's house (actually owned by Beatrice's brother James William Eyre Duff) was one of the old terraced dwellings on top of the steep hill over the railway line and the river, at the end closest to the steelworks surrounding Victoria Station. Beatrice lived with her mother at the shops end, near to Rock Street. Her father Robert, a goods guard, had recently died.

William and Beatrice were married on 22 June 1896, at Holy Trinity church on Nursery Street, overlooking the river Don. Beatrice, tiny in comparison to the six-foot-plus groom, was to be a rock of stability in the relationship. William, possibly recognising his own tendency to waywardness in less crucial matters, had made a good choice of partner. Beatrice was a strong personality and had the social ambition and the organisational skills that were to see the family progress to a more select area, and thence to a successful shopkeeping venture that would provide the wherewithal during William's retirement from football.

William and Beatrice's marriage certificate. (By permission of General Records Office/HMSO)

Their first child, John Robert, was born in Blackwell in March 1897, just two days before Foulke's international appearance.

Back in the world of football, it was in the League that the Blades shone. In those two seasons the FA Cup had brought little cheer. It was Blackburn Rovers who cut short the 1897 run, in a bruising confrontation at Ewood Park. United were without Needham, Cain and Ross, and Rovers forward Nichol laid out Foulke for five minutes by jumping up and kneeing him in the stomach.

The following year it was perhaps overconfidence that led to the astonishing reversal at the hands of lowly Burslem Port Vale from the Midland League. It was only a late, late penalty that kept United in contention at Bramall Lane. In the replay, in a gale-force wind (so strong that one of Foulke's goal kicks was blown back out for a corner!) the Blades were losing 0–1 with ten minutes left. Desperate times called for desperate measures: Needham ordered everybody into the Port Vale half, Willie included. Foulke had a header saved, and then Thickett toe-poked a late equaliser. In extra time Vale broke the siege and, having the run of the opponents' half, scored another. The final score was 2–1 to the Midlands side.

So United had something to learn in the realm of the FA Cup. Now that the forward line was beginning to settle, though, and a consistent defensive line-up anchored by the ever-dependable Foulke was stamping its authority on match after match, the League Championship was becoming a real possibility.

In 1896/97 they were runners-up behind the double-winning Villa. Foulke had conceded just 29 goals throughout the campaign – easily the best defensive record in the League. That season they had drawn twice with the Villa. In the last minute of the goalless draw at Bramall Lane, William had created quite a stir by bouncing the ball as far as the halfway line – as the rules of the time allowed. But the final whistle blew before matters could become more interesting.

The scene was set for the thrilling 1897/98 campaign. The Blades started at a gallop, unbeaten until mid-December. After the home draw (1–1) with Nottingham Forest the top of the table read:

	P	W	D	L	F	A	Pts
Sheffield United	14	8	6	0	32	17	22
Aston Villa	15	9	2	4	37	29	20
Bolton Wanderers	14	8	1	5	17	16	17
Wolverhampton Wanderers	15	7	3	5	27	19	17

Then United lost 1–2 at Stoke. Paradoxically, it was a game in which Foulke played exceptionally well, so that at the end both sets of supporters rose to give him a tumultuous cheer of appreciation. There followed a home draw with

Wednesday (1-1, William beaten by another Spikesley special) and a home defeat at the hands of Liverpool, with their fast orthodox wingers who utterly baffled the United backs. Thickett, in an attempt to clear, put through his own net. Villa gained the lead in the Championship race.

Then, in successive weeks in January, there were the two top-of-the-table clashes. Both sides treated the games as cup finals. Sheffield United spent the week before both of them in special training at Chesterfield House, Matlock Bath, while the Villans partook of the supposedly 'magic cure' of the brine baths at Droitwich!

In the first game at Bramall Lane a single Walter Bennett goal – a dazzling individual effort – separated the teams. Foulke and the backs, in outstanding form, repulsed all opposition attacks. The Villa forwards, over-elaborating on the heavy pitch, played into the defence's hands. 'Foulke stood firm as a rock,' said the *Athletic News*.

The return game was at The Lower Meadows, Aston (the modern Villa Park) where the home side had never tasted defeat since returning there the previous year. It was a match to savour, a thrilling, end-to-end clash in front of 43,000 spectators, in which William, sporting a new haircut, made some spectacular saves from the rampant home forwards. There were no goals in the first half, then Wheldon hit a penalty past Foulke on fifty minutes. Villa now swarmed forward, scenting victory. But the Blades 'keeper wasn't to be beaten again:

> … bringing off a sensational save as the ball appeared to be going from him into
> the corner of the net.
> *Sheffield Daily Telegraph* (17/1/98)

It was the perfect launch pad for United's counterattacks: new forward Cunningham bagged two late goals to ensure a stirring victory. It had been a no-holds-barred, often violent encounter. Towards the end Needham was seen to 'pause… to pick the skin of his knees, where it hung in shreds'. (Match programme 29/1/98).

The Villa's challenge was now seen to be broken. The most dangerous threat, however, was now looming from an unexpected direction: Sunderland, languishing mid-table until Christmas, had put together a recent formidable string of wins, and by February were pushing for the leadership. United had to play them twice within a month.

The first repercussion from those crucial battles with Sunderland was the Rab Howell affair. This was during the first game, on 5 March 1898. United were without Morren, in Belfast with the England team (where he scored in a 3-2 win).

A constant trickle of hysteria accompanied this game. The official gate was 23,500, but an estimated 30,000 crammed into the ground. Corner flags disappeared into the encroaching throng, and at times spectators wandered onto the pitch, even passing in front of Foulke, according to one report. The game was stopped no fewer than four times by the referee until order was restored.

And then there were Howell's two own-goals.

Sunderland winger Morgan sent in a hopeful cross from somewhere near the corner flag. Foulke strode forward to collect and the danger seemed minimal. Then Howell intercepted, slipped in doing so, and sent the ball skewing into the net. Cunningham equalised before half-time. After the interval the Wearsiders regained the lead with an unstoppable swerving shot. Then Howell, racing back in an attempt to forestall a Sunderland forward, merely helped the ball past a mesmerised Foulke for the final goal. So the vital game ended Sunderland 3, United 1.

William was incensed, convinced that a player of Howell's skill and experience couldn't have blundered so dreadfully twice in the same match. There were whispers of backhanders from the home side. Foulke, never one to content himself with whispers, was more outspoken. Whatever the truth, Howell was clearly upset and couldn't settle to his game after that. He played one poor match – the 0-2 defeat v. WBA – and was then transferred to Liverpool for £150 within the month. 'Rab' Howell, the gypsy who lived in a caravan up Wincobank way, hitched a horse to the vehicle and trotted over the Pennines to his new home.

After the WBA defeat the Championship front-runners were:

	P	W	D	L	F	A	Pts
Sheffield United	27	14	8	5	52	30	36
Sunderland	26	15	5	6	39	26	35

The following Saturday, 2 April, saw the return game with the Wearsiders at Bramall Lane.

The Blades released Needham for the England match, against Scotland in Glasgow on the same day. Sunderland, however, hell-bent on winning the League, refused to release their Scottish internationals Doig and Wilson. They also refused to agree to a change of date, despite this being 'recommended' by the Football League.

The match attracted a crowd of some 25,000, with receipts amounting to over £540. It was described as 'a brilliant attack versus a brilliant defence.' Foulke had little to do as the rampant Blades forwards peppered Doig with shots. The Scottish goalkeeper was in equally outstanding form, stopping everything until just thirteen minutes from time. Right half Johnson, a local lad fresh out of the reserves, redirected a corner out of Doig's reach. It was the all-important goal. The result, given Sunderland's stubborn ploys, was seen by some as (to borrow Percy M. Young's phrase) 'a judgment by some high, impartial and supernatural authority'. Perhaps St Barnabas, patron saint of protection against hailstorms, was looking benignly down the hill at his parishioners.

Dovetailing the Sunderland tussles were the two games in contention for the Sheriff of London Charity Shield, otherwise known as the Dewar Trophy. This was a barn door of a shield, six feet by three (so almost as big as Bill Foulke!) played for by the pick of the professionals against the amateur cream. In spring 1898, this meant the Blades *v.* the Corinthians, who had eight present or future England internationals on their team.

The first meeting, 'a grand exposition of the game', took place at Crystal Palace, and was a victory for the defences: 0-0. Only G.O. Smith gave William anything like an anxious moment or two, but the smart shots from that doyen of Oxford strikers were dealt with comfortably enough. The teams were: *Corinthians:* Campbell; Fry, Oakley; Middleditch, Wreford-Brown, Ingram; Gosling, Stanbrough, Smith, Burnup, Alexander. *Sheffield United:* Foulke; Thickett, Cain; Johnson, Morren, Needham; Bennett, McKay, Gaudie, Cunningham, Priest.

The replay took place, again at the Palace, on the Monday following the second Sunderland match. Again honours were even, each team scoring once. The Corinthian goal, however, was from a twice-taken free-kick of dubious validity. Almost constant United pressure meant Foulke was metaphorically twiddling his thumbs for most of the match. Players on both sides wanted to play extra time, but the Sheffield Directors, mindful of the tough run-in for the League title, intervened and opted not to. The Dewar Trophy was thus shared, or, in C.B. Fry's inimitable phraseology: 'The honour of the Shield was bisected.'

During the after-match celebrations the amateurs got to hear about Sunderland's 'win-at-all-costs' attitude, and immediately G.O. Smith and C. Wreford-Brown offered their services to the Blades 'should they be needed.'

Let's freeze the frame for a moment or two. With Corinthians Gilbert Oswald Smith and Charles Wreford-Brown we are in the presence of amateur greatness.

Smith played in the same England teams as Needham, Bloomer and Goodall, collecting 20 caps and netting 12 goals. Wreford-Brown, with just the 4 England appearances, played cricket for Gloucestershire. He is the one who is credited with the invention of the word 'soccer'. Apparently the historic exchange in an Oxford college hall one morning in around 1888 went something like: 'Coming for a game of rugger after brekker, Charles?' 'No thanks old chap, I'm going to play soccer.' The coinage, of course, was a contraction of 'Association'. The offer of help was never taken up, but the fact that it was made at all tells us much about the stage English football had reached and Sheffield United's signal role within it.

We have already seen the class-based dichotomy within the game. It's significant that in this particular case we see evidence of an enormous mutual respect in football terms, that was strong enough to bridge such an ingrained social division.

The next hurdle was the penultimate League match, away to Bolton Wanderers. On the same day Sunderland were away to Bury. Bolton could do nothing against the solid Blades defence (with Foulke at his imperturbable best), and it was left to Needham, playing on the left wing, to hit the game's only goal. The news came from Bury: Sunderland had lost by the same score, so the Championship was Sheffield United's.

Nobody was in any doubt about the indispensable role played in the success story by the Blades' custodian.

We'll allow the last word of this chapter to Corinthian C.B. Fry, not usually renowned for dishing out compliments to professionals:

'Foulke is no small part of a mountain. You cannot bundle him through ball and all; you cannot surprise or humbug him. He has a touch of genius, and in spite of a suspicion of eagerness makes a last defence that is almost impregnable.'

Praise indeed!

5: Per Ardua

*But Benbow did some foolish things. What in the world did he want
to charge Foulke for? Talk about Don Quixote tilting at a windmill,
why, it was like a fly trying to knock an elephant over.*

Athletic News (27/2/99)
(FA Cup quarter-final at Nottingham Forest)

*Bloomer went through towards the Sheffield goal several times – only
to find out the impregnability of Foulke.*

Football in Sheffield
(FA Cup Final 1899)

The following season of 1898/99 possibly outdid even the Championship-winning campaign for heart-stopping drama and heroic struggles against the odds.

Foulke ran a gauntlet of tribulations. According to a snippet in a United
match programme, for a short while at one or two north country grounds it
was considered the done thing – at least, by a lunatic minority – to welcome the
Sheffield 'keeper to his station between the sticks with a hail of 'oranges, pipe
stems, together with the bowls, and other devotional acts of unkindness.' Then
there was the scuffle with Hannigan at Notts County, which resulted in several
home supporters jumping over the perimeter ropes to try and mix it. William
was escorted from the pitch at half and full time. There were the injuries: a minor
one to his hand in September, and a more serious leg sprain – which saw him
carried off the field – perilously close to the cup match with Liverpool. There
was the seismic clash with Allan (see below).

After a promising start, the Blades went into free fall in the League. About the
only palliative in this area was the fact that Wednesday were doing even worse.
They were to finish bottom of the pile, and thus relegated, with United narrowly
escaping the same fate.

On the plus side, there was the FA Cup run. There was a new maturity to
the Blades' approach to cup matches, which paralleled Foulke's development
as a 'keeper. The following September the match programme for the League
game with Derby County contained the following gently satirical piece of
strategic analysis:

The goalkeeper in a team is an immensely important personage. In a negative sense he, being good in his office, wins his side's matches to the extent that he prevents the other fellows' beating his own. Some men there are who seek to do more than this, and bid for victory in a positive sense by going forward – joining the attack. If you desire ampler information as to this departure from conventionality, apply to Burslem Port Vale, and William Foulke. I would make a friendly addendum: – write or telephone to my Sheffield United chum; don't ask him face to face, because he's a muckle mannie, awfu' strong in head and arm; and vaguest reference to his forward 'turn' in a certain historic cup-tie gives elevation to his choler. He has been proselytised, and no longer expounds or practises such behaviour. (16/9/99)

And for Bill Foulke that year, there was an unforgettable moment of supreme goalkeeping skill.

Thanks to television, there are a few more recent saves that glow in the memory with all the glamour of a top-class strike. Some clips from the album: Stepney's courageous block of Eusebio's cannonball in the 1968 European Cup final; Bonetti's full-length dive to fingertip Allan Clarke's exquisitely struck penalty round the post; David James' gravity-defying backward-stretching acrobatics that tipped over Nihat's wickedly placed header (England–Turkey 2003). And the daddy of them all, THAT stop by Banks in the 1970 World Cup. There was Pelé's phenomenal leap, heading his air-to-ground missile that bulleted towards the far corner of the goal. Unstoppable, surely: then Banks suddenly materialising, flinging himself down to whip the bullet impossibly over the bar.

Well, William made a comparable save, regarded by many contemporaries as the jewel in the crown of a lustrous career. It was in the FA Cup (of course), with the Blades under siege in a ferociously fought match. What a pity no camera recorded the feat. Imagination will have to do – and that's perhaps not a completely bad thing. Let's set the scene.

Few teams have had a rockier ride to the final than the Blades that year. They were drawn away to First Division opposition in every round. A swarm of misfortune seemed to follow them around from tie to tie. Injuries accumulated to such a degree that by March the *Telegraph* referred to the 'United cripples'. Inside left Becton was suspended by the club for his part in a pub brawl. Luckily his replacement Almond was well up to the job, scoring in the final.

The first round was at Burnley. The Sheffielders kept their feet better on the frozen pitch, and in a rough game managed a 2-2 draw. The replay was more one-sided than the 2-1 scoreline suggests. Boyle handled the ball within the eighteen-yard line, and Burnley scored from the penalty. After that it was reckoned that Foulke touched the ball about four times, and the Blades progressed without too much trouble. Peter Boyle, later an Irish international, was the departed Bob Cain's replacement at left-back. A hard and uncompromising tackler, he had made his debut the previous December.

Preston North End were next, again away. Again it finished 2-2, but with William giving a surprisingly jittery performance in goal. Both Preston scores looked saveable: the first from a free-kick which Brown touched in while the Blades 'keeper made an ineffectual challenge; the second from an optimistic shot from the wing which appeared to 'glide over Foulke's arm', according to one observer.

Back at Bramall Lane it was the Preston goalie McBride who was to receive the accolades (and generous applause from the home fans). William continued to live dangerously: at one point it took a goal-line clearance from Boyle to save the day. But United were worth their eventual win. Needham's second-half penalty made the final score 2-1.

And so to the quarter-finals, against Nottingham Forest, Cup holders and most pundits' choice to repeat the feat.

Fate had more mischief up its sleeve. United's kit was somehow left behind on the platform at Victoria Station, Sheffield. Frantic telegrams ensured that it arrived at the City Ground a few minutes before kick-off.

The Blades held out against a fierce and almost continuous Forest attack throughout the first half. Foulke was equal to everything flung at him. Then, on the stroke of half-time, Almond injured his ankle, and United had to play the whole of the second half with ten men. The home side threw men forward, sensing that it was 'now or never'. Needham, however, covering extra ground, managed to hold things together, and William was keeping goal safely. Then, with some ten minutes left, Forest forced an opening. Capes let fly with a shot that hurtled for the top corner, with the United goalkeeper earthbound. Surely, at last, this was the winner.

For that vital second or two, Foulke switched over to the superhuman. With astonishing speed of thought and action he flung his nigh on twenty stone across the goal, into the air, and tipped the rocket round the post. It was a save, said the *Telegraph* 'worthy of the greatest goalkeeper in the world.' When he fell to earth, he caused not a few teammates and supporters to feel concern for his welfare as he hit the ground. Not to worry: he stood, shook himself and got on with the game. Centre forward George Hedley, who had sprinted fully sixty yards to congratulate him, joined the defence in clearing the corner.

Forest's spirit was broken now. The job was completed on eighty-six minutes when inside right Billy Beers, a youngster from the Staveley stable, skinned his full-back and swung in a gem of a cross which Priest whacked into the net. United, not until now renowned as cup fighters, had done the impossible – or at least, the highly improbable – beating the holders and favourites on their own ground.

The draw for the semi was up to the season's standard of unkindness, pairing the Blades with the powerful Liverpool side, who had already beaten them twice in the League.

One of the subplots of that titanic semi-final series was the running battle between William and George Allan, the Liverpool inside right. Allan, a high-scoring, combative Glaswegian and Scottish international, was the latest in the succession of forwards who had openly opted for the (usually unrewarding) tactic of the intimidation of Foulke. There was little of the subtlety of a Bloomer or a Meredith in this bull-at-a-gate approach, and it was usually no problem to one who had been a student at the Blackwell Colliery soccer school of hard knocks.

In the League game the previous October, however, there had occurred one of those incidents that has taken on legendary status over the years. It was at Anfield, and the Blades were winning 1-0 from a well-taken Bennett goal. In the second half Liverpool pressed, Foulke collected, and Allan ran at Foulke. What happened next probably took no more than a couple of seconds, and the *Liverpool Daily Post*'s description was unequivocal:

> Allan charged Foulke in the goalmouth, and the big man, losing his temper, seized him by the leg and turned him upside down.
> (29/10/98)

The *Manchester Guardian* paints much the same picture, albeit slightly less damning:

> McCowie shot in from the left, Foulke caught the ball with one hand, and as Allan dashed up, Foulke used his other hand to collar Allan's leg and upset him.
> (31/10/98)

And the *Athletic News*: '…he got hold of Allan by one of his legs, and laid him on the grass.' (31/10/98)

From the resultant penalty McCowie scored; then a late own-goal gave Liverpool the points.

Almost before the crowd had dispersed at the end of the game the tale was growing in the telling. One version depicted the incident as the culmination of a fiery vendetta between the two players, with William catching Allan by the midriff, turning him over, and planting his head in the mud, giving him such a shock that he never played again. William himself describes the collision somewhat differently:

In reality, Allan and I were quite good friends off the field. On it we were opponents, of course, and there's no doubt he was ready to give chaff for chaff with me. What actually happened on the occasion referred to was that Allan (a big strong chap, mind you) once bore down on me with all his weight when I was saving. I bent forward to protect myself, and Allan, striking my shoulder, flew right over me and fell heavily. He had quite a shaking up, I admit.

London Evening News (1913)

It must be said that this has the ring of truth to it. But whichever version you prefer, all of these tales of rough-and-tumble added to the enormous interest in the 1899 semi-final, which turned out to be a run of four classic confrontations that had everything from high drama and suspense to low farce.

For Act One it was back to the City Ground at Nottingham.

The respective styles of the two teams ran like a theme almost throughout the series: Liverpool's finesse and classy cohesion (relying on the typical interplay of their international Scottish contingent), and the verve and pluck of the Blades. Foulke was equal to Allan's rushes, but a couple of errors from his unusually nervy full-backs gave Liverpool a 2-1 lead which they kept until well into the second half. In one heart-stopping incident Foulke sprinted off his line, racing Allan for the ball, and managed to boot clear before the forward could take possession. Then a bold Needham run up the left wing set up Hedley, who netted the late equaliser.

Act Two, the replay the following Thursday at Burnden Park, Bolton, was the epitome of a blood-and-thunder cup tie, the football equivalent of a bout of all-in wrestling. The Merseysiders were leading 1-0 at half-time, thanks to a controversial goal from Walker: the inside right stabbed in a shot between Foulke's legs, despite there being more than a suspicion of obstruction by Allan on Needham. When Allan himself scored with a free-kick that sneaked inside the post, United's cause seemed lost. But then Billy Beers reduced the margin less than two minutes later, also from a free-kick. Bennett equalised for the Blades midway through the half. Game on; but Allan was far from a spent force. With ten minutes left he cracked in a wicked shot which Foulke parried – only for Boyle, unable to deal with the speed of the manoeuvre, to help the rebound agonisingly into his own goal. Then more excruciating bad luck, as Liverpool were awarded a penalty. Allan struck it well, but Foulke dived and pushed it away... as far as right-winger Cox, who swept the loose ball into the net.

Four-two down with eight minutes left. It was time for the Needham speciality in such apparently hopeless circumstances: the Charge of the Blades Brigade. The last time this had been tried in a cup tie, the previous year against

PortVale in a gale-force wind, all eleven players had been ordered into attack, and, it will be remembered, the Vale stole the winner through a breakaway, attacking an empty net. This time Foulke and Boyle were left behind to stand guard, while the remaining nine players invaded the Liverpool area.

Orchestrated by Needham, the attacking was relentless. Bill Foulke would have thrived in such a blitzkrieg, but the Merseyside goalie Storer's game suffered a breakdown. Blades left-winger Priest scored one, as the Liverpool 'keeper appeared transfixed with fear. A minute or so later the same player struck again, and the game ended with the Merseysiders defending feverishly. So, in that most astonishing of matches, the Blades had once again forced a replay.

Act Three was the farcical interlude, complete with Keystone Cops. It took place on the Monday after the Burnden Park game.

Fallowfield, Manchester, already had a reputation for the odd fiasco. The most famous was the Everton *v.* Wolverhampton Wanderers FA Cup final of six years before. An unexpectedly large crowd of over 40,000 broke through the flimsy perimeter wire and overflowed onto the pitch. For a while it was even uncertain whether the result (1-0 to Wolves) would stand, so unruly had the circumstances been.

Alas! the authorities hadn't learned from the experience. A crowd of 30,000, again breaking through the inadequate wire barriers, delayed the kick-off until four o'clock. When the match finally got under way Foulke and Allan had their usual altercations, the Scot on one occasion being 'laid out for a short time'. Liverpool scored – through Allan – then after half an hour another pitch invasion caused the referee to halt proceedings and take the players off.

The contribution of the local police left a lot to be desired, both as regards numbers deployed, and the adequacy of their briefing. A crowd of such magnitude had simply not been foreseen. The Athletic News reported that the police were 'mere animated specimens of a violation of space'. Another account compared them, in terms of mobility and sensitivity to circumstance, to the monoliths of Stonehenge. The teams took the field again at gone half past five. They went through the motions for another fifteen minutes, but with the crowd pressing yet again, it was clear that no meaningful result was to be reached that day. The referee abandoned the game. A meagre posse of desolate characters remained behind to howl abuse at Foulke, but generally, considering the obvious disappointment, the crowd drifted away without too many incidents.

Act Four, on the day before Good Friday, brought a welcome conclusion to the epic. It was on Derby's Baseball Ground, another 'battle brimful of incident'. William's performance received praise from the *Athletic News*:

I never saw Foulke to more advantage than on Thursday. His kicking from goal
was as mighty as ever, and his good right hand, doubled up, banged out incom-
ing shots with the force of a sledgehammer.
(3/4/99)

A dangerous run and shot from George Allan was dealt with unflappably.
William's cool self-assurance communicated itself to the rest of the team: with
three minutes left Priest burst through, and sent a shot flying into a defensive melee. A full-back kicked clear, but Beers followed up and managed to
squeeze the ball past Storer.

The George Allan story was to have a tragically premature ending: just six
months later he would die of tuberculosis, aged twenty-six.

In the other semi, Derby County had made short work of Stoke 3-1, with
Bloomer sending out a warning note by bagging a hat-trick. Indeed 'Paleface'
was at his most fearsome at about that time. He had equalled his own club
record of 24 League goals in the season, had already hit six in Derby's fairly smooth ride to the final, and had scored four in that year's international
matches. He had scored in the previous year's final, and the general opinion
around Derbyshire (and among most neutrals) was that this year he, and his
team, would go one better and win the thing.

United spent the week before the final at Skegness, in that footballers'
favourite hotel, the Sea View.

Preparation had been supervised once again by Tom Bott, who had taken up
the role of team manager earlier that year. Bott was a Sheffield fishmonger, a man
of great good humour and generosity who, incongruously, sported the waxed
and tapering mustachios of a villain in a silent film. George Waller's training (early
morning walks, six-a-side games, and the odd invigorating dip into the briny) had
been supplemented by Bott's entertainments. One of these was a 100-yards challenge race between Bill Foulke and assistant trainer Jack Houseley. Since everybody
apart from Mr Bott and William thought that the proudly fit trainer would have an
easy win, Tom proposed a wager: if Mr Houseley won, Tom would pay for all the
team's outing to the music hall; if the big fellow won, the team would foot the bill.

To general surprise, Foulke thundered down the track and left Houseley for
dead. The genial team manager still paid for the music hall outing!

The Blades party arrived in London on the eve of the big day, and stayed
in the Court Royal Hotel in Upper Norwood, about a mile from the Crystal
Palace ground.

Sheffield Tory MP Sir Howard Vincent took it upon himself to give the
United team a guided tour of the House of Commons. The usual boisterous

good humour, to a large extent generated by Willie, set the tone for the visit. As Vincent left his horse in the care of his groom, William asked if he had any objection to getting on the horse's back. 'Not the least objection,' replied the dignitary, 'but I think the horse would have.' At the end of the tour, as Sir Howard was shaking the players' hands, William was heard to declare in a loud voice that, whoever that fellow was, they'd be a mean lot if they didn't buy him a drink!

As for the 1899 cup final itself, if ever there was a game of two halves, this was it. And once again Foulke played a major role in the result. The teams were: *Derby County:* Fryer; Methven, Staley; Cox, Paterson, May; Arkesden, Bloomer, Boag, McDonald, Allen. *Sheffield United:* Foulke; Thickett, Boyle; Johnson, Morren, Needham; Bennett, Beers, Hedley, Almond, Priest.

Derby had the better of the early exchanges. On several occasions Bloomer shrugged off the policing of Needham and dribbled through to test Foulke. The sharp inter-passing between Allen and MacDonald on the opposite wing was giving United problems too. After twelve minutes Derby County forced three corners in succession. The third concluded with the ball arriving neatly at Boag's feet, and the centre forward 'rushed the ball through'.

So the score remained until half-time. The Blades' attack got no change out of the fiercely resolute Derby defence. It was left to Foulke's immense clearance punches and kicks to shift the focus of the game upfield.

The second half began with Bloomer determined to stamp his mark on this final. With Needham pushing to join the attack, the 'Destroying Angel', clearly faster than both United backs, was allowed a couple of worrying runs at goal. The first ended with him putting his shot wide, as Foulke advanced. The second, a seemingly easy pot from six yards, was kicked hard and low into the corner. William dived and saved. The moment was easily identifiable as a turning point in the game. Another occurred on the hour. Needham sent in a searching, curling centre and Fryer came off his line to intercept. But Bennett's head got there first and the ball looped into the unguarded net.

Foulke had held the fort; now the rejuvenated Blades switched to attack. Five minutes later Beers set off on a mazy dribble that took him into a useful position in front of the Derby goal. His shot was skilfully parried by Fryer, but he followed up and netted anyway.

Now that the famed Sheffield half-back line was freed from the shackles of defending, there was only one way the game could go. Four minutes after Beers' goal there was a 'sharp tussle in front of Fryer' and Almond popped up to make it 3–1. Priest made it four with a minute left.

*Team portraits and cigarette card from 1899 FA Cup Final. (*Athletic News*)*

There was an impressive array of establishment bigwigs present at the match: Lords Kinnaird and Rosebery, Mr Cecil Rhodes, and assorted Lord Mayors, MPs, and a Knight of the Realm. Prime Minister elect A.J. Balfour presented the Cup.

The intelligentsia had pooh-poohed the immense popularity of association football, referring to the 'decadence' of this fairly new sport, as it was so obviously rooted in commercialism. The 1899 final, however, opened a few eyes. *The Times* reworked the cliché of Waterloo being won on the playing fields of Eton, stating that for the rank and file too 'games are pre-eminently schools of discipline.' It was unconsciously the wrong conclusion to come to (and perhaps unavoidably, it reeks of the patronising) as, with hindsight, we can detect in these comments the looming shade of the First World War. But at least the skills on display at Crystal Palace that day persuaded that professional football could be a spectacle every bit as complex and thrilling as the more established sports.

Bill Foulke, not renowned for his political awareness, still had the courage of his convictions. When asked by the left-wing *Sheffield Independent* reporter what was his opinion of Mr Balfour, the goalkeeper's succinct reply was that he 'didn't think much of him.' The reporter concluded that the Tory 'was not the leviathan's ideal of a leader of the House of Commons'.

Early that summer William, his wife Beatrice, and two-year-old son Robert moved from Blackwell into 8 Belgrave Square, Sheffield. The house was in a quiet cul-de-sac five minutes' walk from the United ground.

Foulke's portrait, 1899. (Athletic News)

6: Twenty Stones Between the Sticks

*This majestic man gave a rare display of keeping and kicking, one of his lat-
ter efforts on the wings of the wind being carried from goal line to goal line.*

Glasgow Herald (30/4/00)

*Taylor and Settle [Everton forwards] were endeavouring to paint a living
picture of The Stag At Bay, one on his shoulders and the other hanging on
somewhere else. The worriers, however, might just as well have been tackling
a stone wall.*

Athletic News (7/10/01)

1900. A good enough point at which to take stock. A new century begins,
and Foulke has already reached the halfway mark in his career. Thoughts of
it ever finishing are naturally a million miles away. He now weighs twenty
stones, but is as nimble and strong as ever. He has an FA Cup winners' medal
to go with his international cap and League Championship medal. He will
play cricket for Derbyshire within the year. At Bramall Lane, only Needham's
wage packet can compare with his. He receives a (for then) top-range salary
of £4 a week.

He is married to Beatrice, a Sheffield-born girl of the same age. They have
one healthy son, John Robert, with another, William Redvers, on the way.
The family has moved to 8 Belgrave Square, a large three-storey terraced
house situated in one of the more well-to-do areas of turn-of-the-century
Sheffield, and within walking distance of the ground. The house is one of the
newer ones (built 1888) with gas lighting. They start to receive paying lodgers;
Beatrice sees to the necessary paperwork and logistics.

NAME		MARITAL STATUS, AGE		PROFESSION OR OCCUPATION	WHERE BORN
William Foulkes	Head	M	26	professional footballer (Sheffield United)	Drawley Bank Salop
Beatrice Do	Wife	M	26		Yorks Sheffield
Robert Do	Son		4		Derbys Blackwell
Redvers Do	Son		1		Yorks - Sheffield
Louisa Matthews	niece		13		Derbys Morton
Nellie Lambert	Boarder		24		Scotland

Extract from 1901 Census: 8 Belgrave Square, Sheffield. (Courtesy of the National Archives)

The family has added affluence to the sporting success story. William becomes quite the dandy, liking to be seen around town in his bowler hat, and smart suit and waistcoat with gold watch chain.

Sheffield is a booming turn-of-the-century industrial city whose population has nearly tripled over the past fifty years. The electric tramlines reach out into the suburbs, and new-fangled cinemas have started to offer alternative entertainment to the music hall. The 'horseless carriage' has begun to make its appearance.

Sheffield steel is in demand throughout the world. The names of the steelworks shout confidence: 'Vulcan', 'Etna', 'Cyclops', 'Atlas'. It's a fitting stage for a sporting titan.

Let's gather a few anecdotes.

Of Willie's humour: the inevitable modern-day comparison is with Paul Gascoigne. How Foulke would have rejoiced, for example, at Gazza's hijacking a London bus with a bemused Gary Lineker along for the ride; or the delicious moment when he picked up the yellow card dropped by the ref, and – too good to miss, this one – 'booked' the official. The referee returned the compliment, but for real.

Willie's clowning was a positive force in the Blades' success story. As he was to say in the 1913 interview with the *London Evening News*: 'Ask the old team, the boys who won the League Championship once and the Cup twice, if a bit of 'Little Willie's' foolery didn't chirp 'em up before a tough match.' And as Ernest Needham was to acknowledge in the same year, gratefully recalling such foolery: 'A merry heart goes a long way on a football field.'

It was a mixture of genuine mischievous wit, some painful puns, a dash of what would nowadays be deemed political incorrectness, and, it must be admitted, the occasional spasm of what appears to have been downright rudeness.

There was the time when he turned up for training with Irish international full-back Peter Boyle draped across his shoulders. William didn't always take too readily to training sessions, but this time he appeared to have an excuse: 'I can't train today,' he said to George Waller, 'I've got a painful Boyle on me back.'

The *Athletic News* tells the tale of William tucking into a snack of bread and cheese in a railway carriage. A curate gets in, and rather self-consciously observes: 'I see you are an epicure.'

Foulke, stunned by the word, regained his speech and answered: 'Oh am I? Then you're a —.' The final word was more unparliamentary than that which George Bernard Shaw employed once in *Pygmalion*.
Athletic News (8/5/16)

Another of his one-liners:

'Ah, William, have you seen your colleagues?'
'Don't be daft, tha knows I've nivver been to colleege.'

All right, not exactly Cambridge Footlights material, but this was in an era when the atrocious pun was in vogue, and when the most side-splitting exchange on offer was the following:

'Do you like Kipling, my dear?'
'I don't know, you naughty boy. I've never kippled.'

After an away victory, he would tend to doze on the return journey. After a defeat, there were no holds barred in his desire to work off his own depression and cheer up his despondent teammates. Again the railway is the scene: Willie was known to make his way along the train to the coal tender, black up his face and 'play the minstrel'. Untenably dicey ground these days, of course, but at the time his performance was apparently droll enough to counteract the pain of defeat.

Walter Bennett was sometimes the unwitting half of a double act. The stocky winger was best of mates with William (they once truanted from training together for a day at Doncaster races) and indeed it was after a successful Bennett session at these races that he was the butt of a practical joke. He turned up to training on this particular day with £25 winnings in his pocket. Foulke took £15 and hid it, intending to return it after his friend had been suitably wound up. Bennett, however, possibly not wishing to lose face, didn't even mention the money's disappearance. A couple of weeks later, just before a tough match with Manchester City, William confided in his friend that he knew of a supporter who would give him £15 if he were to score at least two goals that day. Bennett notched a hat-trick, Foulke duly handed over the cash – and only then revealed its source!

It's an appropriate time to have a look at another of the famous legends surrounding our man. David Pickering, subscribing to the view that the incident in question took place while Foulke was at Chelsea, tells it thus:

On one occasion he got into the dining-room before the rest of the team and polished off all eleven breakfasts. In response to the remonstrations of his teammates he only replied: 'I don't care what you call me, so long as you don't call me late for lunch.'
The Cassell Soccer Companion

According to Keith Farnsworth (see bibliography), however, this happened 'during training for the 1899 semi-final, at United's cup headquarters', which would have been Lytham St Anne's. And according to director Tom Bott, Foulke 'wasn't a big eater'. Who to believe? It's a great story, and as Bryan Butler observes: 'We need our legends.' The historian, though, has to sift the myth-making, and run the risk of shaving the nimbus, such as it is, in this case.

First off, that splendid one-liner. It's a clever play on words that may not be original. Apparently it was standard repertoire for the Cajuns of Louisiana 100 years before – and the wordplay works just as well in French. But if William had borrowed the joke from some music hall sketch he'd seen, doesn't this make the whole anecdote more likely to have happened? It's what people do, after all: borrow a well-known punch-line and co-opt it for their own use.

Secondly, I think we can disregard Tom Bott's defence with a smile. The good-humoured, avuncular Bott was a great fan of Willie's, and would often speak up for him in front of the club committee. Such a comment as 'Foulke wasn't a big eater' would be completely in character for him, which means we can take it with a pinch or more of salt.

Tracking down the *when* may help to confirm the *whether*. Another candidate for time and place is the Sea View hotel in Skegness before the 1901 cup final. I have even seen a hopelessly unfeasible version (in a heavyweight Sunday newspaper not so long ago) which has William scoffing the Southampton meals as well, just before the 1902 final. According to this flight of fancy, the United team had brought packed lunches as they'd guessed what was going to happen.

Meanwhile, back in the real world, my own opinion, for what it's worth, is that the incident, or something like it, really did take place, and, as Farnsworth suggests, at Lytham before the 1899 semi with Liverpool. My reasoning is that for the first few days of the seaside stay William was badly injured with a leg sprain through saving a shot from Forest's Benbow the previous Saturday, and was unable to walk for several days. The usual preamble to the tale is that Foulke (traditionally averse to training) had a lie-in through choice while his teammates went on their early morning walk, and then stole down and ate the breakfasts in their absence. Perhaps the point was that he was incapable of joining his fellows on the walk? There's the opportunity and the means, if not the motive!

Strictly speaking the jury has to remain out on this one. I'll stop now, hoping that I haven't flogged the joke to death.

On the pitch, Willie would often exploit his size in order to indulge in the deadpan humour of an Obélix or an Oliver Hardy:

> He performed his duties in an extremely creditable manner, and when a wee, little, diminutive forward runs up against him after he has parted with the ball he doesn't claim a foul, but simply places that paw of his on the shoulder of the

charging gentleman in a most fatherly manner, and pushes him aside with an expression of 'Get on one side, little boy.'
Athletic News (10/10/98)

Again, when Everton's Settle tried to charge him into the net:

> Naturally, the collision had no effect on the custodian, and the diminutive Settle glared up at Foulke, as the massive goalkeeper glanced wonderingly down at his opponent in astonishment at such impertinence. This happened often, to the crowd's joy.
> *Athletic News* (8/10/00)

Such mannerisms would be worth nothing without the talent, of course.

His burgeoning bulk brought with it another useful trait, of which we see increasing evidence round about now: the ability to psych out opposition forwards. The *Athletic News* is once more our source, reporting on the Blades' 3-0 destruction of Blackburn Rovers in September 1899:

> The Lilliputian forwards could scarcely look at this still-growing Gulliver, much less tackle him.

There was one point during the FA Cup battles with Wednesday that year (see below) when three or four of the opposing attack were queuing up for the privilege of scoring. There was just Foulke to beat, yet his very presence appeared to reduce them to a dithering indecision, and he was able to clear. And again, as late as March 1904, in the FA Cup match with Bolton:

> Stokes rushed past both backs and seemed likely to dribble through, but the mountain of flesh which is possessed by Foulke hove in sight, and appeared to paralyse the little Wanderer, who simply shot into the hands of the leviathan.
> *Athletic News* (7/3/04)

The head-to-head tussles with Steve Bloomer now seemed to be constantly won. The Derby man got no change out of William during the September 1899 Baseball Ground League match (won by United 1-0). Memories of the cup final seemed to have scotched 'Paleface's' challenge for good: on several occasions he squirmed through to confront the Blades' 'keeper, but each effort fizzled out into a shot way over the bar, or a tame poke into William's arms. (As we shall see, though, Bloomer was far from finished. It's a tribute to the forward's skills and tenacity that in the corresponding match the following year he was to bounce back with a hat-trick against Foulke.)

Another of the myths clinging to 'Little Willie' is his supposedly short fuse and violent temper. The celebrated specific incidents are looked at elsewhere, but the unsubstantiated generic tales about him losing his rag and pursuing spectators (and the odd match official) can be dismissed without too much trouble. Flamboyance, bravado, yes; raging through the red mist, no. Chasing the ball up the pitch is plausible as well as verifiable. Chasing the boo-boys up the sixpenny bank is neither.

Relationships with figures of authority could sometimes be stretched to breaking point (see the incident with Dr Stokes in chapter 8). His conduct on the pitch, though, apart from the occasional burst of usually justifiable invective, showed in general a commendable *lack* of the more extreme reactions to provocation. Times without number reports refer to him in such terms as 'cool', 'clever,' and 'steady under fire'.

There's an illuminating paragraph from a match programme in October 1901, after a particularly trying time at Everton (see match-by-match analysis):

FOULKE AND HIS TORMENTORS

Big as he is, probably because of it, Foulke has times of sore affliction. He is made the butt of human battering rams on foreign soil, and is called upon to keep his temper through his fear of 'penalties'. He has to take all and give nothing, taking the hottest and unkindest of charges without turning a hair, and has to allow opposing forwards to hit him all over the place and merely smile the smile of peace… Is there one law for the big man and one for the tiny one? (12/10/01)

Furthermore there's evidence that, on at least one occasion, he used his bulky presence as a peacekeeping force. Before the 1902 cup final replay a reporter accosted Boyle and gave his opinion that the full-back was at fault in the controversial Southampton equaliser in the first match. As the argument became more and more heated, William decided to intervene. 'If there's to be a fight,' he told the reporter, 'Then you're about my size.' The man from the press took the hint and beat a hasty retreat.

Foulke could look after himself, which of course isn't the same thing as losing it. 'Giving chaff for chaff' was a necessary string to a 'keeper's bow, given the rough-and-tumble – 'the thicket of hurt' – that was the penalty area in those days.

Nor was he above the odd touch of gamesmanship. Witness his pulling down on the crossbar to give a high shot a marginally smaller target. Then there was the moment, with less than a minute to go in the torrid Sheffield derby in December 1900. A battered and limping Foulke collected the ball from yet another Wednesday attack, then stepped over the dead-ball line with it, conceding the corner. He then feigned a mild concussion, hanging onto the ball until a large slice of that final minute had ticked away, to the fury of the opposition. United won 1-0.

There are indications that he berated his defenders, much as Schmeichel was wont to do a century later. It's a symptom of intense involvement in the game, and as such its root cause is laudable. Those around the blast, naturally, may disagree. There is a resolution in the SUFC committee meeting minutes from September 1901:

> That Foulke be written to as to his habit of shouting to players while playing, requesting him to discontinue this practice.

Such a delicate choice of words! We note the 'shouting *to*' as opposed to '*at*'. We can imagine Tom Bott fine-tuning the final wording of the letter before it was sent off. It had been known for William, with his stubborn head on, to take criticism (to paraphrase Roger McGough) like God takes advice.

*'Foulke remonstrates.' (*Athletic News*)*

The big man was especially popular on Merseyside. Indeed, it's quite possible that the Anfield Kop's long-standing tradition of applauding the visiting goalie originated with Foulke's performances during those years. During the January 1897 match at Anfield (which finished goal-less) one of Willie's long periods of inactivity was enlivened by the present of a packet of toffee from a doting little old lady stationed behind the goal.

Another 'Foulke tale' originated on Merseyside, this time at Everton, early on in the Championship-winning campaign of 1897/98. Home forward Larry Bell, ex-Wednesday, a tricky customer with a useful shot, had scored on four minutes, and had led wave after wave of attacks on the United goal. Willie frustrated them all. Gradually the Blades turned the tide, so that in the second half they were leading 4-1. Back came Bell, and after one clash Foulke (around eighteen stone at the time) fell on top of him, knocking him senseless. The story goes that William rubbed his nose in the mud, then picked him up in one hand and handed him over to his trainer for restorative care.

William's version shows another side to his personality (he had, after all, recently become a father, traditionally a mellowing process):

> It was really all an accident. Just as I was reaching for a high ball Bell came at me, and the result of the collision was that we both tumbled down, but it was his bad luck to be underneath, and I could not prevent myself from falling with both knees in his back. When I saw his face I got about the worst shock I ever have had on the football field. He looked as if he was dead. I picked him up in my arms as tenderly as a babe, and all I could say was 'Oh dear, oh dear.' But I am happy to say the affair was not as serious as it looked, and the Everton man came round all right.
> London Evening News (1913)

That turn-of-the-century season, the one that started like a dream for the Blades but was to end in frustration, contained several memorable moments involving our man.

Those who say he never scored a goal for Sheffield United are unaware of his freewheeling contribution to the match against the black African touring side the Kaffirs, in October 1899. In the friendly at Bramall Lane the tourists, despite their athleticism and enthusiasm, were no match for the skilful United. The score was 4-0 early in the second half, when the cry from the terraces went up: 'Let 'em have a goal!' So Foulke left his goal empty and went and joined the attack. Before too long he dribbled past two defenders and scored with a thirty-yard shot – 'a feat which was hugely enjoyed', according to the *Telegraph* report. Then the tourists, attacking the undefended net, scored twice. William notched another, and the final score in a good-humoured advert for stress-free football was a 7-2 win for the home side. Richard Sparling (see bibliography) relates that a deputation from the Kaffirs went to the United dressing room after the game to marvel at the phenomenon that was Foulke, one of them commenting: 'What a monster – he's a team in himself!'

That same month there was another minor incident during a train journey. The *Independent* reporter, in a dry tongue-in-cheek manner of which William would have approved, described it thus:

> A rather curious accident occurred during the journey of the United team to Nottingham on Saturday. When passing Woodhouse Junction the curve in the line caused the saloon to lurch, the train going at a good speed, and at the same moment one of the seats, on which sat Foulke, Morren, Moran, Bennett, Johnson and Howard, broke down. One or two of them looked as though they thought their time had come, but happily no harm was done. It was suggested that the accident was brought about by Morren having put on weight during the past few weeks.
> (2/10/99)

Tommy Morren was just 5ft 5ins, and weighed in at just over half of our hero's bulk, so the reader can come to his own conclusions as to whether there's any ironic subtext here.

The League campaign started swimmingly for Sheffield United. They were undefeated until January, equalling Preston North End's record of twenty-two consecutive games without a loss. They were six points in the clear after the Christmas programme, which included a 2-1 win at Manchester City, with a lively Meredith bringing out the best from William, and a 5-0 drubbing of Everton.

Then the cruise began to stutter. Bury ended the unbeaten run in late January, albeit with a dubious winning goal, chipped over Foulke's head while he appeared to be impeded. William's comment to trainer George Waller after a tough match would often be: 'Ah well, George, we're badly shaken, but we're not beat.' After this defeat he said: 'We've got beat AND badly shaken.' It's the belief of some football historians that this was the true origin of Bury FC's nickname – 'The Shakers'.

February was given over to a climactic, violent, injury-strewn series of scraps with Wednesday in the second round of the FA Cup. Wednesday were temporarily resident in the Second Division, but were on their way to the Championship of that division. Their attack, headed by the prolific Spikesley, would hit 84 goals, the highest total in England that year. Thus a close battle was predicted, despite the discrepancy in League status.

The *Athletic News* anticipated a 'hot-pot, with sauce piquante'. The weather disagreed: the first match was abandoned in a snowstorm, the referee declaring

his inability to see the ball. A further thick fall of snow caused another postpone-
ment, then the teams set to it once more. On a muddy Bramall Lane pitch The
Wednesday had the better of the exchanges. Foulke was in top form and had
to be; the visitors' first-half goal was a belter, Spikesley swinging over a precise
cross-field pass for Brash to hit in a thunderbolt from the right wing. Attempts
to add to the lead were dealt with by Foulke, who wasn't really troubled again.
As time went on Wednesday were content to kick for touch or dish out fouls
(many of which were returned with gusto). It needed a last-minute goal from
Almond to take the game to a replay the following Monday.

Once again Wednesday's attack started the more dangerously; once again
United had William to thank for keeping the scoresheet blank. The play grew
increasingly violent. Wednesday had two sent off, so with a couple more players having to retire injured, at the end ten men were pitted against eight.
Unsurprisingly, United's greater numbers eventually struggled through to the
worst of Pyrrhic victories by 2-0.

The Blades were to progress no further in that year's FA Cup. In the next
round they lost in a replay, again to Bury, who were the eventual winners.
George Waller and Foulke carried a crippled Thickett off the field. He returned
some thirty minutes later, but remained a hobbling liability that the opposition
clinically exploited. William had little chance with the two shots that beat him.

So with Needham, Morren, Thickett and Priest on the serious injury list, the
Championship lead was gradually frittered away. Too many drawn games (twelve
by the end of the season) allowed Aston Villa to overtake them. Foulke was
made captain in Needham's absence, and the defence, despite Thickett's injury,
remained United's strength. The one bad defeat – and many people pointed
to this game as the one which lost the Championship – was a 0-4 reverse at
Nottingham Forest. Foulke was playing for the Football League against the
Scottish League at the Crystal Palace that day. His place was taken by his understudy, the tall Mexborough man William Biggar making a nervous debut.

After Villa had completed their programme by scraping a 1-0 win against
Wolves on Easter Monday, the top of the table read:

	P	W	D	L	F	A	Pts
Aston Villa	34	22	6	6	77	35	50
Sheffield United	32	17	12	3	61	31	46

In those days, of course, it was goal average rather than goal difference that
separated teams that finished level on points. From this, the mathematicians
or those with a pocket calculator handy will deduce that the Blades had to
win both their remaining games (both away), scoring eight goals without

reply in the process. To underline the near-impossible task that United had set
themselves, the reader is asked to remember that the team was riddled with
injuries, and to consider the following Easter itinerary:

Thursday 12 April	0700 dep. Midland Station, Sheffield, for Manchester.
	Base: Albion Hotel, Piccadilly
Friday 13 April	0925 dep. Victoria Station, Manchester, for Blackburn.
	Lunch at the White Bull. Blackburn Rovers 3, United 3.
	1745 dep. Blackburn for Manchester
Saturday 14 April	1200 dep. London Road Station, Manchester, for Stoke.
	Stoke 1, United 1. 1930 dep. Stoke. 2310 arr. Sheffield
Monday 16 April	0920 dep. Midland Station, Sheffield, for London.
	Corinthians 0, United 4. 2000 dep. Paddington
	Station for Birmingham. Base: Colonnade Hotel
Tuesday 17 April	0915 dep. Birmingham for Wolverhampton.
	Wolves 1, United 2. 1815 dep. Wolverhampton for
	Birmingham.
Wednesday 18 April	0845 dep. Birmingham for Cardiff. Base: Alexander
	Hotel. South Wales XI 0, United 2.
Thursday 19 April	Aberdare 2, United 1
Friday 20 April	1232 dep. Cardiff. 1823 arr. Sheffield
	Sheffield Independent (16/4/00)

The 2-1 win over Wolves meant that mathematically they were back to
square one: only an implausible 8-0 win at Burnley would secure them the
Championship. Needham took Thickett's place at right-back. Perhaps his
verve might have better employed up front: United failed to score, but Burnley
notched a suspiciously offside goal a couple of minutes from the end.

Once more we have to note the invaluable contribution of Willie Foulke
to the season. United finished – yet again – with the best defensive record in
the division. The *Sheffield Independent* gave the big man due praise for his role
in that final match with Burnley:

On several occasions only the dexterity of Foulke in goal saved his side from
disaster.
(24/4/00)

And so to the 1900 summer, during which, for the four months of the football close season, William was to make waves in another sport.

7: Cricketer

Foulke to be allowed to play with Derbyshire next Monday, Tuesday and Wednesday, provided he returns home to sleep each evening.

From the minutes of Sheffield United FC's Committee meeting 15/8/00

Foulke then went on and got two wickets in his first over, amid scenes of great enthusiasm.

Derby Express (20/8/00), Derbyshire v. Notts. at Queen's Park, Chesterfield

In many ways the cricketer was his alter ego. In the more placid world of cork ball and willow he put his great strength and appetite for sport to good use, demonstrating some eye-catching skills as batsman, fast bowler and fielder.

He had represented Blackwell Colliery in the Derbyshire League-winning season of 1895. Ernest Needham played in the same League, for Staveley, and the match between the two village sides that summer produced an entertaining tit for tat: Needham was caught and bowled by Foulke, and then in the Blackwell innings the Blades captain returned the compliment, catching William out.

More eventful for Foulke personally was the following year, with six wickets against Chesterfield, 6 for 29 in the match with Riddings, and some alert fielding in the slips (five catches *v.* Morton). His batting had so far suffered from an extravagance easy to out-think: he would often be caught out for single-figure totals.

Of marginal interest is the August 1895 footballers-only match with Wednesday. United had the theoretical advantage with three players of pure cricketing ability: Needham, who was later to represent Derbyshire as a fine batsman; Thickett, whose stolid strength translated itself perfectly to the game at this level; and of course, Foulke. William was delighted to be given a chance to show his prowess at the summer game. His batting was a disaster, though: in a single-innings match his happy swipe at a loose ball saw him caught out for a duck. United finished on 138 for 9 (Needham 40, Thickett 32). On that day it was William's bowling that marked him out as a serious cut above most of the other non-specialists. He took six wickets for just five runs, and also brought off a spectacular one-handed diving catch. He was a major factor in the dismissal of The Wednesday footballers for 33.

By 1897 both the Foulke brothers were playing for the Colliery team. Their batting remained a bit of a lottery, but their close fielding developed into a great double act. William bowled or played in the slips, and Tommy (as we have seen, no mean goalie himself) was wicketkeeper. Thus against Grassmoor that year we see the following:

S. Cooper 12, caught Foulke, bowled Foulke.

The following summer there is the first evidence of a maturity in William's batting. Taking the field as third wicket in the Derbyshire League match with Sheepbridge Works he hit a solid 43 not out. This was the backbone of the colliery total of 97 for 1, enough for a comfortable win.

The 1899 season had two major highlights. One was an innings, the other a memorable catch. The innings was a rollicking 62 against Sutton, which contained a six walloped onto the Blackwell hospital roof. The catch was on the end of a straight drive from a Chesterfield opener. The shot appeared to be heading safely for a wide open space, until William arrived at speed, and leaping into the air caught the ball one-handed.

As we have seen, Foulke and family had by now moved to Sheffield, but ironically the call to action now came from his native county. Derbyshire cricket had recently been rocked by the tragically early loss of one of its heroes: the all-rounder (but especially brilliant bowler) George Davidson. He had died of pneumonia in February 1899. A committee member wondered: 'How to recover from this crushing blow?'

Derbyshire had returned to the elite County Championship in 1894, but this position looked in danger as the 1899 season progressed, with the side struggling near the foot of the table. They needed a new figurehead, an injection of enthusiasm that would kick-start the side into a new era.

1900 was a grand season in general for the English cricket fan. The MCC, in an attempt to curtail the large number of drawn games, decreed six balls per over instead of five, and introduced the follow-on option. It was all part of a drive for brighter cricket. The West Indies were here on tour. W.G. Grace, by now in his fifties, was still hitting his centuries, as were the glamour boys of the game, Prince Ranjitsinhji and the ubiquitous C.B. Fry.

W.H. Foulke's case for County honours had been plugged by 'the forcible representation of a Sheffield journalist'. The journalist in question – 'J.H.S.' – wrote for the *Yorkshire Telegraph and Star* under the pen-name of 'Looker-On', but it was in a persuasive behind-the-scenes capacity that he eventually convinced the Derbyshire selection committee that their currently weak attack could be strengthened by the inclusion of the United 'keeper. That spring Foulke had joined the Sheffield United cricketing ranks as a professional, so now had a more prominent showcase for his skills. Memorable early season feats in the

Hallamshire League were a 20 not out against Barnsley ('free hitting, including one stroke for 5'), and a 58 against White Lane ('hitting the bowling to all parts of the field'). He was to finish the season with the best batting average in the club. He took a few wickets too, usually about two or three per game. So it was that in 1900 William played four games of cricket at top-rank County level.

There were the expected jokes: 'Foulke comes to the crease and there's an appeal against the light.' His appearance on the first-class scene did wonders for crowd numbers, nevertheless.

His debut was at Leyton, Essex, at the end of June. He had been placed seventh in the batting order, the selection committee no doubt reasoning that the newcomer with a reputation for a flamboyant style (in batting as well as keeping goal) shouldn't take a traditionally 'steadier' opening role. A sound decision in theory, but in the event, an unfortunate contributory factor to the comparatively disappointing result. What should have been a glorious firework display of a convincing victory fizzled out into a draw. Once again the weather played its part: play didn't commence until three o'clock on the third day. At the close Derbyshire were luxuriating in a massive 424 for 5, night watchman Storer on 136 ... and our William on 39!

But what was this? Foulke was batting as carefully as any opener. When the tactics should perhaps have been to hit out and amass runs in the shorter amount of time available, the big man was immovable at the crease, painstakingly doing his bit for the ultimate Derbyshire total of 508. He was eventually dismissed for 53, stumped. He had scored 10 in a single over.

Essex scored 368 in reply. Foulke injured his hand with a badly split finger while fielding in the slips, and retired from the game. This incident gave rise to criticisms of his ability in this domain, and yet towards the end of this, his sole season in first-class cricket, the *Athletic News* was to describe him as 'a smart fielder and a safe catch'. Derbyshire's request to forfeit their second innings was refused, so they declared when they lost a wicket on the second ball. Essex played out the remaining time, with the desired result.

William didn't represent his county again until the end of July. It was another drawn match, this time against Warwickshire at Edgbaston. A lapse of concentration saw him caught and bowled for 1 in the first innings, then in the second he was still there at the death, on 1 not out! This was the match, ultimately drawn, that saw John Devey of Aston Villa fame hit a phenomenal 246.

In the remaining four innings Foulke played for Derbyshire, the scores were 0, 5, 4 and 1. It seemed already clear that his mind was elsewhere. However, he still had one decent shot in his locker. His bowling had yet to impress at first-class level, but in the torrid match with Nottinghamshire (towards the end of

August, just before being recalled for football training) he took two wickets in his first over. The Chesterfield crowd were in raptures. For the man, it was a more than adequate swansong. For the team, it was another defeat, the Derbyshire batting being ripped to shreds by the fierce bowling of Wass.

W.H. Foulke's full career stats. are given in the appendices.

William remains in the record books as the heaviest ever first-class cricketer, anywhere in the world. A rival for this title emerged in the early 1970s, when in what was then Rhodesia a slow bowler by the name of R.H. Kaschula came to prominence. But Mr Kaschula (by all accounts a mediocre batsman, and 'not a good fielder') weighed in at just over twenty stone, leaving Willie the winner by a couple of pounds.

Foulke's cricket promised a lot, and would undoubtedly have delivered more had the minor matter of a full professional Football League programme not been his first priority. An injury to the hand is usually of scant importance for an outfield player, but obviously an undamaged pair of hands is a goalkeeper's stock in trade. It was the memory of that sobering June injury that finally made up William's mind: from now on his more serious energies would be devoted to football.

The cricketing story isn't quite over, though. The next summer, possibly no longer feeling inhibited by the need to prove himself at county level, he played some dazzling innings for Sheffield United CC. Pick of the bunch was his unbeaten 123 against Collegiate in July, a joyous knock which included 2 sixes and no fewer than 21 fours. He was partnering football trainer George Waller, who hit 78 not out. United, who had been struggling on 46 for 3, declared on 244 for the loss of no more wickets. Once again he was to finish the season with the club's highest batting average, marginally beating Waller (also a fine spin bowler) into second place. His tally for the season was 483.

Meanwhile, Ernest Needham had been selected for county honours for Derbyshire. He was to prove himself a dependable middle-order batsman, and would keep his place for many seasons to come.

A resolution from a committee meeting (May 1902) reads:

That when Foulke's injury is cured he be permitted to play for the cricket section.
(6/5/02)

From now on his appearances on the cricket pitch were few and far between. By the summer of 1904 they had stopped altogether. With his goalkeeping first-team place by no means certain, he couldn't risk any more injuries to his hands. By then he was about to embark on his final season with the Blades.

8: The Road to Pie Saturday

All along Manchester Road, through which traffic has been suspended,
stalls, containing huge stocks of all kinds of delicacies, have been erect-
ed, while yards and all open spaces have been utilised for the purpose
of supplying refreshments. Flags are floating gaily, and the day is one
which will long live in the memory of Boltonians.

Bolton Evening News (27/4/01)

Foulke could not be blamed for the defeat by any means.

Athletic News (29/4/01)

As every football buff knows, Tottenham Hotspur occupy a unique place in
FA Cup history. They are the only team from outside the Football League
to carry off the Cup. This they accomplished in 1901 as members of the
Southern League, beating Sheffield United after a replay in the final.

Superficially the Spurs' success looks like a phenomenal feat of giant-killing.
Imagine a side from the Dr Martens League accomplishing the same today!
Except that the Southern League wasn't always the domain of the likes of Bath
City and Chippenham Town (no disrespect intended). The Dr Martens League
is the descendant of the early Southern League, but not its equivalent.

In its earliest years it almost rivalled the Football League in glamour and
as a reservoir of playing ability, especially among its top half-dozen clubs.
Accomplished players had been lured south to where wages were higher, and
the likes of Southampton, Portsmouth, Reading, Millwall, and Spurs had built
teams that could at least hold their own against the Midlands and Northern
elite. Between 1898 and 1908 Southampton reached the FA Cup final twice,
Millwall the semi-finals twice; Portsmouth beat Grimsby Town, who were
then a First Division outfit, as well as Manchester United; and Reading had
defeats of Bolton and Notts County to their credit.

This is not to belittle Spurs' achievement that year: on their way to the final
they eliminated the best the Football League could throw at them. Preston
North End, holders Bury, and renowned Cup fighters West Brom all succumbed to a powerful and skilful blend of football which in many ways was
something new on the scene.

In the final, the pundits sided with the Blades. True, the London-based team had four international players in it, but the Sheffielders could boast nine, and Needham and Foulke especially were at the height of their powers. An upset was unthinkable.

That season hadn't been the smoothest of rides for Bill Foulke. Incredibly, in a puzzlingly erratic autumn, both he and Bennett had been the object of some barracking from the fans. There are fewer organisms fickler than the football crowd, and as Nick Hornby observed, a cynical century later: 'The natural state of the football fan is bitter disappointment, no matter what the score.' In the official Blades programme we see the following attempt to come to terms with the comparatively new phenomenon of terrace rage:

> The attention of the committee has been drawn to a most iniquitous and scandalous treatment of our players by certain sections of the crowd behind the Bramall Lane goal. Their language is most dirty, to say nothing of the bitterness with which they taunt Foulke and Bennett. It has become so warm that today a large staff of detectives has been engaged to catch the delinquents, and it will go hard with the wrongdoers.
> *Sheffield Football: A History, Vol. 1*

Then there was the leg injury which caused William to miss several games around New Year. A blazing row with club medic Dr Stokes didn't help. The 'keeper turned up for an examination, took exception to some of the doctor's comments, and amid a good deal of effing and jeffing (not all of which, apparently, issued from the player) Foulke stormed out. An interview with the committee and a written apology seemed to cool things off. William was booked into Allison's, a specialist in sports injuries who practised in Manchester, and who charged an arm and a leg. The bill for treatment in this case came to over £7 – or nearly £1,000 in today's money.

Amid the club's stuttering performance in the League there were signs of better things to come. In December 1900 the Blades travelled to Merseyside and brought off an inspiring 2-1 win against Liverpool, who that season were to go on and win the Championship for the first of their many, many times. Thus was demonstrated an ability to rise to the big occasion – traditionally a useful weapon in the 'one-off' battles that make up a knockout tournament such as the FA Cup. And so it proved. Drawn away at Sunderland in the first round, the Blades withstood almost relentless pressure from the Wearsiders to scrape home 2-1. The tie was of great significance for William, as it was the occasion of his first ever penalty save – as opposed to the kicker missing the target.

Ferguson hit a hard spot kick, but too close to Foulke. The ball rebounded off the 'keeper's knee, and there followed a race between the two men for the loose ball. Ferguson got there first, and cracked in a shot which hit the post and went behind. It was something of a turning point: William had been criticised for his lack of success facing penalties, but he was to save another crucial one within a few weeks. By the time he got to Chelsea (see chapter 12) he was to save ten in a season. Before the rule was changed in 1905, the goalkeeper wasn't obliged to stay on his line until the ball was kicked. In another dying echo of the rugby game, the goalie was allowed to start his run out immediately after the kicker began his run at the ball. A hard-struck, well-placed penalty would still almost invariably result in a goal, but Willie, combining a fair measure of speed with his increasing width, was becoming more adept at rapidly reducing the target area!

The second round brought Everton to Bramall Lane. There were the expected robust challenges on the United goalie, culminating on this occasion with Foulke falling on the ball, and half the opposing attack, by accident or design, falling on top of him. He managed to shake the worriers off and clear his lines. Two fine saves – one from Turner, the other from Settle – were instrumental in the Blades' 2-0 win.

There was a trip to Molineux next, and most neutrals were forecasting a win for the Wolves, traditionally doughty cup fighters. Sheffield United took the lead through Priest, then soon afterwards the home side were awarded a penalty. Harper, possibly succumbing to the Foulke psyching-out (or rushing out), shot straight at the goalkeeper. It was another pivotal moment: United went on to rout their opponents 4-0.

Their adversaries in the semi-final were old rivals the Villa. In a game that was in marked contrast to the previous week's spiritless league encounter, both sides attacked from the off. It took two excellent goals to beat Foulke. The first, after some nifty approach work by Devey, was an unstoppable rising drive from Garratty. The second was claimed by Devey himself, bulleting a header into the top corner of the goal. United hit back through Priest and Lipsham, and despite late pressure from Villa, the Blades held on for a replay.

The United squad spent the week at Skegness, following George Waller's regime of walks, sea dips, skipping and hefting dumb-bells. On the Thursday the teams met again at Derby, and this time Needham's men registered a clear 3-0 win. One of the highlights of the game was an acrobatic save by William from a Templeton thunderbolt, touched over the bar for a corner. The *Independent* reporter couldn't resist a display of parochial pride: 'Foulke astonished the natives by fisting the ball over the halfway line.' (12/4/01)

Meanwhile Tottenham had sounded out a warning by demolishing West Brom in their semi by 4-0. Bustling and improvisational centre forward Sandy

Brown, one of the Spurs' Scottish contingent, had bagged all four. His total for all the competition that year would be fifteen, which was to remain the twentieth-century record.

So who were these Southern Leaguers, and how had they risen to the heights so quickly? They had turned professional less than six years before, and had won their League Championship the previous season. Prime mover behind the success story on the field was inside right John Cameron, ex-Queen's Park, who took on the role of player-manager some years before anybody else had thought of it.

Backed by plentiful finances, he had cast his net across the kingdom in his search for a winning team. From Stoke came goalkeeper George Clawley; from Preston the tough and uncompromising full-back Sandy Tait; and Welsh international Jack Jones, team captain and ex-Blade, was in the half-back line. There was a formidable attack, Tom Smith and Irish international Jack Kirwan on the wings complementing Brown and Cameron, with subtle assists provided by yet another Scot, Dave Copeland at inside left.

For the week before the final United returned to Skegness, where the tone of the light training, according to the *Sporting Chronicle*, was 'regular diet, short walks, and being kept together.' Meanwhile Spurs repaired to their Epping Forest retreat. Here they practised sprints in the morning, and for afternoon relaxation they had a choice of golf, billiards, whist or woodland rambles.

The London newspapers had been waging a psychological war. A headline in the *London Evening News* proclaimed 'A TEAM OF CRIPPLES', and proceeded to enumerate the walking wounded that were supposed to make up the United team. Foulke, according to the article, had a badly injured right thigh, and was only able to kick with his left foot 'to avoid breaking down'. William had in fact hurt his thigh during the League match with Villa at the end of March, having to leave the field for ten minutes, but the problem had cleared up in time for the final. (Bott's telegram from Skegness read: 'Players all well.') The counter-propaganda was pushed further in an article in a match programme a fortnight before the final, describing the relaxed atmosphere of United's seaside sojourn. An extract:

> After tea we while away the time, and another visit is paid to the Piers, and Foulke throws, and nearly knocks a gull from its perch... The cripples are certainly looking and feeling A1, while Foulke says he could eat the 'blooming ball'.
>
> (5/4/01)

A comparison of the bonuses on offer is illuminating. The Football League team were on £10 for a win, and £5 for a draw. The Spurs' incentives were a mammoth £25 a man if they won the Cup, and £10 if they lost!

It was a nominal north–south battle that captured the imagination of the public. Actually no Spurs player hailed from south of the Trent, and United's Charley Field, ex-Brentford, was the only southerner playing in the 1901 final. Nevertheless the Palace final was to attract a world-record crowd of 110,820 paying customers, although the real total of those present on that warm and sunny spring day, including those watching for free from tree-tops and other vantage points, was certainly far higher.

United had travelled down the day before, and had spent, according to Tom Bott, a less-than-perfect night in what turned out to be a converted loft in the Bedford Hotel, Covent Garden. Confidence in a fairly unproblematic victory was still high. The teams were: *Sheffield United:* Foulke; Thickett, Boyle; Johnson, Morren, Needham; Bennett, Field, Hedley, Priest, Lipsham. *Tottenham Hotspur:* Clawley; Erentz, Tait; Morris, Hughes, Jones; Smith, Cameron, Brown, Copeland, Kirwan.

United started well, and most of the early play was in the Tottenham half. Priest opened the scoring on ten minutes with a fast low shot from eighteen yards, which Clawley spotted too late. Midway through the first half Spurs were awarded a series of free-kicks some twenty yards from their opponents' goal. The final one found its way to the unmarked Sandy Brown, whose well-directed header, easily out of Foulke's reach, equalised.

The tempo now increased, and both defences had lively manoeuvres to deal with. Foulke had to save a high speculative shot from Kirwan. Smith, bringing out the best from Boyle, nevertheless managed to outwit him and squeeze in a hard shot which William turned round the post. At the other end United's combination approach work was keeping Clawley on his toes. Half-time came with honours still even. Tottenham attacked from the off in the second half, and it took five minutes for their efforts to pay off. Cameron took the ball out towards the right corner flag, then turned and rolled a pass inside to that man again Sandy Brown. Despite close attention from Thickett and Boyle, the centre forward hit a fierce rising diagonal shot that rebounded into the net off the underside of the bar. The sheer speed of the whole manoeuvre had given Foulke no chance – in fact it would have probably beaten any 'keeper in the game.

Within two minutes the Blades were on level terms again, but with a goal that would be fervently debated for at least a generation to come. It was the 'Hurst World Cup goal that hit the crossbar and bounced down' of its time. If anything, Bennett's equaliser was probably argued over more heatedly and

'*The scene at the Palace.*' (Athletic News)

for longer, as at least, as we all know, Hurst went on and scored another just to make sure. The United goal was crucial, in that it took the tie to a replay.

Lipsham went off on one of his runs down the left wing, and centred. Clawley grabbed the ball, but Bennett weighed in, causing the Spurs goalie to turn and drop the ball behind him. It was then 'fetched out smartly' by the 'keeper and pushed round the post. Did Clawley drop the ball behind the line? Most of those present thought he didn't, not by at least a yard. The referee Mr Kingscott thought he did, and so awarded a goal. The linesman had flagged for a corner, but this was overruled.

The rest of the game was played out with Mr Kingscott the butt of the Spurs fans' anger. Every United shot was accompanied by ironic shouts of 'Goal!' To complete the picture:

> The Tottenham supporters did not let Mr Kingscott off the hook. They kept up
> a running commentary that was rustically to the point, on his looks, walk, man-
> nerisms, and parentage.
> *The Giant Killers*

About the only further memorable items from that second half were a couple of fine saves by Foulke, and his twice running nearly fifty yards from his goal line to pick up and clear. (So much for his damaged thigh!) There were no more goals, and the final score remained at 2-2. And so to Pie Saturday.

Bolton Wanderers' new home since 1997 has been the strikingly hyper-modern Reebok stadium, out on the semi-rural north-western town limit. With its bracing backdrop of the Rivington hills it's a far cry from the old centrally located Burnden Park, the dark brick edifice that used to stand alongside the main Manchester Road, and the club's home ground for over a century.

The *Manchester Guardian* reporter, up there for the 1901 cup final replay, puzzled over the epithet 'Park', and described 'some dingy shedding... a railway embankment, some slate roofs, half a dozen smoke stacks, two pit-mouth wheels'. The weather was grimmer than the previous week, too, with overcast skies, showers and a chilly wind. Sheffield United had spent the week at Lytham, and according to Tom Bott, another less than comfortable night in a nearby hotel adjacent to a sewage farm. For the superstitious, the omens were gathering – plus the fact that Needham had only just passed an eleventh-hour fitness test.

Another huge crowd had been predicted. Famously, local caterers had worked long and hard at supplying:

> ... a mountain of meat pies baked, acres of sandwiches cut and buttered, hundreds of hams roasted and spiced, tons of German sausage, black puddings and saveloys... and sufficient beer to float a line of battleships.
> *London Evening News* (27/4/01)

The authorities, worried that the ground capacity of just 40,000 would be nothing like enough to accommodate the expected multitudes, had drafted in 300 foot and mounted police, as well as the fire brigade, ready with hoses should any of the crowd decide to run amok. These were unnecessary precautions: the actual official attendance that day was a mere 20,470. Nobody appeared to have taken into account the fact that Bolton station was undergoing alterations, and that Lancashire railways had declined to run football specials, or reduced 'excursion' fares. To arrive on time for the match, Londoners had to take a train that departed in the wee small hours of Saturday morning. The poor weather no doubt put a dampener on many people's cup fever too. So, in a half-full ground, the cup finalists locked horns once more.

Spurs showed early superiority. It became clear that the wily Cameron had done his homework, and he had the added benefit of the previous week's dry run. The hard pitch suited his team's close passing game, reminiscent of Preston North End at their invincible zenith, and it's significant that Clawley in their goal didn't touch the ball until twenty-five minutes had elapsed.

Foulke, on the other hand, was kept busy. The edited highlights: he kicked a shot from Copeland right off the line, caught a long shot from Kirwan ('brushing aside' the encroaching Smith as he did so), and ran out to kick clear as Brown was shaping up for a shot.

Yet it was the Blades who took the lead, five minutes before the interval. Part of the Tottenham strategy was to deny Needham possession. When the Blades' inspirational captain finally had the space and opportunity to set up an attacking move, there was a rich, if brief, harvest. After drawing opponents to him, he fed Lipsham on the left, who set off on a classic wing run and whipped in a low centre. Priest met the ball on the half-volley and the shot beat Clawley just inside the post.

It was a temporary respite. Spurs began the second half as they had played most of the first, with rapid inter-passing and dangerous build-ups. It took just seven minutes for the quick-fire approach work to pay off. After a move which had involved all five forwards, Cameron applied the coup de grâce with a cracking ground shot which Foulke hadn't a hope of reaching.

United hit back. Bennett struck the side netting, and Hedley had a fine shot well saved by Clawley. Foulke repulsed attempts by Smith and Brown.

Then, with less than a quarter of an hour left, Spurs got the lucky break their attractive play deserved. Brown sent in a fierce shot which Foulke did well to reach and fist down. Boyle appeared to be about to complete the job with a hefty clearance kick, but the ball hit Needham and rebounded to Smith, who was in a plum position in front of goal and had little difficulty in hitting it past the badly placed 'keeper. Now the London side sensed victory, and for the remainder of the game it was mostly one-way traffic. A series of corners conceded by the Blades towards the end resulted in a marvellously opportunistic header from Brown, who had eluded any marker and cleverly directed the shot well away from Foulke's sphere of attention. It was a fitting climax to Spurs' win.

Nobody felt that William had been to blame for any of the goals. The *Sheffield Independent*, bemoaning the fact that United's attack hadn't been at its best, considered that:

> Foulke had a lot of work to do, and cleared with great power. He had not the ghost of a chance with any of the three shots that scored, while by his skill and judgment he helped to save his side from a heavier defeat than they sustained. (29/4/01)

And the mountain of food that had been prepared? The unexpectedly small attendance had resulted in mounds of unsold leftovers. Later that evening in the centre of Bolton you could pick up a dozen of the meat pies for a penny (half a penny today). This entrepreneurial desperation still failed to shift all the eatables, and an orphanage round the corner from the ground had an unexpected windfall on the Sunday morning.

From the Blades' point of view it was almost symbolic: the anticipated feast that dwindled away into a loss.

They would be back in the final the next year, with Willie Foulke, despite being yet another stone heavier, having one of his greatest ever games.

9: Twice More to the Palace

Foulke was a host in himself, and the Leviathan's one-handed saves of short, sharp, low, deceptive shots were like sleight of hand.

> The Sporting Chronicle (21/4/02)

The outstanding feature of the match was the grand goalkeeping of Foulke. He made a number of good saves, and on two or three occasions cleared the ball from what appeared impossible positions. Once, near the end, from a corner, he effected an absolute miracle with four or five men right on to him.

> C.B. Fry on the 1902 cup final, quoted in the *Southern Echo* (21/4/02)

Bill Foulke's benefit was scheduled for October 1901. What with the £4 maximum wage and strict control of bonuses, professional footballers (often with the end of their career on the horizon) in those days needed all the financial parachutes they could get. In the twenty-first century, when top players can earn more in a week than most of us can in a year, the need for planning for a life beyond football at that level perhaps isn't quite so pressing. A hundred years ago clubs' one-off reward system for loyal players was crucial.

Foulke's benefit match was theoretically an attractive fixture with Glasgow Celtic, Scottish Cup finalists and League runners-up the previous season. However, the necessity of playing it on a Monday afternoon reduced the attendance to around 2,500. It was nonetheless a combative, attacking match, ending in a close-fought 2-2 draw. William rose to the occasion and made several fine saves.

To supplement the takings from the match, a 'smoker', or evening of informal entertainment, was organised at the Bramall Lane pavilion. Around 300 people packed into the function hall. The repertoire was certainly varied, and William, a music hall fan, would have appreciated the wide range of *divertissements* on offer. The evening was enlivened by, among others:

Staff, Wadsley Asylum, quartette;
Mr J. Dillon, comic;
Miss Marshall, soprano;
Miss A. Myra, assisted by Mr A. Oliver, experiments in second sight;

Mr E.S. Maxfield, tenor;

Mr J. Harrison, comic;

Mr F. Flintham, handbell ringer;

Mr R. Poulter, female impersonator;

Mr Farron Sumner, baritone;

Mr H. Heath, humorist;

Mr H. Jervis, ventriloquist;

Mr Jasper Redfern, cinematograph exhibition.

This last item would no doubt have included footage from the 1901 cup final.

Contributions to the Foulke fund came from far and wide. The Blackwell community naturally made a considerable addition to the cause. It was recorded in the Sheffield United committee meeting minutes that a fan in South Africa had wired £11 – no mean sum at the time. The committee themselves clubbed up with a donation of £25. There would be more generosity from that direction after the 1902 cup final: William had been fined £4 the previous year for 'failure to keep an appointment', but it was decided to repay him following his sterling performance at the Palace!

Once more an injury dogged Foulke during the winter. He sprained his knee in the match with Notts County in November, and didn't play again until after Christmas. There were also the worrying first inklings of the great man's fallibility. Forwards were beginning to compile an arsenal of ploys that would at least stretch and perturb, if not invariably beat him. He was finding it increasingly difficult to get down to fast low shots, although, paradoxically, not necessarily the ones placed furthest from him. The full-length dive was still well within his capabilities, but as many goalkeepers will admit, the most difficult shots to stop are often the ones that streak into that tantalising area within a yard or two of the shins. Foulke's tactic of kicking clear still came in useful, but times were changing, opponents were getting wise to it, and a comprehensive clearance couldn't always be guaranteed. A case in point was in the October 1900 League match with Derby County. William's booted clearance was straightaway returned by Bloomer with a swerving volley for a sensational opening goal. Also very difficult to deal with were the attacks whose focus was rapidly shifted, for example a head on from a corner, like Brown's goal in the 1901 final replay or for that matter a fluky deflection, like the one that gave Wednesday victory in the November 1901 derby.

Small Heath (soon to become Birmingham FC), newly promoted from the Second Division, shocked everyone by hitting five past Foulke in the October 1901 League game. Once again the consistency necessary for success in this competition was to elude the Blades. The FA Cup that year, though, was another glory road, and William had his usual vital part to play.

Before the turn of the year, however, he underwent the unusual experience of having to fight for his first-team place. Understudy William Biggar took over between the sticks during Foulke's enforced lay-off through injury. Almost two years after his nervy beginning, Biggar had gained confidence by playing well in United's successful reserve side. He received fully merited praise for his performances in the next three games: a 5-0 rout of Manchester City, a fighting 1-1 draw at Wolves, and a 2-1 defeat of Liverpool.

By mid-December Foulke was back in action, playing in the reserves, no doubt savouring the 9-0 win over Hinckley Town. On the same day, at Newcastle, Biggar was instrumental in holding the Tynesiders to a 1-1 draw. Now the committee had a dilemma: did they bring back Foulke, who despite his eccentricities had proven himself to be the best in the kingdom when fully fit, or did they stick with the fellow who had anchored a mini-run of success?

On the Saturday before Christmas the Blades played a friendly with Glasgow Rangers at Bramall Lane. Foulke was selected and, obviously seeing this as a golden opportunity to return to first-team favour, duly went out and played a blinder in the 1-0 win. Still the committee hesitated: Biggar was preferred for the League game at Stoke on Boxing Day. Here, however, the Mexborough man committed a glaring schoolboy error which gave the home side an early lead. Stoke went on to win 3-2, and Foulke regained his place.

Sheffield United now hit another winning streak. William was back at his confident best, Needham's half-back line was once more the fearsomely inventive unit of old, and up front £350 new boy Alf Common was boosting the firepower of Bennett, Priest and Hedley. The results of all games, League and cup, in which Foulke played in the first couple of months of 1902 read as follows:

P	W	D	L	F	A
12	8	4	0	27	8

It was the perfect time to peak for an FA Cup run.

The first round was a trip to Northampton, and a relatively straightforward 2-0 win. William performed the two or three textbook tasks that befell him without breaking too much of a sweat.

Next was a home tie against Bolton Wanderers. The visitors took a first-half lead when McKie was left unchallenged a dozen yards out, allowing him the time to pick his spot and hammer a rising shot into the net. And if truth be told, the United 'keeper had a generous slice of luck with the match poised at 1-1 in the second half. Foulke had gone on one of his forays, and Bolton forward Williams was put through in front of an empty goal with a barn door to aim at. As he strove to bring the ball under control Thickett got his foot in and conceded a harmless throw-in. With a quarter of an hour to go Priest hit the winner, after a tricky Bennett run had drawn the opposing goalie out of position.

For the third round the Blades had to travel to Newcastle. This 'other United' had yet to develop into the formidable cup warriors of the twentieth century, but were tough opponents all the same. They would finish third in the League that year, stealing Sheffield United's record of the best defence in the First Division. They employed the one-back game, whose purpose was to catch out forwards under the older, more cumbersome offside rule.

It was the attack, though, that gave Needham's team most headaches that day (apart, possibly, from the state of the pitch – see Appendix). The major irritant was the diminutive, marauding Orr, dwarfed by Foulke but unworried by the big fellow's bulk. Priest had beaten the offside trap to give Sheffield a half-time lead, but on seventy-five minutes Roberts shot hard and low, bringing a fine scooping save from Foulke. But he was unable to hold the ball, and the hovering Orr, accompanied by Stewart, swept in the equaliser.

Back at Bramall Lane, in a rattling good cup-tie chock with incident, Needham put the Blades into the lead after twenty minutes. Newcastle, unbowed, attacked with increased vigour. An equalising goal before half-time was almost inevitable, and a cracker it was, McColl belting a twenty-yarder through a crowd of players and way out of Foulke's reach. In the second half Thickett came to the rescue again, robbing Gardner of the ball when the Tynesider forward appeared to have a tap-in chance. Then Common settled matters with a late winner for Sheffield.

Another semi-final: this time against old adversaries Derby County. The Rams were hungry for revenge, and were in the mood, having just beaten Portsmouth 6-3, with Steve Bloomer hitting a hat-trick. The first game, at the Hawthorns, saw 'Paleface' at his most active. It was one of his speedy low shots that led to the Rams opening the scoring. Foulke, running across the goal, pushed the ball clear, only for Warren to lob back the return into the far side of the net. United were lucky to survive: Bloomer headed just wide of the post, and for most of the game it was Derby hammering at the gates. A late equaliser from Hedley, which County goalkeeper Jack Fryer allowed to run in as he was convinced it was offside, gave the Blades a lifeline.

The replay was at Molineux. After five minutes Wombwell attempted a cross from the right, but the strong wind took hold of the ball and directed it into goal, much to Foulke's incredulous disgust. The *Derby Daily Telegraph* told of a 'clever screw shot', and indeed Wombwell carried it off rather well, his celebrations masking his surprise. Priest equalised, and the score remained at 1-1 throughout the second half and the half-hour of extra time.

Foulke earned his £4 many times over that day. Boyle, assigned to police Bloomer, was having a nightmare, and as the game progressed more and more Derby attacks found their way through to crash against the United goal. William saved another low shot from Bloomer, then fisted out a dangerous header from the 'Destroying Angel' from right under the bar. In diving full length to stop a shot from Warren the big man knocked his head against the post. He was back in action after a couple of minutes' recovery. Three cracking shots in the final minute of normal time were fielded with the usual aplomb. Yet again William had shone and saved the day, with the rest of the team below par.

Needham was injured late on in this match, so was unable to turn out for the second replay, the following Thursday, at Nottingham. The young reserve Billy Parker took his place at left half, and in a reshuffle, it was he who was designated to try and subdue the mercurial Bloomer, with Boyle as the fail-safe man. The plan worked well. Yet again Derby, despite their clear advantage in territory and possession, were unable to translate it into goals. Warren and Boag fluffed easy chances, and Foulke was alert enough to repel Bloomer's usual testing contributions. In the Blades' only attack throughout the first half, Priest put his team into the lead for the first time. Then in what was to become time-honoured semi-final style, United hunkered down in defence and played out the second half. In the face of such a pragmatic approach, a tiring County's attacks were repeatedly thwarted, and a furious Bloomer started to hurl abuse at his colleagues. Not for the first time in those years, Sheffield United grit and brio, typified by and founded upon the goalkeeping of Bill Foulke, had overcome a theoretically stronger, classier outfit.

In the final the Blades would meet another team from the Southern League. On the way to the Crystal Palace Southampton – 'that veritable Klondyke for professional footballers' – had seen off such daunting prospects as Nottingham Forest, holders Spurs, League Champions Liverpool, and 1900 winners Bury. Their team was a glittering mosaic of internationals and seasoned players, lured by the more substantial wage packets that the newer League was able to offer.

There was a crowd of over 74,000 at the Palace, and, obsession in such cases being nine points of the law, means were found to watch the game for free. An observer 'counted fifty men in one elm behind the grandstand'. Elsewhere, necessity giving birth to invention:

> One man carried a hook, a rope, and a board. He made a sort of boatswain's chair, and hooked himself to the top of a high post.
> *Manchester Guardian* (21/4/02)

The teams were: *Sheffield United:* Foulke; Thickett, Boyle; Johnson, Wilkinson, Needham (capt.); Bennett, Common, Hedley, Priest, Lipsham. *Southampton:*

Robinson; Fry, Molyneux; Meston, Bowman, Lee; A. Turner, Wood (capt.),
Brown, Chadwick, J. Turner.

It was a stiflingly hot day, and despite the huge interest, overall it was a drab,
shapeless game with neither team showing enough attacking verve to stand
out as worthy winners. Alf Common scored for United early in the second
half, and as full time approached, it appeared that the Football League side
had done just enough to scrape an unremarkable victory. Both Bennett and
Common sustained injuries, so that eventually the entire right-sided attack
was reduced to virtual spectators.

The Southern League team were growing increasingly frustrated as attack
after attack broke down. Their strategy of long passes and shots from relative distance – an attempt to circumvent United's powerhouse of a midfield
and resolute defence – played into Foulke's hands. Master of his goal area, he
would leave his line to collect or clear. Time was nearly up, and Southampton
fans had started to drift out of the ground. Then, with a minute or so remaining, there was a gift from the gods. Yet another Southampton offensive had
been repulsed, but this time only as far as right-winger Arthur Turner, who
sent in an optimistic shot (or perhaps a cross – it was that sort of ball) which
found the immobile Harry Wood a few yards in front of the Sheffield goal,
with just Foulke to beat. As Wood himself was to admit later, it was a clearly
offside position, but in a reflex reaction he dribbled the ball on and placed it
in the net. The United 'keeper, naturally, didn't bother to attempt a save.

The referee Tom Kirkham ran across to the linesman, and they embarked on
a seemingly interminable discussion. Foulke stood shielding his eyes from the
low sun, with the ball in his hand, ready to place it for the free-kick. Then, to
universal amazement and the goalkeeper's angry disbelief, the referee pointed
to the centre. A goal had been awarded.

Unfortunately film of that incident, if taken, hasn't survived, so an interpretation of the officials' thought processes will have to rely on eyewitness
reports. The crux of Mr Kirkham's argument was that the ball had touched
Boyle on its way forward, and this – according to the rules then in force – put
Wood onside. Boyle was later vehemently to deny any contact. One version of
events has Wood tying his bootlaces at the moment the pass was made. If true,
this would arguably render him 'not interfering with play'. The Southampton
captain, by the way, with a track record as respected ex-Wolves captain and
England player, and at thirty-four towards the end of a blameless career, can
be exonerated from any suspicion of sneaky play-acting.

In any case, whatever happened during those crucial few seconds, without
the benefit of action replays we'll probably never be sure of the precise details,

and the goal stood. Some of the more neutral observers saw it as poetic justice after United's highly dubious equaliser in the previous year's final. But for those with more partisan interest, the shenanigans were far from over.

As the teams made their way from the pitch, a Southampton fan decided to vent his frustration on Needham, hitting the Sheffielder in the face. Perhaps he chose Needham because of the half-back's small stature. If it were so, it were a grievous fault. Nobody present – with the single obvious exception – could have been a more redoubtable opponent in such a confrontation than hard-as-nails Needham. Normally the soul of diplomacy, the United captain retaliated with a left-right combination that wouldn't have disgraced Bob Fitzsimmons. At this point the spectator, concluding it might be a good idea to make himself scarce, turned and ran – into the arms of a couple of policemen.

The next day back in Sheffield there was a rumour that it was Foulke who had hit back. But as the Monday's *Telegraph* wryly commented: 'The assailant may be glad it was only Needham.'

Foulke's anger at Wood's last-minute goal was still smouldering as the teams reached the dressing rooms. Were the moneyed southerners about to steal a march as they had done the previous year? In broad terms, the South equalled London and the establishment. Jack Robinson, the Southampton goalie, was the usual choice for international honours, getting the nod over Foulke every time. And there was right-back C.B. Fry, landed gent and lauded amateur, the Corinthian whose well-bred insults directed at the professionals and the proles in football were well known. All these ingredients no doubt added to the cocktail of resentment simmering away inside the big man.

Journalist and author David Randall takes up the story, subscribing to the version usually given:

At the end of the 1902 cup final he left the field huffing and puffing with indignation at a decision by Mr Tom Kirkham which allowed Southampton to equalise and earn a replay. In the dressing room Foulke got more and more worked up so that by the time he was stripped, his entire mass was wobbling with rage. With a great roar Foulke swore vengeance on the little official and went looking for him. Fortunately Kirkham saw him first and he dived for cover into a nearby boot cupboard. But Foulke was not to be thwarted. He seized the cupboard door and began trying to wrench it from its hinges. It was in this rather compromising position that the naked goalkeeper was discovered by the secretary of the Football Association and several other worthies. They somehow managed to soothe the savage Foulke and shepherd him gently back to his dressing room.

Great Sporting Eccentrics (1985)

It's a mini-drama that has entertained for over a century. Once again, though, we have to ask: how true is it? Mr Randall paints a colourful picture, but, if I may say so, he wasn't there. We could do a lot worse than listen to somebody who was, namely the linesman J.T. Howcroft:

> Foulke was exasperated by the goal and claimed it was miles offside. He was in
> his birthday suit outside the dressing room, and I saw F.J. Wall, secretary of the
> FA, pleading with him to rejoin his colleagues. But Bill was out for blood, and I
> shouted to Mr Kirkham to lock his cubicle door. He didn't need telling twice.
> But what a sight! The thing I'll never forget is Foulke, so tremendous in size,
> striding along the corridor, without a stitch of clothing.
> *Sheffield Football: A History, Vol. I*

There are a number of significant differences between this account and Randall's extrapolation. The ideas of pursuit of, and confrontation with, the referee aren't made explicit. The ignominy of a 'boot cupboard' has become the official's changing quarters, and the FA secretary's intervention occurred at the beginning of the episode, rather than at its supposed climax. Besides, is it likely that a professional footballer would risk his livelihood and probable litigation by terrorising a ref in this way? Despite the burning sense of injustice that was no doubt tingeing the atmosphere of the United dressing room, we know that the experienced Foulke (reputed short fuse and all) was basically a canny enough character not to be suckered into such a performance as the one commonly related. The evidence appears to point to a fuming, rumbling volcano, rather than a Krakatoan attempted assault on an official.

The replay, one week later, was in many ways a great contrast. The teams were the same, except that the young Billy Barnes took the injured Bennett's place on the right wing. It was a better contest, more open and attacking, and for our William, the best possible antidote to the tribulations of the first game.

There had been a couple of initial skirmishes at either end, and the game was less than two minutes old. The Blades 'keeper walloped out an immense clearance kick that tickled the stratosphere, and when it next made contact with the earth was but twenty yards in front of the Southampton goal. Lipsham brought the ball under control then embarked on a bold, tricky run that left Meston and Fry in his wake. The unbalanced Saints' defence was caught napping, and a precise pass to Hedley gave the centre forward a simple chance, which, almost nonchalantly, he took. The Southern-biased crowd raised scarcely a murmur.

With Needham virtually running the show from midfield, and the Blades full-backs showing a toughness and ingenuity that nullified any potential danger, it looked as if the Sheffielders could win as they pleased. Long shots were dealt with by Foulke in the usual confident manner, and the tactic employed by Wood of charging the goalie was, as expected, an exercise in futility. Well, it amused the crowd. United attacks were plentiful enough in that first half, but too many of them culminated in a shot off target. So half-time was reached, with Needham's team just the one goal to the good.

It was against the run of play when Southampton grabbed an equaliser midway through the second half. A fast low shot from an oblique angle by Albert Brown gave the United 'keeper no chance. Now the crowd erupted, and for a worrying ten minutes or so it looked as though the reanimated Southerners might steal it.

But William was not to be beaten again. The more the shots rained in on him, the more he appeared to relish the attention. 'Foulke was invincible,' said the *Athletic News*. With ten minutes to go a combined Blades effort gained the winning goal. After some interplay between the forwards, Common laid the ball back for Johnson, who, seeing that Needham had joined the attack, lobbed it forward. The United captain sent in a crafty high shot that was curling for the top corner when Robinson, at full stretch, pushed it out, but only to Barnes, who rammed the ball into the unguarded net. The Saints' effort duly collapsed, and United played out the final few minutes by easy and confident man-to-man passing across the midfield. So the Cup returned to Sheffield.

The recently installed maximum wage also entailed a ban on win bonuses, which ruling extended to any special reward bestowed upon players. After the celebration banquet at Sheffield Foulke somehow conjured up a crate of champagne. So as not to appear to be recipients of an illegal inducement, it was arranged for one bottle to be consumed at one man's house, another at someone else's, and so on. As the next few years were to show, this light-hearted ploy was the forerunner of more serious attempts by League clubs to evade the maximum wage straitjacket.

Jasper Redfern, pioneer of the cinema in the region, had shot footage of both matches, as well as of training at Skegness. Foulke wielding Indian clubs, and the team practising leap-frog – now that would have been worth seeing!

The advert in the *Telegraph* read:

EMPIRE PALACE
JASPER REDFERN'S FOOTBALL PICTURES
THE RE-PLAYED ENGLISH CUP FINAL
at the Crystal Palace, showing Southampton's one goal, Sheffield's winning goal, fine saving by Foulke, etc., etc., Box Office open daily 11 to 3. Sat. 11 to 1
Sheffield Daily Telegraph (30/4/02)

This film was shown on Saturday 3 May, with Marie Lloyd performing at the same venue in the evening. It's interesting to note, in the midst of the celebrations, the speed with which politicians can nail their colours to the mast:

> …our giant goalkeeper Foulke, with his tremendous smite and prodigious kick, the best goalkeeper football has ever seen. May he live a thousand years.
> Sir Howard Vincent, Sheffield MP

For once, no one was likely to contradict him!

The 1902 FA Cup final replay, a lively affair as seen by cartoonist Frank Gillett.
(Football Association)

10: 'Twixt Cup and Lip

Liverpool fairly bombarded the United goal, but Foulke performed marvels, at which the crowd cheered most impartially.

Athletic News (30/3/03), reporting on Liverpool 2, Sheffield United 4

Mind you, he [Foulke] was often a bit nervy before a big game, and when he was feeling jumpy he'd point to my little whisky flask and say 'Now, Father, I'll be better for a drop,' and after a toothful he'd be right as rain.

Tom Bott (from *Sheffield Football: A History, Vol. 1*)

Sheffield United would have won the 1902/03 League Championship, were it not for an injury to Bill Foulke in the first game of the New Year. A tenuous claim? Let's see.

In the match itself, a 1–3 defeat at Bury, the United goalkeeper wrenched his left knee in the first half, damaging a cartilage. Rudimentary on-the-pitch massage brought an illusory, short-lived relief. Thereafter the Bury attack exploited the limping Foulke. In the second half he was drawn out to the right, then the ball was switched to the other wing, and it was a relatively easy matter for Wood to put the home side into the lead. As William had tried to run across to cover, his leg had given way completely, and in great agony he had to leave the field. While United were re-arranging their defence – Boyle was eventually to take Foulke's place on the day – Sagar walked the ball into an empty net for Bury's third.

So at least a point had been lost in that particular game. William was now out of action for the next seven league games, and the two FA Cup ties. 'The lean Lewis', his new understudy, took his place.

Albert Lewis, who also batted for Somerset, had performed superbly in the Blades reserves, and indeed there was a faction on the club committee that had been pushing for regular first-team status for the newcomer. His performances at this level, though, were erratic. At his best he displayed an agility and a daring equal to his mentor. He received praise for his contribution to the 2–1 win over Blackburn Rovers, as well as the fine goalless draw at Sunderland. The *Sheffield Daily Telegraph*, not usually given over to wild praise, stated: 'If Lewis stands the test of time, there will come a period when he will be the leading goalkeeper in the League.' (2/2/03). Then a crucial blunder in

the home FA Cup match with Bury, which led to United being knocked out
of that year's competition, and a succession of error-strewn League games,
made his supporters reconsider.

If we include the two games earlier in the season when Lewis had taken
Foulke's place when the big man was suffering from a bad cold, the results of
the league games in which Lewis kept goal are as follows:

P	W	D	L	F	A	Pts
9	2	2	5	9	13	6

Which gives Foulke's games for 1902/03 as:

P	W	D	L	F	A	Pts
25	15	3	7	49	31	33

Although 'nothing is certain in football', translating Foulke's games' record to
the entire season suggests the trophy would have gone to Bramall Lane – by a
considerable margin.

The Championship race of 1902/03 was a close-run thing, the pendulum
swinging several times during the campaign. In the event it was Wednesday
who stole it after a nail-biting run-in. Just seven points covered the top ten
teams at the end.

The major innovation that season had been the introduction of the new
penalty area, which is pretty much the design that has survived until today.
Out went the pitch-wide 12-yds line with the 'kidney' arcs in front of goal,
and in came the more compact 44 yds x 18 yds box. In an oblique way, it was
symptomatic of a changing world. A new monarch was on the throne, and
suffragettes and powered flight were about to make their appearance. The war
in South Africa was over, but concern was already being expressed about the
accelerated build-up of armaments over in Germany. The twentieth century
was already well into its stride.

It was tempting to look at Willie Foulke as an emblem of a disappearing
age, the soccer equivalent of the Wild West. His rough-cut ebullience, some
held, had served its purpose, but now in the increasingly super-subtle modern
world, there would come a time soon when he would have to bow out.

Critics pointed to the occasional fine shots that found their way past him
(as if this was something completely new). 'Not the force he was' was the
whispered leitmotif. Yet time and again, after an indifferent performance, he
would launch himself back into favour with some astonishing saves. Even
in the 2-4 defeat against the Villa, in which, according to the *Telegraph*, he

was 'far from at his best', he still managed to stop a last-minute penalty from Garratty. Some said he was finding it more difficult to get down to low shots: the Nottingham Forest attack, having peppered the United goal with around a dozen such attempts in the league game that October – all of them held or knocked away by Foulke – would have had to disagree.

Not all the attempts to beat the big fellow were blessed with legality. In front of a howling partisan crowd at Middlesbrough, several of the opposing forwards borrowed a tactic from American football and wedged William up against a post, while the ball was put into the net. Not surprisingly the 'goal' was disallowed, much to the fury of the home fans. United won 2-0.

Despite the loss to Wednesday on the opening day of the season, the Blades had begun the campaign well, and were in contention until Foulke's injury. Just before Christmas the top of the table read:

	P	W	D	L	F	A	Pts
West Bromwich Albion	19	12	2	5	39	23	26
The Wednesday	20	12	1	7	35	23	25
Sheffield United	19	11	2	6	32	21	24

United had gained their revenge by winning 1-0 at Owlerton, a game in which 'Foulke's constant magnificence' (*Telegraph*) was a deciding factor.

Herbert Chapman – he who was to gain far greater fame as the seminal club manager of the twentieth century – had made his debut for the Blades. For a time, oddly considering his comparative lack of height, he was deployed at centre forward. His football skills were actually nothing special: about his only memorable attributes on the field of play were his banana-yellow boots. As soon as he was moved to inside right, and the slightly taller, lightning-fast Alf Common switched to spearhead, the winning combination appeared to have been achieved. And then came that fateful clash at Bury.

Typically, though incapacitated, William refused to remain idle. He accompanied the team to Plumstead for the FA Cup first round tie with Woolwich Arsenal.

When United arrived at the ground they had an excellent reception, especially Needham and Foulke, the latter perhaps being the general favourite.
Sheffield Daily Telegraph (9/2/03)

The capital's adulation was prophetic, in that within a couple of years he would be playing for a London club.

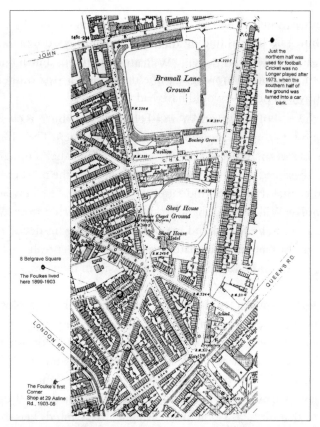

Map of the area around Bramall Lane in 1903, based on the contemporary
Ordnance Survey map 'Sheffield Park'.

On the Foulkes' home front, too, there would be significant changes. It was
in early 1903 that William invested his benefit monies into his and Beatrice's
first shop, a general store and 'beerhouse' on Asline Road, two minutes' walk
from Belgrave Square. Given the great popularity of the player, it's not surprising that the shop was a success, and that by the time of his retirement the
family were able to buy larger premises on the more central Matilda Street.
One story goes that William was landlord of a pub called The Duke, but this
turns out to be only part of the truth (see chapter 14).

Bill Foulke's relationship with alcohol has fuelled many a tale. The stories
of him turning up for a match once so drunk he had to be hosed down can
only be dismissed as apocryphal. Firstly, he was too much of a professional to
indulge in such folly, and secondly the ethos of strict abstention maintained
by the Bramall Lane committee would have resulted in severe disciplinary
measures, had this Fred Karno-like incident really taken place. His traditional pre-match snack was supposed to have been a round of toast and a glass

of beer, and as Tom Bott was to reveal, a secret snifter from the committee member's hip flask sometimes steadied the 'keeper's nerves before a really important game. There's no denying William liked his ale, but he never let it interfere with his football. Once again, it would appear that some tales have grown in the telling.

Towards the end of his lay-off, in mid-February, Blackburn Rovers reserves beat Heywood 3-0 in a Lancashire Combination match. The *Athletic News* sang the praises of the Rovers' new 6ft and 14st 7lb goalie: 'Though at times he was hotly besieged, he performed very well, clearing the most dangerous of the shots in capital style…' Sound familiar? It ought to. The new acquisition was Jack Foulke, William's younger brother, just transferred from Wellington Town. Like Tommy, he had played in goal there, making his debut at the pre-cocious age of thirteen! Unfortunately the promise wasn't realised, Jack didn't settle in the north, and returned to Shropshire within the year.

The Blades had sunk to mid-table during William's absence. Now, in mid-March with just seven games remaining, his return inspired the team to a stirring chase of the front-runners. Realists saw it as a forlorn hope: but although six points adrift of the leaders, with Sunderland and Villa having matches in hand, United weren't going down without a fight.

Foulke gave a flawless performance at Newcastle in the 0-0 draw. Then Wolves were demolished 3-0 at Bramall Lane, the United 'keeper virtually a spectator. A tough proposition at Liverpool was transformed into a great 4-2 win, with Foulke giving one of his virtuoso displays which was loudly appreciated even by the home fans. Derby County, cup finalists, were next, albeit after a scare: 0-2 down, the Rams fought back to equalise (Warren's searing shot on seventy-four minutes giving the United goalie not a ghost of a chance) before Archie Needham dropped a craftily placed header beyond Fryer for the winner.

By now United were among the leaders, although they had played more games than the other contenders. Sunderland were looking the best bet, three points behind leaders The Wednesday, but with two games in hand. And their last match would be away against Newcastle United, who had never beaten the Wearsiders in a League game at St James' Park.

Sheffield United could only plough on, hoping their opponents might slip up. Two of their final three games were won, both by the convincing margin of 3-0. The Blades dominated in both, but when called upon, William gave his usual formidable display of skill.

It still didn't seem to be enough. By the middle of April both Sheffield sides looked ready to concede the title to the previous year's winners:

	P	W	D	L	F	A	Pts
The Wednesday	33	18	4	11	51	35	40
Sunderland	31	15	9	7	47	29	39
Sheffield United	33	17	5	11	56	40	39

Wednesday won their last game and went away on tour in the West Country. Sunderland won one and lost one. United's heroic and unlikely bid for glory came to an emphatic end after their return from their Irish tour (in which William had saved a penalty in a cracking 3–3 draw with Dublin's Bohemians). They played Aston Villa, away, and were completely outclassed. Three out of the four goals conceded in the 2–4 defeat were similar in approach and execution: a fast wing run, a head-high swerving cross that entered the no man's land between Foulke and his backs, and a thumping header directed out of the goalie's reach. On the day, the Blades had no answer to this.

Villa leapfrogged over United and Sunderland, finishing on 41 points. Now it seemed a simple matter for Sunderland, also on 41 points, to gain at least a draw at Newcastle, and since their goal average was marginally superior to Wednesday's, to take the trophy back up to the North-East. Unfortunately Newcastle had read another script, and won 1–0. So Wednesday heard of their 1902/03 Championship win while away in sunny Devon.

Bill Foulke spent the summer building up the Asline Road shop. His daughter, Selina, was born later that year. When he returned refreshed for football training in August, he wasn't prepared for the blow which would put him out of action again for the first four games, and would see Albert Lewis back in the first team.

11: 'His Royal Mountainousness'

*His Royal Mountainousness … went through the gamut of his duties
with that fixedness that mountains suggest so well.*
Athletic News (21/3/04)

*Foulke's weakness is his inability to capture low shots. He got low ones
on Saturday…*
Athletic News (14/11/04) after Bury 7, Sheffield United 1

It was a routine practice game, a week or so before the opening match of the
1903/04 season. William dived full-length for the ball, gathered up and kicked
clear. Before the end of the game he felt a pain in his shoulder. Upon examination it was discovered he had damaged his collarbone, and would be out for
a month.

The Blades had put their four-figure profit from the previous year to good
use, and had built up their squad. An addition to the ranks during the summer
had been the nineteen-year-old Joe Leivesley, yet another Staveley product
spotted and recommended by Needham. Now United could boast three top-
class keepers. With Foulke nursing his injury, Lewis took over the first-team
spot, and Leivesley kept goal for the high-achieving Blades reserves in the
Midland League.

The first team started well too, enjoying four straight League wins before
William's return. His comeback match was the most difficult imaginable:
away against Manchester City, joint leaders, also on 100%. Meredith and
Co., who were to carry off the FA Cup that season, had cooked up a storm
for the Sheffielders, and threw everything into an early spate of attacks. But
Foulke, despite a minor injury to his wrist, was on song, and eventually it was
Common who profited from a breakaway to net the only goal of the match.

The Blades went on to win their next three league games, thus setting a
record for the time of eight straight wins at the beginning of a campaign. As
usual, William was in the thick of it, never more so than in the nail-biting 1-0
win at Newcastle. For the first fifteen minutes United were prisoners around
their own goal, but the defence performed heroics. Foulke was elbowed
painfully in the ribs by a Newcastle forward, but recovered enough to leap
and turn a forty-yard scorcher over the bar. Young Arthur Brown scored for

'Sheffield have a group taken.' (Athletic News)

Sheffield, then back came the home side in their droves. With minutes left, Howie cracked in a tricky shot which the United 'keeper managed to push away. Templeton followed up, and Foulke smothered his effort. But the ball squirmed out from under him – the pitch being 'a curious mixture of the sticky and the slippery' – and Templeton had another go. This one William pushed round the post, and the corner came to nothing. The top of the table immediately after that record eighth win read as follows:

	P	W	D	L	F	A	Pts
Sheffield United	8	8	0	0	24	10	16
The Wednesday	9	6	2	1	14	6	14
Everton	9	6	1	2	20	11	13

It was Aston Villa, often the party-poopers for the Blades, who burst the bubble, winning 2-1 at Bramall Lane on the last day of October. Ominously, Foulke fell heavily in saving a shot, and injured his knee.

He was back for the next game, but that winter injuries were a recurring theme. He had to miss a couple of matches in December with a groin strain, then hurt his wrist again in stopping a fierce shot from Billy Meredith just before New Year. Almost imperceptibly, age and avoirdupois were at last taking their toll.

The Blades started to slip down the league. They were to win just seven more games after that dazzling opening. Bad luck played its part. Team injuries accumulated, so that seven reserves had to be played against Liverpool in March. Two extraordinarily unlucky goals were conceded against Blackburn Rovers in the same month: Foulke was about to gather up an easy loose ball when Thickett, not seeing his 'keeper approach, attempted to clear, slipped in the mud, and sent the ball skewing into the net. Then the referee appeared to disallow the final goal through offside, then inexplicably changed his mind.

Thickett, incidentally, had started to put on weight almost as fast as his 'keeper. Nippy wingers could now easily outpace him, which contributed to the fall in League form. Sheffield United finished a disappointing seventh in the First Division that year. The Wednesday were once again Champions, nine points ahead of United.

In the FA Cup, after a memorable 2-1 win in a pell-mell game at Bury, there followed a surprising 0-2 home reverse against Second Division Bolton Wanderers. On the day, the Lancastrians were well worth their win.

A typically hammer-and-tongs Sheffield derby match, December 1903. The teams occupied the top two positions in the league at the time. (Athletic News)

William fluffed a centre, seeming to take his eye off the ball, which simply struck him and fell nicely for Yenson, who had an easy tap-in from a couple of yards for the first goal.

It was on Wednesday 20 April 1904 that the famous photo of Sheffield United's array of twelve internationals was taken. The line-up was:

Foulke, Thickett, Boyle, Johnson, Morren, Needham, Wilkinson, Brown, Common, Bennett, Priest, Lipsham.

It was the final memento of the golden era. Thickett, Boyle and Common wouldn't start the next season at Bramall Lane, and Foulke wouldn't keep his first-team place beyond November. Walter Bennett would be transferred to Bristol City (where Harry Thickett had been appointed team manager) the following April. The times they were a-changing.

Early games in the 1904/05 season highlighted the sudden paucity of decent full-backs available. Groves and Annan were good enough, but no substitute for Thickett and Boyle. Their marking was haphazard, and lack of consistent covering support for Foulke's eccentricities meant that the Blades were vulnerable to the swift counterattack. After the 1-2 defeat at Stoke the *Telegraph* noted: 'Occasionally he had to run right out of goal in order to clear when the backs were beaten.' (10/10/04).

The nature of the game was subtly shifting. That season saw the introduction of the direct free-kick and the advantage rule. As William's youthful speed was starting to fade, so the game itself was becoming quicker, and more demanding on defences. In an attempt to keep pace with the new conditions, even lively winger Fred Priest had been given a trial run at left-back. But things got worse, reaching a lowest ebb in November, with successive defeats of 1-7 and 0-3.

After the debacle at Bury ('Now we are seven', gloated the caption to a cartoon in the *Athletic News*) the United committee were philosophical. It had surely been 'just one of those days.' The Bury attack had hit a probably unrepeatable streak of power play, and Sagar had played the game of his life. The team, then, remained largely unchanged, and Foulke was given a chance to redeem himself. A two-edged sword: the next match was against traditional bêtes noires Aston Villa.

Although the game was at Bramall Lane, on that fateful day the Villa completely outclassed the Blades, in all departments. The fearless nineteen-year-old Hampton was inspirational, hitting the first goal with a shot that gave Foulke no chance, then two minutes later setting up Bache whose optimistic stab found its way between William's legs. A penalty finished the job. The writing was now

on the wall, in six-foot high playbill script. Bill Foulke had just played his last
League game for Sheffield United.

Enter Joe Leivesley, who had been pushing for a regular first-team place for
some time.

Here was a new breed of 'keeper: precise, dependable, cutting down attack-
ers' options through his reading of the game and keen sense of position. It was
modern thinking: the eye-catching save meant that something somewhere
along the line had been less than perfect. To quote Gordon Banks: 'The mark of
a good goalkeeper is how few saves he has to make during a game. A spectacular
save is the last resort when all else – positioning, anticipation, defence – have
failed.' (*Banksy*, p.1). Moreover, reflecting a general trend in the first decade of
the twentieth century, the commonsensical was replacing the romantic and the
devil-may-care.

The two keepers, both brilliant in their own way, were as different as chalk
and cheese: Leivesley the correct theoretician and cool pragmatist, and the zesty
calorie-replete Derbyshire-with-nuts that was Foulke.

Joe Leivesley had waited long enough in the big fellow's shadow. Suddenly
finding himself centre stage, he wasn't going to blow the opportunity. The
Blades hit a winning streak, and within a few weeks were at the top of the First
Division. All William could do was bide his time in the reserves.

The Midland League side was an unbeatable mix of talented youth and more
mature characters who in any other club would have been regular first-team-
ers. Besides Foulke as anchor, Walter Bennett and Archie Needham were prime
movers in a rampant attack. Some of the games were stunningly one-sided:

26/11/04: Sheffield United Reserves 9, Gresley Rovers 1
7/1/05: Sheffield United Reserves 10, Derby County Reserves 0
28/1/05: Sheffield United Reserves 15, Lincoln City 0

Such was the strength in depth of the Blades' overall squad, that on one day they
were able to field three decent teams. Foulke on that day played for the reserves
side that beat Doncaster Rovers 3-0.

In the semi of the Sheffield Challenge Cup, he was up to his familiar tricks:

Foulke caused a roar of laughter by holding the ball in one hand, and gazing at
three comparatively diminutive Denaby men, who were careful to avoid charging
him.

Sheffield Daily Telegraph (6/1/05)

United reserves won that one 3–0, and went on to beat The Wednesday reserves 3–1 in a fairly unproblematic final, at Owlerton, no less. Significantly, the crowd that day was 7,000, which was higher than at the first-team fixture over at Bramall Lane!

The Midland League was also won in emphatic style. The final leading positions were:

	P	W	D	L	F	A	Pts
Sheffield United Res.	32	22	4	6	107	33	48
Nottingham Forest Res.	32	20	5	7	85	49	45

Although he was unable to return to first-team favour, it's noteworthy that for friendlies and benefit matches that year, it was Foulke who was requested rather than Leivesley. He was, as ever, a major box-office attraction.

Walter Bennett's benefit was a match with the Corinthians. It was, of course, unthinkable for anyone other than best mate William to turn out as 'keeper for that one. He also appeared in friendlies against new club Leeds City, West Ham United and Hull City. Only at the very end, for the two-match tour of London at the end of April, was Leivesley preferred.

There followed a fortnight's suspense, before the following paragraph appeared in the *Independent*:

FOULKE GOES SOUTH

William Foulke, the famous giant goalkeeper, who has played a prominent part in many of the greatest deeds of the Sheffield United Football Club, has been transferred to Chelsea, a newly formed club. Presumably the transfer and the fee (which I hear, is not an exorbitant one) became necessary in view of the intention of Chelsea to apply for admission to the Second Division of the League, for Foulke, who declined less than the maximum wages, had not signed for United. He is to receive the maximum from Chelsea.

(15/5/05)

The transfer fee was actually a very reasonable £50. Chelsea must have thought their Christmas had come early.

12: Chelsea

The captain is Foulke. He is already one of the most popular players
in London. When people first come to Chelsea, they fall to admiring
the proportions of the ground, then the proportions of Foulke, and next
his unquestionable skill as a goalkeeper.

J.T. ('Jock') Robertson, Chelsea's first ever manager.
The Book of Football (Nov. 1905)

Sheffield people will be interested in knowing that their old goalkeeper
took eight flights of hurdles (without, of course, the water jump) at
Stamford Bridge the other day.

Athletic News (4/9/05)

Londoners had never seen the like.

Stamford Bridge. Saturday 23 September, 1905. Around 4.30 p.m. Chelsea,
the new kids on the block, were hanging on to a precarious one-goal lead
notched by centre forward McRoberts. West Bromwich Albion, still smart-
ing from their recent demotion from the top flight, decided to launch a
sustained attack that would blow these southern upstarts out of the water.
Who did they think they were; Spurs?

The Throstles poured forward. Shot after cross after shot bombarded the
home goal. The exhausted Chelsea backs, wilting under the onslaught, could
do little more than stand and watch. For fully fifteen minutes the blitz continued. It was surely only a matter of time before at least the equaliser arrived.
That Chelsea withstood the storm, the scoresheet unblemished, is almost
entirely due to the fact that Bill Foulke was in their goal. As those in the
know could have predicted, this bombardment was the very sort of warm
attention that he revelled in. Without the slightest ruffle in his calm demean-
our he flung himself to left and right, saving the day with his customary
mobility and certainty. Any lingering local doubters were won over on that
day: Foulke was every bit as good as they said he was.

And that poker-faced prediction of manager Jock Robertson, the one
which had his side 'halfway up the table' by the end of the season, perhaps
that needed revising too? As it turned out, Chelsea would be pushing for

promotion till the end. Remarkable considering that six months beforehand, this feisty team, captained by Foulke, didn't even exist!

Fate had seemed to postpone the birth of Chelsea FC until, by a generous serendipity, Bill Foulke became available.

Initially the Stamford Bridge ground was an athletics track, built in 1877 on the site of old allotments and a market garden. The London Athletic Club started holding its meets there – and the perimeter track, in its time used for greyhound and speedway races too – lasted until well into the next century. It was the Mears brothers who conceived the idea of transforming the ground into one fit for a major football club. Gus and Joseph Mears, both football daft and neither short of a bob or two, bought the ground, but had to wait until 1904 before launch. Mr Stunt, the previous owner, had had a clause inserted into the contract whereby the London Athletic Club would remain owners until two years after his death. That most illustrious of architects of football stadia, Archibald Leitch (whose CV already included Villa Park, Hampden, Ibrox and Goodison) was commissioned to design the new ground. Building started before the end of the year, with a projected capacity crowd of 70,000.

Once again, then, the stadium predated the team. With a breathtaking speed and near-blind faith in the power of positive thinking, Chelsea FC held their first meeting in March 1905. They had no players yet, save player-manager John Tait ('Jock') Robertson, an ex-Glasgow Rangers star with 16 inter-national caps to his name. Director Frederick Parker attended the Football League AGM in May, and was given three minutes to convince the executive that the new club was worthy of inclusion in that September's Second Division of the League. (Note that already Chelsea's ultimate ambitions were trained on higher echelons than the Southern League.) By now Robertson had assembled something resembling a squad, and with the superb new stadium weighing heavily in the club's favour, Chelsea FC were duly elected to the Football League.

The sceptics were legion. The *Athletic News* sat on the fence between admiration and incredulity:

> Mr. Mears evidently does not believe in doing things by halves, and has spared no expense in the furtherance of his hobby – for hobby it undoubtedly is – as it is obvious that it is a matter of impossibility for many years at any rate that he can receive anything like an adequate return for the money he has spent.
> *Athletic News* (14/8/05)

The pessimists pointed to the fact that there was already a thriving club in the area: Fulham, in their new riverbank home of Craven Cottage, less than a mile away. But Fulham were in the comparatively less vigorous Southern League (for two more years, at any rate); Chelsea were potential challengers to the nation's elite clubs via the League's promotion system; and perhaps most crucially of all, Stamford Bridge was just round the corner from a railway station.

And of course, there was the team. Given a massive financial backing from the directorate, Robertson cannily crammed his squad with 'name' players. Foulke, not overjoyed at his first-team position being usurped by Leivesley back at Bramall Lane, became available. By early May Robertson had swooped, and William was a Chelsea man, costing the new club just £50.

By the summer the squad included: Davie Copeland and Jack Kirwan from that 1901 Spurs team; Small Heath striker R. McRoberts; from Hearts came full-back R. Mackie, international half-back G. Key, and right-winger M. Moran. A last-minute addition to the attacking jigsaw was Pearson, late of Manchester City, where he had combined in a lethal partnership with Billy Meredith.

The connoisseurs of the game knew these players well. With Foulke as the major attraction, the crowds flocked to Stamford Bridge. The 6,000 for the first home game, a 5-1 drubbing of Hull City on a Monday evening, had swollen to five figures by the end of the month, on the occasion of Foulke's heroic performance against West Bromwich Albion. Twenty-five thousand watched the top of the table clash with Bristol City in December. An astonishing 67,000 came to see the home match with the other promotion rivals, Manchester United, on Good Friday.

William, by now used to the odd train journey, would commute down from Sheffield to St Pancras Station, where the club provided a car to take him across the city. Selling up the shop and moving south was out of the question.

Chelsea FC knew the value of selling oneself. To begin with (and many would say, to go on with ever since) the club had an eye to the image, to the razzamatazz. Ball boys made their first ever appearance behind the goal at Stamford Bridge this year: not just to fetch the ball if it strayed onto the track, but also further to emphasise Foulke's bulk!

One cornerstone of this self-promotion was the *Chelsea Chronicle*, a match-day programme in some ways ahead of its time. Besides giving the usual information on kick-off time and composition of teams, the four-page publication (printed in blue ink) was a treasure-pot of news snippets, gossip, match reports and comments, portraits of the players, and the odd competition and poetical offering. Choice items from that first season include:

At Stockport in September a 'four foot urchin' approached William and declared: 'Ye'll get licked today!' To which Chelsea's new captain replied: 'It'll be the first time this year, then.' A statement you couldn't argue with, as it was the new club's first ever game!

The young Leicester Fosse forward Haycock, trying to cope with the, for him, new phenomenon of Foulke:

'I have never seen that big goalkeeper before. When he came out and put his arms out, it was as though darkness had come over the goal.' (7/10/05)

Where there's a Will (Foulke) there's no way to the net. (4/9/05)

In an interesting variation on a famous theme (see chapter 6):

Foulke says he doesn't care how much they charge him, so long as they don't charge him too much for his dinner. (2/12/05)

On the 'goal' awarded in favour of Stockport County in December (see Appendix 'Match By Match'):

Foulke's face when the referee pointed to the centre was a study. Transferred to canvas, and labelled 'Amazement', it would be the picture of the season at next year's Academy exhibition. What he thought would fill a volume – in several languages. (6/1/06)

The relevant lines from a parody of a contemporary song, celebrating the 2-0 win at Chesterfield:

Foulke led the way, so slim and spare…

The whistle blew, Bill hoisted his slacks,
Prepared to meet the home attacks,
But Chelsea stuck to the ball like wax…

The game was scarcely twelve minutes old
When number two was safely goaled
And big Bill cried, 'I'm catching COLD'
At the football match on Saturday.
(3/3/06)

There was a series of competitions, which turned out to be very popular. The first one was to compose a limerick on the subject of Irish boyo Jack Kirwan. The second was to write a sentence of six words, the initial letters of which were to spell out F-O-U-L-K-E. Unfortunately the winning entry appeared in a programme which has since been lost, but the example given by the competition setter was:

Fairly

Often

Unchallenged

Long

Kicks

Energetically

(10/3/06)

And finally, after the 0–2 defeat at Burnley, a few weeks before his departure from Stamford Bridge:

> Foulke says that the foul given against him with three opponents roosting on his back must belong to a new breed. (31/3/06)

Partially thanks to the relentless Chelsea publicity machine, the hype surrounding Foulke was already threatening to take on a life of its own. The team travelled to a northern ground (possibly Blackpool) and William came out of the railway station to see a couple of locals who had been employed to carry sandwich boards announcing 'COME AND SEE THE TWENTY-FOUR-STONE GOALKEEPER.' Feigning anger at such a personal observation, William growled a threat or two and shuffled his feet as if to give chase. The terrified two dropped their placards and took to their heels.

Another tale – this one more difficult to corroborate – from the Chelsea year involves an alleged misunderstanding on a London railway station. Blades historian Denis Clarebrough gives the popular version:

> Willie nipped off to the buffet to get himself a pie. When he tried to rejoin the rest of his team the ticket inspectors wouldn't let him back on the platform because he could not produce a ticket. He tried to explain that the club secretary had his ticket but they would not let him through. So Little Willie is said to have picked both men up and carried them to the station master's office to sort it out. *The Star* (19/10/1998)

By now, incidentally, Willie's fame as the heaviest ever football player had spread across the Channel. The gastronomically unchallenged French, never ones to take this sort of thing lying down, as it were, wheeled out a competitor: one G. Soulié, centre half for the works team of Parisian journal *Les Sports*. Monsieur Soulié weighed in at 24st 7lb. The *Daily Express* observed: 'When he starts to put on flesh they will possibly permit him to keep goal – sideways.'

Not that European fame was anything new. A team from Liverpool called the Xaverians had gone on an Easter tour of Holland back in 1902. Their

Amsterdam opponents had a 'keeper by the name of Blöte, six foot plus and weighing in at around eighteen stones. The Liverpudlians, of course, were quick to nickname him 'Foulke'. To their surprise Blöte replied in halting English:'Yes, me Foulke. Sheffield United, yes?'Apparently his resemblance to William was already a well-worn joke over there, and the Dutchman took it as a great compliment.

In November and December of his year with Chelsea, Foulke enjoyed nine consecutive clean sheets. By Christmas Day (0-0 away to Manchester United) the top of the table read:

	P	W	D	L	F	A	Pts
Bristol City	18	15	2	1	35	14	32
Manchester United	18	14	2	2	37	12	30
Chelsea	17	11	3	3	32	8	25

It will be noted that the strength of the London club was in its defence. Being awarded a penalty against Chelsea was usually no guarantee of a goal, as Foulke saved ten of them during the season. The pick of the bunch would be a double whammy against Port Vale in March. The Potteries side were awarded two penalties within a couple of minutes of each other. William stopped them both with almost insolent ease, plucking them out of the air to the huge delight of the crowd. The penalty rule had just been changed, so that the 'keeper now had to remain on his line until the ball was kicked. Clearly this had not restricted Foulke's ability.

Four days after the Port Vale game, on the way to the League encounter at Barnsley, the Chelsea roadshow reached Buxton in Derbyshire. The players attended the Buxton v. Newton Heath match in the Manchester Wednesday League, William fulfilling his role of visiting celebrity by kicking-off. The glorious spring weather and the presence of the First Division players ensured a record crowd. On the Saturday over at Barnsley, at a game which Chelsea won 2-1, the attendance again broke the ground record.

Foulke's FA Cup career with the Pensioners was short-lived, and ended with a number of might-have-beens. It started auspiciously enough in the first qualifying round in October, with a cakewalk of a 6-1 win over a team of Grenadier Guards. William had a bit of a sinecure that afternoon.

In the next round Chelsea were drawn against Southern League team Southend United, a new outfit drawn together mainly by the financial interest of one Baron von Reiffenstein (a London poultry magnate, an inveterate football club committee man and, surprisingly, a Scot). There would have been an intriguing clash with old Wednesday rival Fred Spikesley, newly acquired by Southend. Unfortunately Foulke was carrying an injury that day, and his place was taken by full-back Mackie. Chelsea scraped home 1-0.

The date of the third qualifying round against Crystal Palace was 18 November, but this clashed with an important League match against Burnley. Palace refused to move the FA Cup date, so Chelsea had no alternative but to play two matches on the same day. Foulke played against Burnley, and had an easy time of it in a 1-0 win. It was mostly a reserve side that went to south-east London and were swamped 7-1. It was a direct result of this game, incidentally, that the Football Association introduced the ruling that clubs must play their strongest possible teams in FA Cup ties, or risk heavy fines.

'So goodbye now to Foulke meeting the competition proper,' lamented the *Athletic News*.

Stamford Bridge was also used as a venue for other sports, which was of course part and parcel of the new club's money-spinning schema. In October 1905 the all-conquering rugby team of the All Blacks came to town to play Middlesex. Although the tourists won as expected, there was a shock: the county side had the effrontery to score a try against the New Zealanders, the first one since their arrival in the UK. Willie Foulke immediately offered his services. All concerned got the joke, and unsurprisingly nothing came of it. But even in imagination it was a wondrous vision: the Jonah Lomu of his day – only bigger – barrelling down the pitch with the ball tucked under his arm, would-be tacklers flying off like so many loose chippings.

The home game with promotion rivals Bristol City (whose line-up now included old friend Walter Bennett) took place just before Christmas. Chelsea desperately needed the two points, but in a cracking end-to end tussle no goals were scored. Foulke was on top form, at one point advancing to confront the lone City forward Gilligan, forcing him to deliver a square ball out to the wing instead of attempting the shot. The winger was tackled, the ball was cleared, and the visitors were never granted such a gift horse again.

The criticism directed at the Chelsea attack was that the wealth of talent on display had a tendency to over-elaborate, or unnecessarily 'finesse' as contemporary observers put it. Where a direct approach might have reaped a richer harvest, especially against weaker teams, territorial superiority was often frittered away. On song, the forwards were unstoppable. Wins of 6-0 (Blackpool), 4-2 (Stockport County, Bradford City, and Lincoln City), and 7-0 (Burslem Port Vale) are, needless to say, the stuff of promotion. In some games Chelsea's domination was so pronounced that now and again William, ever the showman, would lean on his goalpost and feign sleep. But the team's inability to score in crucial games, plus storming runs from their two top-of-the-table rivals, baulked Chelsea's progress into the First Division that year. They would succeed the following season, but by then Foulke would be long gone.

William made the most of his brief time in London. Sometimes Beatrice would travel down, and a Saturday night would be spent at the beloved music hall. Such was Foulke's fame and popularity that his presence would be announced to the audience before the show. He made the acquaintance of George Robey – 'The Prime Minister of Mirth' – and was invited to play in a charity match representing George's showbiz XI. The game, however, clashed with Chelsea's away fixture against Leeds City, so the invitation had to be declined.

Foulke was also spotted watching the wrestling at the Lyceum, when star grapplers Tom Jenkins the US champion and Ahmed Madrali ('the terrible Turk') were on the bill. A reporter posed the mischievous question of whether the goalkeeper was picking up some hints as to how to deal with rival forwards. The sports editor of the *Sheffield Telegraph*, writing Foulke's obituary in 1916, was to recall one of his visits to Stamford Bridge:

> The writer well remembers being present at one of the League games at a time when Foulke was at the height of his popularity. He had been having a particularly good time that afternoon, and at the close the juvenile portion of the crowd, as was their custom, rushed on to the ground, and surrounding the giant a thousand strong, cheered him to the echo. Then Billy amused everyone by good-naturedly tucking a couple of the smaller boys under each arm and allowing another to climb his broad shoulders and be carried pick-a-back off the pitch.
> The 'Green 'Un' (6/5/16)

Despite all efforts, William could not be persuaded to up sticks and move to the capital. His heart was in still in Sheffield, and if United had no more use for him, then a move to a club not a million miles away from Bramall Lane was about to be considered. The break with Chelsea came in April 1906, just after the Easter programme.

13: The Bantam Heavyweight

*There is no doubt that the mighty goalkeeper is doing a great
deal in the direction of inspiring confidence in the team.*
Bradford Daily Argus (25/8/06)

A letter published in the *Argus* the day before William's debut for Bradford City
in April 1906 captured the local mood of the moment. It was signed ONE
WHO WILL BE AT HEADINGLEY UNLESS FOULKE IS TO PLAY.

The gist of the letter was that rumours of top players showing up at Valley
Parade had been current before, but each time the punters had been let down.
Rumours were all they had been. If William Henry Foulke really was going to
turn out for City, then the writer, along with thousands of others, would gladly
forego the Rugby League Cup final (Bradford v. Salford) over at Headingley
so as to watch the big man perform. Could he be given a cast-iron guarantee
that Foulke would be in goal against Barnsley?

A swift and certain reply was given by Peter O'Rourke, the club secretary whose efficient information system and speed off the mark had secured
William's signature the Saturday before. The tom-toms had reached Yorkshire:
Foulke was not going to sign up for Chelsea for the following season. He
hadn't settled in London (despite Chelsea's claims that he had) and Beatrice
and the children can't have been too happy about the gaps of time he'd spent
away from them in the capital.

O'Rourke did the necessary paperwork, establishing that the FA had set
Foulke's price at £50, the same as Chelsea had paid for him the year before.
The secretary hopped on a train to London and tracked down his man at
Stamford Bridge. An hour or so was spent discussing terms (one proviso was
that William be allowed to train at Bramall Lane with his old club – this
request was granted by the FA) and by the end of the afternoon the 'keeper
was a Bradford City man.

It was just the shot in the arm the club needed. In a part of the world where
the dominant sport had for more than twenty years been rugby, the effect on
the association club was little short of galvanic. Despite the fact that Foulke's
debut was the last match of the season, between two fairly mediocre Second
Division sides, and that it clashed with that Rugby League Cup final, the

crowds flocked to Valley Parade. The attendance that day was 11,000, around 3,000 more than at the previous home game. William was first to jog out onto the pitch, to a storm of cheering. The result was a goalless draw, breaking the run of desultory losses. There was a new verve and confidence about the team, with Bradford City doing most of the attacking. Within the club, there was now an almost palpable feeling that the bad days were over.

The club's first three years of existence had had its share of teething troubles. As with Chelsea two years later, City had been elected to the Football League before they were even certain of their team. The League had been keen to promote the association game in the rugby heartland of the West Riding, and the directors of Manningham FC (Bradford City's earlier incarnation) had been seeking to make the switch from rugby so as to adopt a 'game which would pay'. Two thousand pounds had been pledged from promoters, and the 'Robins' or 'Wasps' – the nickname of 'Bantams' would be bestowed several years later – started the 1903/04 season in the Second Division. Promotion was promised 'within two or three years'.

When City seemed destined to languish around mid-table, the initial enthusiasm started to dissipate. There had been the occasional high spot. There was the beating of First Division Wolves 5-0 in the FA Cup in February 1906. The acquisition of Scottish international winger Jimmy Conlin boosted the firepower up front, as well as bringing the crowds in. Then Conlin was sold to Manchester City for the then-huge sum of £1,000, so that when Willie Foulke arrived, finances were sound but morale was low.

Foulke was no stranger to Bradford. Indeed he had been a vital component of the package used to help spread the gospel of association in the area. Sheffield United had played a friendly at Valley Parade back in April 1903, and had beaten a West Yorkshire amateur XI 8-5 in a rollicking attacking exhibition that must have gone a long way to convincing the 7,500 crowd of the viability of the new game. Then a year later, at the end of the new club's first season, the Blades fulfilled a promise by playing Bradford City in another friendly.

The 1906/07 season began with a new, robust optimism. The pre-season charity practice matches attracted the crowds as never before: nearly 10,000 turned out for one of them.

It was on a bakingly hot day – 33°C in the shade – that Bradford opened their League campaign in a potentially tough derby over at Leeds. Foulke had two new backs in front of him: Fred Farren and Robert Campbell. Although not quite in the Thickett and Boyle bracket, the duo were generally safe enough, both firm tacklers with sound positional sense. The game was far more one-sided than predicted. Bradford completely suppressed their opponents, but had just the one goal by half-time to show for it. 'Foulke had nothing to do but count the shots at the other end,' said the *Argus* report. Leeds City, in one of their rare attacks, scrambled a messy, possibly offside equaliser on eighty-five minutes, giving the match a wholly unrepresentative final score of 1-1.

Nevertheless the team had displayed its potential, and the next game, on the following Monday afternoon at Burnley, brought its first victory, 1-0. William was lord of his area, 'treating the bustling and funny efforts of the Burnley forwards with almost humorous contempt'. The big fellow was back in business.

Next was the first home game of the season, again against Barnsley. The attendance was still growing: 13,000 this time, pretty good for a Second Division match. This was, incidentally, the first time in the history of Bradford City that the same team had been fielded three times in succession! A lot of this new stability and confidence was surely down to the arrival of the charismatic new goalkeeper. The line-up was: Foulke; Farren, Campbell; Mellor, Kirk, Robinson; Garton, Montgomery, Newton, Smith, Clarke. This one was won 2-0. Already City were among the front-runners for promotion.

Unfortunately, Chelsea were still in the frame.

William was to return to the capital twice in quick succession. He was by now something of a national institution, trailing clouds of recognition and publicity wherever he went. The night before the Chelsea match the team were making their way to Earl's Court in a charabanc. Their passage was treated with indifference until suddenly a bunch of young men spotted and recognised Foulke. They cheered and applauded his presence, and word travelled like wildfire. The team's return journey to their hotel was triumphal.

The next day William was given a rousing reception by his former fans at Stamford Bridge. Before the game the paparazzi – or 'camera fiends' in the jargon of the day – were buzzing around William's goal. Those with a premonition for goalmouth action would have stayed there, as Chelsea hit five past their former 'keeper. Obviously the forwards' knowledge of Foulke's Achilles' heel came in handy, as they cracked in one fast low shot after another.

A fortnight later the City were back in London. Once again, William was in the spotlight:

CAB HORSE IN PERIL
NEARLY COLLIDES WITH FOULKE

The team spent last evening at the Tivoli, and on leaving the place of amusement there was an exciting episode. Foulke was endeavouring to cross the busy Strand, and when he slipped behind a motor, a bus came by in front of a passing

hansom. The horse luckily recognised its danger when the leviathan goalkeeper loomed ahead, and it stopped with such suddenness that it reared up within inches of the City giant. It seemed impossible that he could escape injury, but he tripped lightly aside, and dodged through to the safety of the sidewalk, amid cheers. It was a narrow escape for the cab horse. Foulke regarded the incident with apparent indifference, and simply remarked: 'I would have jumped on the beggar's back before I would have let him come into me.'
Bradford Daily Argus (29/9/06)

The game with Clapton Orient had a happier result (1–1) than the one with Chelsea, even though Bradford were aggrieved by what they thought was a highly arguable equalising goal from the home side. The ball appeared to hit the inside of the post and rebound back into play. Inspired by this generous slice of luck, Clapton threw everything into a final attempt to steal the winner. This late attacking frenzy was quelled and nullified by Foulke's unruffled 'keeping.

William and the capital worked an effervescent chemistry on one another. The return train from St Pancras, due to depart at 11.30 p.m., was over an hour late. On the platform, besides the disgruntled City team and committee members and sundry late-night travellers, were a couple of brass bands who had spent the day giving a concert at Earl's Court. These fellows had partaken freely of London ale, and to pass the time were rendering highly informal versions of various musical standards. It was pandemonium. Secretary Peter O'Rourke took it upon himself to make enquiries about the departure time, but couldn't get a useful reply. William decided to get involved, and went on the prowl up and down the station accompanied by a small crowd, seeking the necessary information. This arrived at the same time as the train: 12.40 a.m. They chugged into Leeds at 7 a.m., where a special had been hired to take them the rest of the way. It's not recorded when William got back home to Sheffield: probably in time for Sunday lunch.

On the morning of the Clapton match Foulke had paid a visit with Peter O'Rourke to the FA offices in High Holborn. Here the player and the secretary were told that the Sheffield United committee had expressed their displeasure with their former goalie training at Bramall Lane. If a reason was given it hasn't survived, but it was possibly because the management of the club were trying to create a new playing ethos, keeping pace with the new order that was threatening to leave them behind. And Foulke was too obviously a symbol of the old ways, and a reminder of how far the club had fallen since the years of plenty. Whatever the reason, William's brief month of training in the company of his former team was at an end, and a daily trip to Bradford was now necessary.

Then there was another clash with an opposing forward, but this time the tale left no humorous legacy. It was in the League match at Stockport that Foulke and winger 'Teddy' Bardsley raced for a loose ball, kicking it simultaneously. The lighter man came off much worse, badly damaging his leg in the collision. At first it was thought that his leg was broken, and he was taken by horse ambulance to the nearby infirmary. Here it was determined that the limb, although 'lacerated just below the knee', was unbroken. Bardsley was allowed home later that day, but wouldn't play again for several months. Henceforth Stockport players and fans found it hard to see the funny side of William's bulk.

Bradford City hit a four-game winning streak in October and November, which lifted them to within two points of division leaders West Brom. This was partly due to a revamped attack, but also in no small way to Foulke's contribution. During the run he was beaten just once in six hours' play. The single goal came in a rough game at Glossop, Rowbotham hitting a fast low shot out of his reach. However, William was in the wars that day, receiving a bone-cracking kick on the shin early on, and then hurting his shoulder in making a diving save.

There was the usual crop of winter injuries. On Christmas Day against Port Vale he played with a painful stiff neck, which was so bad that he was unable to turn his head without moving his entire upper body. For New Year he was rested, which gave the committee the chance to try out Albert Wise in goal. The younger man was impressive, but the club preferred Foulke for the FA Cup ties with Reading and Accrington Stanley.

The evening before the first-round match at home against Reading, it was still undecided which of the two City 'keepers would get the nod on the morrow. Then the word filtered through from the Reading camp that the Southern League team would rather not play against William! The Bradford committee, assuming that this wasn't a bluff, duly chose Foulke, and a fairly comfortable 2-0 win was achieved.

In the Second Round tie at Valley Parade against Accrington William had an even easier time of it, having to deal with just one shot of any note throughout the game, which was a lot more one-sided than the 1-0 scoreline suggests.

The main talking point of the day was what went on before the kick-off. William had mislaid his kit bag on the train from Sheffield, so was wearing his blue Chelsea jersey. The Accrington team and committee objected to this, as the rules of the time stated that if a goalkeeper opted to wear a different colour shirt from that of his teammates – in this case, Bradford's claret and amber stripes – then said shirt had to be of a lighter colour 'so as to make the wearer more conspicuous'. This was no doubt the first and only time that Foulke had run the risk of being hard to spot.

The referee was prepared to accept the darker jersey, but the Lancastrians stuck to their guns, so William was sent in to change. He solved the problem of finding an article of clothing pale enough and big enough by wrapping a huge white bath towel around himself, covering neck to shin. One observer said he looked like 'one of Kate Greenaway's boys'. The most famous of the popular Kate Greenaway artefacts was a cylindrical pepper pot in the shape of a little boy, chubby cheeks atop a close-fitting ground-length frock coat.

Obviously William couldn't play trussed up like this, so he took the towel off – to reveal an upper body swaddled in reams of snugly fitting bandages. All of this – tantamount to a surreptitious two fingers to the pedants – was of course greatly enjoyed by the crowd.

It was to be his last spot of devilment on a major sporting stage. The very next Saturday he injured his leg at Gainsborough, let in a couple of soft goals in the sea of mud, and lost his place once more to Wise. The disability lasted until the next round of the cup, which pitted Bradford against the mighty Liverpool, at Anfield. How William would have loved to have turned out against the old adversaries one last time. Alas, it was not to be. His leg was getting worse, with what was reported as 'rheumatic complications'. This was probably a recurrence of the old unresolved cartilage problems, the result of general wear and tear. City put up an heroic resistance that day, deserving at least a draw. As it was, international winger John Cox snatched a scrappy, fortunate winner for the Merseysiders. They went on to lose to eventual winners The Wednesday in the next round.

As for William, he now disappeared from view, or at least from selection and the Bradford newspapers. He spent some time in Nurse Cullen's hospital in Manningham, before – it is assumed – returning to Sheffield when it became obvious he wasn't going to play again that season. Bradford finished fifth, after a rousing 6-3 victory over promoted Chelsea. The Bantams would themselves rise to the First Division the following year, winning their League in style. The FA Cup would follow in 1911. Once again a club's success story had been kick-started partly through a massive contribution from William Henry Foulke.

However, over the next few months the big fellow's fitness deteriorated. The problem with the leg didn't abate, and it must have been hard to shift the general feeling of indisposition brought on by comparative inactivity, increasing weight, and the beginnings of what was to be diagnosed several years later as cirrhosis. It was in November 1907 that William at last bowed to the inevitable, and announced his retirement from playing the game he loved.

14: Extra Time

*...a significant minority of individuals were able to take pubs or
shops and move into the relative safety of the lower-middle class.*

Football and the English

*Foulke was a man of the people and loved the people's pastime.
He will not be forgotten.*

Athletic News (8/5/16)

One version of Foulke's retirement years is that he spent them as landlord of
a pub in central Sheffield. However, closer examination shows that this wasn't
the whole story.

By 1908 the Foulkes had moved from the Asline Street shop, via a brief
sojourn at 363 Bramall Lane, to a beer house known as The Duke, at no. 11
Matilda Street. The pub tenure, though financially successful, was short-lived
for a number of reasons, and within a couple of years William and family
would be moving across the road to another corner shop at 10 Matilda Street.
The circumstances of the Foulkes leaving the pub, and the attendant antics,
are narrated below.

Incidentally, a famous sporting name wasn't an automatic guarantee of success in the world of commerce. The great Billy Meredith, for example, came a
cropper in his first three enterprises: a sports shop, cinemas, and pleasure boats.
It was only his later ventures into the public house business that met with better fortune. This uncertainty of the sports–commerce switch underlines the
Foulkes' achievement in maintaining a flourishing trade in their pub and shops.
For William there was every promise of a pleasant and affluent retirement.

Then in April 1908 there came some shocking news from Denaby Main
Colliery.

Walter Bennett had returned from Bristol, and had turned out for
Mexborough and Denaby football teams. He worked as a miner during the
week. On 6 April part of the roof of the main colliery collapsed, and Bennett
was one of the fatalities. He was a couple of weeks shy of his thirty-fourth
birthday. We can imagine the blow this must have been to William. Apart from
the loss of a firm friend, here was a devastating indication of the mortality of

sporting heroes. He must have felt that the old world had begun to crumble around him.

Yet his passion for football remained undiminished. He was a regular fixture at Bramall Lane on match days, sitting in his specially constructed chair on the front row. Still of course very much the hero, he would be allowed in for free. The usual comedy played out on such occasions was for Foulke to mutter 'press' to the gatekeeper, who would pretend to be fooled into believing that this well-known twenty-five-stone giant was a journalist and therefore eligible for a free pass!

Nor did he forego his enthusiasm for horse racing, making frequent trips to Doncaster, his and Bennett's old stamping ground. He was also a familiar figure at the illegal – and for the winners, highly lucrative – pitch and toss meetings atop Sky Edge, a plateau a mile or so to the east of Sheffield centre. Thanks to a well-organised system of lookouts, these immensely popular sessions were for a long time pretty well safe from police raids. Certainly William was never caught out. He would get his comeuppance though, perhaps unjustifiably, later on and closer to home.

The Foulkes' affluence could now run to domestic servants. William was ever the dapper man about town, sporting his gold watch chain, silk scarf and gold pin.

But William never forgot his poorer roots. One of the family tales is that one night he heard a disturbance downstairs in the pub yard, and arming himself with a baseball bat or something equally serviceable, he went down to investigate. He discovered someone he knew, down on his luck and just looking for a roof for the night. William's reaction was immediate, and to those who knew him, typical: he gave the intruder some food and what was eventually to be long-term accommodation. When the family moved over the road to the shop, the man, one Charles Valentine Mettam, accompanied them. He was still there at his death in the 1930s!

Reinventing himself to some extent, no doubt he had the opportunity now to be the full time family man. Two more sons were born: James Rigby in 1907, and Stanley in 1909.

Naturally William had high hopes for his sons to carry on the sporting tradition. In later years eldest son Robert was to recall the occasion he was discovered smoking as a ten-year-old. His father administered a tanned backside and a stern lecture on the harmful effects of the cigarette habit on the lungs and stamina of the aspiring athlete.

In happier mood, one family outing would have been to the music hall, which was a booming leisure industry in Sheffield, as elsewhere, at the time.

In early 1910 at the Hippodrome on Cambridge Street, as part of their immensely popular national tour, Fred Karno's Mumming Birds had a twelve-week run. One of the more memorable comedy sketches – later to be turned into a short silent film – was called *Skating*. It featured a tramp with a deadpan expression who roller-skated showily and clumsily round the stage, oblivious to the chaos and pile-ups he was causing among the others on the rink. Star of both sketch and film was a Mr Charles Chaplin, and one of the minor roles was taken by a Stan Jefferson, later to achieve much greater fame as Stan Laurel. Given the length of the run, we can be fairly certain that on at least one evening, Mr Foulke and family were among the audience.

It was in autumn of the same year that for a few weeks The Duke seemed to become the focal point of inner-city mischief.

In midsummer a hawker by the name of Patrick Hagan had turned up outside the pub with a pony and trap. Seeing William outside taking the air, Hagan offered to sell him the apparatus for £13. As Foulke embarked on negotiating the price, another man came up and revealed that the horse and cart weren't Hagan's to sell, as he'd just stolen them from a fruit stall on Sheffield market! William stabled the pony and kept the cart in his yard until the fruiterer was able to come and collect.

So William was due to appear as a witness in Sheffield City Court on Friday 30 September 1910. As it turned out, he made a dual appearance that day, as on the previous afternoon The Duke had been the object of a police raid.

The premises had been used – frequently and openly – as a venue for illicit betting. It had been organised by an old friend of William's, bookmaker Frank Greaves. Foulke was to profess no knowledge of the activity, a claim that, it must be said, is difficult to believe. Plain-clothes officers armed with a warrant had joined the lunchtime crowd in the main pub room, and a uniformed policeman was stationed on the front door. Noticing this, William went to the door to ask what was going on. The policeman replied: 'I am acting under orders. I don't want anyone to go out.' 'No more do I,' was the big fellow's waggish response. 'I want them to come in so I can sell 'em some drink!'

The reaction was typically William: an almost childlike certainty that any problem could be surmounted by a mixture of good humour and the force of his reputation and personality. This time though, there were larger issues at stake. His pockets were searched, and no less than forty-five apparently incriminating betting slips were found on his person. His excuse: 'I've no idea how they got there.'

He pleaded not guilty, and the trial of Foulke and Greaves was fixed for 19 October.

It never rains but it pours. Two days after the well-publicised raid, The Duke was burgled. The criminal element was possibly attracted by rumours of the pub being a hiding place for ill-gotten gains. At around 10 p.m., with the Saturday night festivities in full swing down below, a domestic servant was putting the Foulke children to bed when she noticed that a rear upstairs window had been forced, and was wide open. In another upstairs room, a wardrobe, normally kept locked, was open, and its contents strewn on the floor. She raised the alarm, and William and Beatrice made an inventory of what had been stolen. Among the missing items were two football medals (the League Championship medal from 1898 has been recovered, and is now in the Hall of Fame at Bramall Lane), some jewellery, and over £3 in cash.

There was evidence of inside collusion in the burglary. The thieves seemed to know the layout of the upstairs rooms, and had a key for the wardrobe at the bottom of which the money was kept. It was no doubt this incident, with the children being potentially at risk, that hastened the Foulkes' decision to relinquish the pub and move over the road to the shop.

Later that month the illegal betting trial took place in a packed city court. It wasn't without its moments of humour, there often being a showbiz subtext where William was concerned. A couple of choice extracts from the report of the four-hour-long trial:

> Chief Inspector Harrison proceeded to relate the circumstances of his raid on 29 September, and said he went into the bagatelle room, and saw Foulke.
> Mr Neal [defending]: You could not well have missed him. (Laughter.)

> Police Constable Scott also related the result of his observations at the Duke Inn, where he also went disguised as a labourer. This officer said he was a teetotaller, and called for a 'stone ginger'.
> Mr Lang Coath [prosecution]: Who brought it?
> Witness: No one, sir. (Loud laughter.)
> *Sheffield Daily Telegraph* (20/10/10)

None of this was enough to mollify the court chairman's stiff sentences: Foulke was fined £25, and Greaves £50. There was no need for the brewery, Messrs. John Richdale Ltd, to take any further action, as Foulke had already quit The Duke.

Now is a good time to deal with that apocryphal tale that has stubbornly attached itself to William's retirement years: that he ended them in poverty as a sad sideshow on Blackpool beach, earning a pittance saving shots from holiday-makers at a penny a go.

The apparent primary evidence for this stems from the final paragraph of a hastily composed obituary in the *Sheffield Daily Telegraph* the morning after his death. As far as contemporary sources go, the story appears absolutely nowhere else. There's nothing – neither photo nor press snippet nor oral recollection – from the Blackpool local history archives. And there's clear evidence from the Sheffield Directories of 1899-1916 that Willie Foulke never moved from that city in all those years. He was a local hero and owner of a thriving corner shop: why would he need to grub for pennies at a Lancashire seaside resort? Was the pressure to meet the morning *Telegraph* deadline the reason for the error? If so, an apology and correction later in the week would have been in order, but nothing of the sort appeared. The fuller obituary in the *Telegraph* sports special – the 'Green 'Un' – the following Saturday night makes no mention of Blackpool. So how did the tale begin?

Foulke's descendants relate that William and family were strolling down Blackpool promenade one bright summer's day when they came across a 'penny a shot – beat the goalie' booth. It wouldn't have been on the sands themselves, incidentally, as all commercial activities had been banned from the resort beach some years previously.

William, an immediately recognisable celebrity pretty well anywhere across the length and breadth of England at the time, was offered a jokey challenge. Naturally – one would have been more surprised if he'd refused – the big man took off his jacket, rolled up his sleeves, and proceeded to demonstrate the skills of goalkeeping. And then stayed for a while, as the crowd gathered on the promenade on that sunny holiday afternoon.

Eventually his family tore him away from his nostalgia session, but evidently not before yet another spiral of Chinese whispers had been set in motion.

In those immediate pre-war years the Foulke family sustained two cruel blows: neither of the two younger sons was to survive infancy. Stanley, just eighteen months old, died in October 1910, a matter of days after the move from The Duke. James Rigby passed away three years later, aged five.

In 1913 the *London Evening News* published the text of an interview with Foulke. Use was made of his potted autobiography – see Appendix. Looking back at the glory years which had started just fifteen years before must have seemed like chatting about ancient history. And of course the changes were about to accelerate brutally as the old European world was ripped apart by the First World War.

The Foulkes, like many in their position, were hit hard by the outbreak of war. Fortunately, none of their immediate family was a casualty during the overseas conflict. But the Defence of the Realm Act, an ever-burgeoning and mutating series of home-front restrictions that at times were to touch on the surreal, almost immediately curtailed shop and pub opening hours. It became illegal to buy a round in a pub. Working class leisure activities seemed to be targeted more than most, and out went the apparently frivolous and non-productive: by 1915 it was against the law to keep pigeons, fly kites, 'loiter by railway lines', and buy or sell binoculars. Entertainment or amusement tax, eventually set at fifteen per cent, was introduced. By degrees, individual freedom was controlled and encroached upon.

Football was tolerated for the 1914/15 season, as it was seen as a rich source of recruits. As the season progressed, though, it became increasingly clear that the nationwide professional game couldn't survive under war conditions.

One of Foulke's former clubs, Bradford City, were forced to play their FA Cup third-round replay with Norwich City at Lincoln in March in front of completely empty stands, 'so as not to disrupt vital war work'. One of the last big games to be played before the curtain fell was the 1915 FA Cup final – the 'khaki final' – at Old Trafford between William's two other clubs, Chelsea and Sheffield United. Naturally favouring the Blades, he travelled to Manchester to lend his support.

On the right wing for United was a Blackwell lad, one Jimmy Simmons, a nephew of William's. He gave his uncle something to talk about, hitting the first goal after thirty-six minutes, a cracking oblique shot that rebounded into the net from the far post. Sheffield went on to win 3-0.

Simmons was declared 'Man of the Match' by several newspaper reports. William's reaction to his nephew's displays of attacking talent was: 'I didn't know the little beggar had it in him.' The surface gruffness of the remark was, of course, a thin disguise for a genuine pride in the youngster's achievements. (On the subject of keeping it in the family, William's great-grandson Richard was to play in goal for the Blades some sixty years later.)

The 1915 FA Cup final was the last top-class football match that Bill Foulke was to attend.

For the 1915/16 season the nationwide game was chopped up into war-time regional competitions. Sheffield United raced Grimsby Town for the Midland League title, the crucial match between the two leaders taking place on the last Saturday of the season: 29 April. Foulke was at Bramall Lane to watch the game. The Blades had to win to lift the title, but the result was goal-less – which was perhaps appropriate as it was to be the great 'keeper's last ever visit to the ground.

He took ill over that weekend. At first it was thought to be a chill, but as his condition rapidly worsened, he was admitted to Sister Tate's nursing home on Glossop Road (on the site of the present Royal Hallamshire Hospital).

By early Monday evening, 1 May, William Henry Foulke was dead. The deterioration and passing away were so quick and unexpected that Annie Crick, the Foulkes' neighbour on Matilda Street, was the only non-medical person at his bedside when he died. Beatrice and the children were possibly planning to visit him later that evening, or were perhaps even expecting him home before too long!

The death certificate gives 'cirrhosis' as major cause of death. It had been diagnosed two years previously. Whether William had paid too much heed to the doctor's advice, though, given the big fellow's typically cavalier 'live life to the full' temperament, is open to question.

The funeral took place at Burngreave Cemetery, Sheffield the following Thursday. Despite the vile weather and the suddenness of Foulke's passing away, a substantial crowd came to pay their last respects. From the old team there was Ernest Needham, Joe Davies, Tommy Morren and trainer George Waller. Among the many others with Sheffield United connections there was John Nicholson the secretary, and Joseph Tomlinson, the man who had first secured the twenty-year-old William's signature in the Ilkeston dressing room all those years ago.

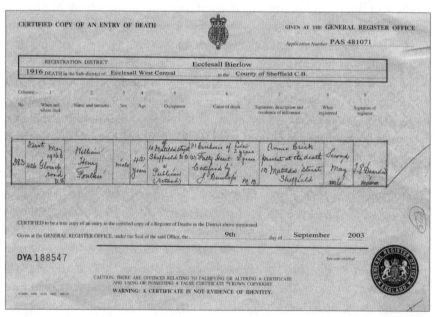

William Henry Foulke's death certificate. (by permission of General Record Office HMSO)

The inscription on the headstone reads:

AT
REST

In Loving Memory of
WILLIAM HENRY FOULKES,

LATE GOALKEEPER, SHEFFIELD UNITED FOOTBALL CLUB
THE BELOVED HUSBAND OF
BEATRICE FOULKES,
WHO DIED MAY 1ST 1916,
AGED 42 YEARS.

And then, poignantly:

ALSO OF THE ABOVE NAMED
BEATRICE FOULKES,
WHO DIED FEB 3RD 1933,
AGED 58 YEARS
RE-UNITED

*'WE CANNOT LORD THY PURPOSE SEE,
BUT ALL IS WELL THAT'S DONE BY THEE!'*

It's tempting to finish the story here, at the graveside, since William's time in Sheffield appears to have come full circle. Marcus Street, his first place of residence in the cutlery city, was about half a mile to the south, and like the cemetery high above the railway and the bustle. The big man's mortal remains may be at rest here, but his genial spirit is surely still at work on the other side of the city, at Bramall Lane. So we'll make the trip down to United's ground, to discover that the story has never really ended. An essential port of call is the Hall of Fame.

Willie Foulke's portrait grins down at us from the middle of the back row in Alan Damm's 'Dream Team' painting. Despite the tradition, launched by the big fellow over 100 years ago, of great Blades goalies, none of them has dislodged our William's place as the best of the lot. There have been worthy contenders galore: Joe Leivesley, Harold Gough, Jack Smith, Ted Burgin, Alan Hodgkinson, Jim Brown, Alan Kelly, and Simon Tracey present a remarkable dynasty of goalkeeping talent. Foulke was the fountainhead, and most Blades fans have enough of a sense of history to continue to appreciate the fact.

In the Hall of Fame is a life-size photo of the man, alongside those of Ernest Needham and other Sheffield United immortals. His shirt, medals and international cap are here, along with all the famous photos and line drawings. One corner of the room is almost his shrine. Mention his name anywhere within several miles of the stadium, and you're fairly certain to prompt a stirring of interest and a gleam in the listener's eye. In Sheffield he is still an icon, still the hero of those glory years when the Blades took on and beat the finest sides in Britain.

And on match days, as the Bramall Lane roar swells and lifts over Foulke's adopted city, your imagination can easily travel back to those all-too-few seasons of long ago. Forever vivid in the mind's eye are the action replays of his goalkeeping feats, of his giant form hurling itself around in defiance of the laws of physics, serving up the spectacular on a weekly basis.

In every positive and meaningful sense of the word, Willie Foulke was, and probably always will be, the greatest.

Match-by-Match Analysis of Foulke's Career

More detailed reports of many of these games may be found in the text. These statistics are based on reports in contemporary newspapers, the *Athletic News*, and pp 159-169 of Denis Clarebrough's invaluable Sheffield United FC: The First 100 Years, although where there is a discrepancy eg. in crowd numbers, unless there is a precise figure to hand I have generally preferred the information given in the *Athletic News*. I have also used Paul Carter's Chelsea stats. from the website www.cfchistory.co.uk.

I have not necessarily included all the friendlies, tour games, and minor trophy matches, just mentioning those with intrinsic interest.

(A) SHEFFIELD UNITED FC

1894/95: FOOTBALL LEAGUE FIRST DIVISION

Sat. 1/9/94   H   West Bromwich Albion   10,000   W 2-1

William Foulke's debut for Sheffield United, aged twenty. He acquitted himself well. McLeod put a (dubious) penalty wide for WBA. 'United's new, tall, cool goalkeeper.' (*Sheffield Independent*)

Mon. 3/9/94   A   Wolverhampton Wanderers 4,000   W 3-0

Wolves' forwards were lively, but Utd defence of Foulke, Thickett and Cain proved unbeatable.

Sat. 8/9/94   A   Preston North End   6,000   L 1-2

Preston North End scored two late goals, snatching a largely undeserved win. Cain was at fault for the second. 'Foulke was here, there, and everywhere, and saved his charge in nice style.' (*Sheffield Daily Telegraph*)

Sat. 15/9/94   H   Burnley   5,750   D 2-2

'The one bright exception to the poor show of the home team was the brilliant exhibition given by the lengthy Foulke.' (*Sheffield Daily Telegraph*)

Sat. 22/9/94   A   Stoke   3,000   W 3-1
'Perhaps the most notable feature of the day's play was the excellent goalkeeping of Foulke.' (*Sheffield Independent*)

Sat. 29/9/94   H   Nottingham Forest   7,250   W 3-2
This win placed United second in the League, behind Everton.

Sat. 6/10/94   A   Liverpool   12,000   D 2-2
William was kept busy, 'bringing off some wonderfully clever saves' (*Liverpool Daily Post*). His second half was especially good.

Mon. 8/10/94   H   Blackburn Rovers   5,000   W 3-0
'Foulke, served by his height, never gave the opposing forwards a chance of getting at the numerous high shots sent in.' (*Sheffield Daily Telegraph*)

Sat. 13/10/94   H   Preston North End   10,000   L 0-1
Cain's miskick set up Preston forward Barr for the only goal.

Mon. 22/10/94   H   Aston Villa   6,000   W 2-1
An exciting, attacking game. William on form again.

Sat. 27/10/94   A   The Wednesday   14,500   W 3-2
'Foulke's superiority to the Wednesday custodian was the main factor in the success of his team.' (*Sheffield Independent*)

Sat. 3/11/94   A   West Bromwich Albion 3,250   L 0-1
Albion rained shots on United goal. Foulke was equal to nearly all of them. 'But for him the Albion would have run up a big score.' (*Sheffield Independent*)

Mon. 12/11/94   A   Aston Villa   7,000   L 0-5
At Perry Bar; bitterly cold wind and sleet. After half-time 'men collapsed one after the other.' United finished with seven men. Even Foulke succumbed. Referee criticised for completing match. See text.

Sat. 17/11/94   A   Nottingham Forest   6,000   L 0-3
United generally outfought by a lively Forest, especially in midfield. Nonetheless, two or three eye-catching saves from William.

Sat. 1/12/94   A   Small Heath   5,000   L 2-4
'Foulke was loudly applauded, and his display was really grand.' (*Birmingham Saturday Night*)

Sat. 8/12/94   H   Liverpool   8,000   D 2-2
Needham headed out from under the bar, with Foulke beaten. United showed fighting spirit.

Sat. 15/12/94   A   Derby County   2,000   L 1-4
Bloomer scored the third goal, and had an excellent game as link man. Jack Robinson, future England goalkeeper, played for Derby. 'Foulke stands out most prominently, and his goalkeeping was one of the features of the afternoon.' (*Derby Daily Telegraph*)

Sat. 22/12/94   A   Burnley   2,000   W 4-2
Freezing gale force wind. Foulke adapted well.

Tue. 25/12/94   H   Derby County   12,000   L 1-4
Bloomer scored number two for Derby. Best players were Foulke, Thickett, John Goodall and Bloomer.

Wed. 26/12/94   A   Blackburn Rovers   4,000   L 2-3
First goal went in through William's legs. Second goal was a lucky rebound off Thickett's back.

Sat. 12/1/95   H   The Wednesday   12,000   W 1-0
United wore rubber studs which were better suited to frozen ground. 'Foulke, who had not a great deal to do, did what fell to his share admirably.' (*Sheffield Daily Telegraph*)

Mon. 14/1/95   A   Bolton Wanderers   1,000   L 2-6
Pouring rain. Pitch 'abominable'. United 2-1 up at half-time.

Sat. 19/1/95   H   Wolverhampton Wanderers 2,000   W 1-0
Sawdust sprinkled over wet pitch. 'Foulke performed brilliantly, while Thickett and Cain were hard to beat.' (*Sheffield Daily Telegraph*)

Sat. 26/1/95   A   Everton   15,000   D 1-1
'In goal Foulke did his work so well as to earn repeated encomiums from the crowd, who – until Sheffield appeared likely to win – were delighted with his display.' (*Sheffield Daily Telegraph*)

Sat. 9/2/95   H   Stoke   3,000   W 3-0
'The backs have learned to place the utmost reliance in Foulke's ability, and he certainly justified them.' (*Sheffield Daily Telegraph*). Clawley in goal for Stoke.

Sat. 23/2/95   A   Sunderland   6,500   L 0-2
Wharton in goal.

Tue. 26/2/95   H   Everton   12,000   W 4-2
William's display up to the usual standard, with some great saves. Everton were 2-0
up. 'Splendid goalkeeping.' (*Sheffield Independent*)

Sat. 9/3/95   H   Sunderland   9,000   W 4-0
'Foulke played an admirable game in goal, though once or twice giving examples of
his rashness by running out of goal.' (*Sheffield Daily Telegraph*)

Sat. 13/4/95   H   Small Heath   4,000   L 0-2
United fielded a depleted team. First goal was a fluky ricochet off reserve full-back
Hill.

Mon. 15/4/95   H   Bolton Wanderers   7,500   W 5-0
All goals scored in the first half. 'Foulke did his work well.' (*Bolton Evening News*)

1894/95: FA CUP

First Round:
Sat. 2/2/95   H   Millwall Athletic   2,000   W 3-1
An easy win over the Southern League leaders. 'What Foulke had to do was done in
his usual smart style.' (*Sheffield Independent*)

Second Round:
Sat. 16/2/95   H   West Bromwich Albion   14,600   D 1-1
Two brilliant saves from Foulke, who 'kept goal grandly'. (*Sheffield Independent*)

Second Round replay:
Wed. 20/2/95   A   West Bromwich Albion   10,025   L 1-2
Controversial winning goal. Albion went on to reach final.

1894/95: FRIENDLIES AND OTHER MATCHES

Sat. 20/10/94   H   Chirk   1,000   W 5-1
Chirk team contained Billy Meredith, who scored to make it 1-1.

Sat. 10/11/94   H   Derby County   3,000   L 4-5
United Counties League. John Goodall, Derby captain, had a superb game. This was
Foulke's first encounter with Steve Bloomer.

Sat. 24/11/94   Sheffield *v.* London   4,500   W 10-0
Played at Bramall Lane. Foulke had little to do apart from hold a couple of long-range
shots.

Thu. 27/12/94   H   Corinthians   1,500   L 3-7
G.O. Smith had an excellent game for Corinthians.

Mon. 18/2/95   English XI *v.* Scottish XI   4,000   W 3-1
William Hendry's benefit match, played at Bramall Lane. Foulke selected. Each player
received an item of steel cutlery.

Wed. 24/4/95   A   Blackwell   1,000   W 3-2
Benefit match for Cockayne, one of William's former teammates.

1895/96: FOOTBALL LEAGUE FIRST DIVISION

Mon. 2/9/95   H   Small Heath   7,000   W 2-0
'Foulke and his backs worked hard and successfully.' (*Sheffield Daily Telegraph*). At
one point Foulke misjudged his run out, and Mobley had an open goal to aim at.
Needham headed clear.

Sat. 7/9/95   A   The Wednesday   15,000   L 0-1
On twenty-five minutes Thickett miskicked a clearance, and Bell scored. 'Foulke once
more showed what a genuine custodian he is.' (*Sheffield Independent*)

Sat. 14/9/95   H   Aston Villa   10,000   W 2-1
Villa's goal was a spectacular flying header from Hodgetts, scored while Thickett
was off the field receiving treatment. 'Foulke kept goal in his usual cool, clever style.'
(*Sheffield Independent*)

Sat. 21/9/95   A   Bury   7,000   L 0-1
Just the one error from William on five minutes: he fluffed his fisted clearance, and
Plant had an easy chance in the corner. With a few minutes left, the United goal-
keeper went upfield to take a free-kick.

Sat. 28/9/95   H   Stoke   7,000   W 1-0
A fine win over the League leaders, hitherto undefeated. Stoke's goalkeeper Clawley
had a good game too. 'Only a miraculous save from a lightning grounder by Schofield
on the part of Foulke stretched on the ground prevented a score.' (*Football World*)

Mon. 30/9/95   H   Preston North End   5,000   W 2-1
A thrilling game. Pierce scored equaliser for Preston North End with a fast low shot.
Three tremendous saves during enormous North End pressure in last few minutes.
'A victory in which the brilliant goalkeeper Foulke had a great and glorious share.'
(*Sheffield Independent*)

Sat. 5/10/95   A   Everton   11,000   L 0-5
United team depleted through injuries. 'Foulke undoubtedly saved his side from a
very much more severe defeat.' (*Sheffield Daily Telegraph*)

Mon. 7/10/95   H   Sunderland   8,000   L 1-2
First Sunderland goal was an unstoppable thunderbolt from Harvey just inside the
post. Then Campbell scored a rare success in a 'one on one' against Foulke. The United
goalkeeper went upfield near the end to take a couple of free-kicks – to no avail.

Sat. 19/10/95   A   Wolverhampton Wanderers 5,000   L 1-4
United weakened by injuries again. First Wolves goal: Griffin and Beats both bundle
William into net.

Sat. 2/11/95   A   Stoke   8,000   L 0-4
United team mostly youngsters from the reserves. Two goals in two minutes from
Hyslop, great shots that gave Foulke no chance.

Sat. 9/11/95   H   Everton   7,500   L 1-2
'With a less capable custodian the two goals might well have been increased to five.'
(*Sheffield Daily Telegraph*)

Sat. 16/11/95   A   Aston Villa   12,000   D 2-2
Cowan's shot was miskicked by Foulke, leading to first goal. This was his only error in
a fine performance. Strong goal-to-goal wind.

Sat. 23/11/95   H   Nottingham Forest   7,000   W 2–1
Forest scored first, against run of play, then United started to dominate. William dealt with most shots without any problem.

Sat. 30/11/95   A   Preston North End   3,000   L 3–4
Very slippery pitch, to which the United goalkeeper had difficulty in adjusting.

Sat. 14/12/95   A   Nottingham Forest   6,500   L 1–3
'Foulke was only beaten at close quarters, and saved any number of excellent shots.' (*Sheffield Daily Telegraph*)

Sat. 21/12/95   H   Derby County   7,000   D 1–1
Goodall and Bloomer had a good attacking game for Derby. 'The visitors tried the long shooting game, but Foulke seemed to be everywhere.' (*Sheffield Daily Telegraph*). Jack Robinson in goal for Derby.

Thu. 26/12/95   H   The Wednesday   26,000   D 1–1
Wednesday were the better team. Foulke had more work to do than his opposite number. United's goal debatable.

Mon. 30/12/95   H   Bolton Wanderers   5,750   W 1–0
'On the day Foulke was the superior of Sutcliffe, whatever the selection committee may do when the teams are picked.' (*Sheffield Daily Telegraph*). Sutcliffe was preferred for the England team against Ireland and Scotland.

Sat. 4/1/96   H   West Bromwich Albion   5,500   W 2–0
A pleasing victory for United, to which William made a major contribution with a range of crucial saves, including one from Banks at point-blank range.

Sat. 11/1/96   A   Sunderland   3,000   D 1–1
Foulke gave a fine display which drew applause from home fans. The following Monday it was discovered that he had broken his finger.

Sat. 25/1/96   A   Blackburn Rovers   3,500   L 0–1
Bradshaw in goal.

Mon. 3/2/96   A   Burnley   3,000   L 0–5
Bradshaw in goal.

Sat. 8/2/96   H   Wolverhampton Wanderers 6,000   W 2-1
A low shot from Beats on thirty-one minutes scored for Wolves. Otherwise, Foulke
had little to do.

Sat. 22/2/96   A   West Bromwich Albion   3,900   L 0-1
Error by Cain led to WBA's goal.

Sat. 7/3/96   H   Blackburn Rovers   8,000   D 1-1
William beaten by a fast low shot from Turnbull, a couple of minutes into the second
half. 'With the exception of one occasion fumbling a shot, he kept goal very well
indeed.' (*Sheffield Independent*)

Sat. 14/3/96   A   Derby County   8,000   W 2-0
United's first ever League victory over Derby. Foulke, who 'gave a capital exhibition
in goal' (*Football World*), saved several times from a lively Bloomer.

Mon. 30/3/96   H   Burnley   2,000   D 1-1
Burnley equalised on eighty-six minutes.

Fri. 3/4/96   A   Bolton Wanderers   5,000   L 1-4
An open, attacking game, with Bolton sharper in front of goal.

Mon. 6/4/96   H   Bury   5,500   W 8-0
United's half-back line, although without Needham, dominated the game. Bury's
long-ball tactics rarely troubled Foulke.

Tue. 7/4/96   A   Small Heath   6,000   L 1-2
An appalling error from the referee led to Small Heath's first goal. 'Very fine work in
goal by Foulke.' (*Sheffield Daily Telegraph*)

1895/96: FA CUP

First Round:
Sat. 1/2/96   A   Burton Wanderers   4,000   D 1-1
Bradshaw in goal.

First Round replay:
Thu. 6/2/96   H   Burton Wanderers   8,000   W 1-0
William's return after injury. 'His inclusion was more owing to his extreme anxiety to
be in harness again.' (*Sheffield Daily Telegraph*)

Second Round: Sat. 15/2/96   A   Everton   20,000   L 0–3
Nil-nil for sixty minutes, then Everton scored from a disputed penalty. Bell scored
after a close-in melee. 'Foulke could not be blamed for any of the shots that scored.'
(*Football World*)

1895/96: FRIENDLIES AND OTHER MATCHES

Mon. 14/10/95   H   Glasgow Celtic   2,000   L 0–1
Rapid and accurate inter-passing of all five Celtic forwards noted. Foulke received
praise from visiting observers.

Wed. 20/11/95   London *v.* Sheffield   1,500   W 2–0
Played at Leyton, Essex. Foulke was rarely troubled, apart from a 'slashing' last-minute
shot from Drake that he turned over the bar.

Sat. 7/12/95   Glasgow *v.* Sheffield   3,000   L 1–3
Played at Glasgow. Again, superior technique of Scottish forwards was in evidence.

Sat. 8/2/96   A   Walsall   6,000   W 5–2
Birmingham Cup second round. William injured pre-match by wooden ball (see
text).

Mon. 9/3/96   Derby County   4,000   W 2–0
Birmingham Cup semi-final, played at Olive Grove. 'Foulke had practically nothing
to do.' (*Sheffield Daily Telegraph*)

Sat. 28/3/96   Aston Villa   4,500   L 0–3
Birmingham Cup final, played at Perry Barr. A one-sided game in wretched weather,
although Foulke gave a good display towards the end.

1896/97: FOOTBALL LEAGUE FIRST DIVISION

Sat. 5/9/96   H   Burnley   4,000   W 1–0
'Foulke brought off smart saves from Hill and Bowes... Needham and his phalanx of
defenders.' (*Athletic News*)

Sat. 12/9/96   A   Aston Villa   5,000   D 2–2
'Foulke gave a grand display.' (*Athletic News*). A shot rolled between his legs, but it
stopped just before the goal line.

Sat. 19/9/96   H   Sunderland   9,000   W 3-0
'Foulke kept goal magnificently, and made not the semblance of a mistake.' (*Athletic News*)

Sat. 26/9/96   A   Nottingham Forest   5,000   D 2-2
Under constant pressure, the Blades goalkeeper performed well. Fred Forman scored a soft goal for Forest. 'The sprightly Foulke… made no mistakes.' (*Sheffield Independent*)

Sat. 3/10/96   H   Aston Villa   12,000   D 0-0
'Just before time was called, Foulke, as a last resort, bounced the ball right up to the halfway line, amid some excitement… but the whistle blew before any damage was done.' (*Athletic News*)

Sat. 10/10/96   A   Derby County   8,000   W 3-1
'The lengthy Foulke somehow got down to Stevenson's shot.' (*Athletic News*)

Sat. 17/10/96   A   Everton   15,000   W 2-1
William fisted the ball into his own goal from a free-kick. Otherwise in excellent form against great pressure from Everton attack. 'Milward shot strongly, but Foulke was on the alert, and cleared in grand style.' (*Liverpool Daily Post*)

Mon. 19/10/96   H   Liverpool   6,000   D 1-1
'Bradshaw's shot was good enough to beat the smartest of all custodians.' (*Sheffield Daily Telegraph*)

Sat. 24/10/96   A   Preston North End   10,000   L 0-1
Foulke beaten by a high shot well out of his reach. 'A fine game in the mud.' (*Sheffield Independent*)

Sat. 31/10/96   H   Derby County   9,000   D 2-2
'Near the finish, Foulke, yards out of his goal, pulled Bloomer down.' (*Athletic News*). Derby scored two late goals in quick succession.

Sat. 14/11/96   A   West Bromwich Albion   5,700   W 1-0
United's first ever League win at WBA. A slow game on a quagmire of a pitch. Foulke made a couple of athletic saves, and one bad error: he kicked a clearance straight to Flewitt, who panicked and shot wide.

Sat. 21/11/96   H   Bury   6,000   D 2-2
United 'keeper beaten by two fine well-placed shots. 'Again Foulke has to be thanked by supporters of United for brilliant services.' (*Sheffield Daily Telegraph*)

Sat. 5/12/96   H   West Bromwich Albion   6,000   L 0-1
WBA scored on eighty-three minutes, with a 'capital goal from a lightning shot' (*Sheffield Independent*) from Bassett.

Sat. 26/12/96   H   The Wednesday   30,000   W 2-0
Wednesday attacked with a will, but Foulke repulsed shots and attempts to dribble through. Heavy pitch.

Tue. 29/12/96   H   Bolton Wanderers   12,000   W 1-0
'A game of goalkeepers.' (*Sheffield Daily Telegraph*). Sutcliffe in goal for Bolton. Foulke gave an uninhibited performance: at one point he ran out to clear, slipped, and allowed a forward a free shot. Cain conceded corner.

Fri. 1/1/97   H   Everton   10,000   L 1-2
Taylor dribbled through United defence and scored from close in. His second goal was disputed.

Sat. 2/1/97   A   Liverpool   15,000   D 0-0
'Foulke did not have much to do.' (*Athletic News*). Old lady handed him sweets when play was at other end!

Sat. 9/1/97   H   Blackburn Rovers   1,000   W 7-0
Heavy, slushy snow. William had little to do in goal.

Sat. 16/1/97   A   Burnley   6,000   D 1-1
'Several capital attempts were made to score, but Foulke was able to deal with them all.' (*Athletic News*). Burnley's goal came from a free-kick, with a hint of offside.

Sat. 23/1/97   H   Wolverhampton Wanderers 5,000   L 1-3
Foulke beaten by a fast low shot for first goal after two minutes; second goal rebounded off Thickett through his hands. First time United had conceded more than two goals in a match that season.

Sat. 6/2/97   A   Blackburn Rovers   5,000   W 3-1
Revenge for the FA Cup defeat. Chippendale was on his own in front of goal, but his low shot was stopped by a quick-reacting Foulke.

Sat. 20/2/97   H   Nottingham Forest   8,000   L 0-3
All three goals in last fifteen minutes. William was drawn out of position to challenge Capes, and Richards headed first goal. Third goal a penalty. 'Foulke, Thickett, Morren and Bennett showed individual excellence.' (*Sheffield Independent*)

Sat. 27/2/97   A   Sunderland   4,000   W 1-0
Sunderland forwards continually outwitted United backs, but Foulke gave one of his best displays of the season.

Tue. 2/3/97   A   The Wednesday   11,800   D 1-1
'It was Foulke's goalkeeping more than anything else which saved United from defeat at Olive Grove on Shrove Tuesday.' (*Athletic News*)

Sat. 6/3/97   A   Wolverhampton Wanderers 5,000   D 1-1
Another exceptional game from Foulke. 'But for his brilliant goalkeeping the Bramall Lane club might not have been so high up the League ladder as they are.' (*Athletic News*). However he was criticised for his one bad error, running out of goal when staying put was wiser.

Sat. 13/3/97   H   Preston North End   6,000   L 0-2
Foulke drawn out into 'scrimmage', Boyd hit into unguarded net on sixty-five minutes. Five minutes later the Blades 'keeper tipped a shot onto the crossbar; it rebounded to Eccleston, who scored.

Sat. 20/3/97   A   Bury   8,000   W 1-0
William in good form: long shots, high and low, easily gathered.

Sat. 27/3/97   H   Stoke   2,000   W 1-0
Foulke's outstanding save from W. Maxwell.

Thu. 15/4/97   A   Stoke   3,000   L 0-2
Hingerty scored with an easy shot a couple of yards out. Foulke generally sound.

Fri. 16/4/97   A   Bolton Wanderers   7,000   W 2-0
'The home forwards gave Foulke plenty to do, but he was in grand form.' (*Sheffield Daily Telegraph*). United finished with the best defence in the League, conceding less than a goal a game.

SHEFFIELD UNITED: FOOTBALL LEAGUE RUNNERS–UP 1896/97

1. *Above:* Primrose Hill, Blackwell. Foulke lived in this row of purpose-built miners' houses until his marriage and permanent move to Sheffield. The wall surrounding the cricket ground may be seen on the right. *(Blackwell Parish)*

2. *Left:* A slim and youthful William, possibly in his Blackwell Colliery FC days.

3. Blackwell 'A' Winning Colliery, where William worked full time between the ages of thirteen and twenty. *(Peak District Mines Historical Society Bulletin)*

William Foulke

4. The earliest shot of Foulke in Sheffield United colours (1894). *(SUFC Hall of Fame)*

5. *Above:* 1894/95 team photo. William is already prominent! Joseph Tomlinson, the director who secured Foulke's signature, is standing, far right. *(SUFC Hall of Fame)*

6. *Below:* The Blades 1895/96. *(SUFC Hall of Fame)*

Trinity Church, Sheffield.

7. Contemporary print of Trinity church, Sheffield, where William and Beatrice were married in June 1896. *(Sheffield Local History Library)*

8. Ernest 'Nudger' Needham – the original Captain Marvel, prince of half-backs, with 16 England caps to his credit. *(SUFC Hall of Fame)*

9. Walter 'Cocky' Bennett, lively winger, an unerringly accurate crosser of the ball, and scorer of remarkable goals. He gained 2 England caps. Best of mates to William. *(SUFC Hall of Fame)*

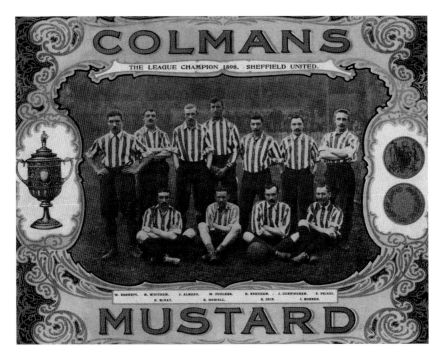

10. Sheffield United League Champions 1898. *(SUFC Hall of Fame)*

11. Team and club directorate with the Dewar Trophy (see chapter 4). Players standing (left to right): Cunningham, Johnson, Bennett, Foulke, Needham (with Thickett behind and between these two), Hedley, Almond, Priest, Morren. Dr Charles Stokes is seated, left of centre. *(SUFC Hall of Fame)*

12. The 1899 FA Cup final team. *(SUFC Hall of Fame)*

13. Return by charabanc from the 1899 cup final victory. Needham is holding the Cup up front, and William as usual is unmissable. *(SUFC Hall of Fame)*

14. Cricketing pose (1900).
(SUFC Hall of Fame)

15. 'The Team at Skegness'. April 1901: Sheffield United at the Sea View Hotel, the professional footballers' favourite. Relaxing listening to phonograph music. George Waller (trainer, and William's cricketing partner) looking after the team's boots. *(SUFC Hall of Fame)*

16. The 1901 FA Cup semi-final against Aston Villa (first match). A sedate pre-match train journey to Nottingham. A pensive-looking Needham, Hedley, Morren, Beers, and Foulke take the field. Scenes from the match, a thrilling 2-2 draw. In the central picture, Foulke is about to make a save. *(SUFC Hall of Fame)*

17. 1901 FA Cup final. Spurs take a corner. Note the old 'kidney' shape of the goal area. *(Illustrated London News)*

18. A Spurs forward discovers – the hard way – how best not to try and discomfit Foulke. *(Illustrated London News)*

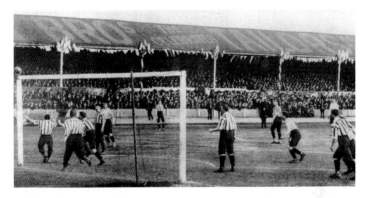

19. 1901 FA Cup final replay. Relentless pressure on the Blades, just prior to Spurs' third goal. *(Illustrated London News)*

20. Sheffield United team and entourage outside the Grand Hotel, Tynemouth. In case you spend too long trying to locate William, he's pretending to be the cabby! *(SUFC Hall of Fame)*

21. Another bit of role–play: Foulke as club milkman! *(SUFC Hall of Fame)*

Our Team emerging from the Dressing Room

22. From a match pro-gramme, 1902. Note that the diminutive Needham follows closely behind Foulke, a psychological ploy that emphasised the 'keeper's bulk. *(SUFC Hall of Fame)*

An anxious wait at Wolverhampton.

23. A scene from the 1902 FA Cup semi-final with Derby County. Foulke and Thickett await the onslaught from Bloomer and Co. *(SUFC Hall of Fame)*

JOHNSON   BARNES   THICKETT   COMMON   FOULKE   HEDLEY   BOYLE   PRIEST   WILKINSON   LIPSHAM   NEEDHAM

24. 1902 cup final replay team and match report. *(SUFC Hall of Fame)*

25. Sheffield United 1903/04: the team that narrowly missed the Championship in 1903, and that set a record of eight straight wins at the beginning of the 1903/04 campaign. *(SUFC Hall of Fame)*

26. The Blades all-international line-up 1904. The number of international caps won by each player is given in brackets. From left to right, standing: Jack Houseley (Assistant Trainer), Harry Johnson (6), Harry Thickett (2), William Foulke (1), Peter Boyle (5 for Ireland), John Nicholson (Secretary), Ernest Needham (16), George Waller (Trainer). Seated, middle row: Walter Bennett (2), Alf Common (3), Arthur Brown (2), Fred Priest (1), Bert Lipsham (1). Seated, front row: Tommy Morren (1), Bernard Wilkinson (1) *(SUFC Hall of Fame)*

W. FOULKE.

27. *Opposite below, left:* August 1905: Foulke at the beginning of his eight-month stint at Chelsea. *(EMPICS)*

28. *Opposite below, right:* William in Bradford City's colours. A cigarette card.

29. *Right:* Part of Bradford City's line-up, August 1906. Players visible are: Newton, Foulke, Campbell; Smith, Robinson, Bartlett.

30. *Below:* Sheffield United FA Cup winners 1915. Jimmy Simmons, Foulke's nephew and scorer of the first goal in the final, is seated, bottom left. *(SUFC Hall of Fame)*

In Loving Memory of
WILLIAM HENRY FOULKES,
LATE GOALKEEPER, SHEFFIELD UNITED FOOTBALL CLUB
THE BELOVED HUSBAND OF
BEATRICE FOULKES,
WHO DIED MAY 1ST 1916,
AGED 42 YEARS.
ALSO OF THE ABOVE NAMED
BEATRICE FOULKES,
WHO DIED FEBY 3RD 1933,
AGED 58 YEARS.
RE-UNITED.
WE CANNOT LORD THY PURPOSE SEE,
BUT ALL IS WELL THATS DONE BY THEE.

31. *Above:* William and Beatrice's headstone in Burngreave Cemetery, Sheffield.

32. *Below, left:* The Foulke's corner shop, 10 Matilda Street, Sheffield, around 1925. In the doorway are Robert, William's eldest, and his foster sister Mary.

33. *Below, right:* Foulke's portrait in the Hall of Fame, Bramall Lane.

Opposite, clockwise from top: 34. Foulke's shirt, and other memorabilia.
35. Foulke's England cap.
36/37. FA Cup winners' medal 1899.
38. The League Championship medal that was stolen in the 1910 burglary of The Duke, and recently recovered.

The Sheffield United Hall of Fame Dream Team
Back row, left to right: Len Badger, Graham Shaw, Bill 'Fatty' Foulke, Joe Shaw, Jimmy Hagan
Front row: Tony Currie, Keith Edwards, Ernest 'Nudger' Needham, Billy Gillespie, Brian Deane, Alan Woodw...

39. Part of Alan Damm's 'Dream Team' oil painting. Players visible are: Len Badger, Graham Shaw, William Henry Foulke, Joe Shaw; Keith Edwards, Ernest Needham, Billy Gillespie, Brian Dunne. *(Reproduced by permission)*

40. Willie takes pride of place in the entrance hall of the National Football Museum, Preston. Pushing twenty-five stones, he is here captain of Chelsea in August 1905. *(Reproduced by permission)*

1896/97: FA CUP

First Round:
Sat. 30/1/97   A   Blackburn Rovers   10,000   L 1-2
Rough game. United without Needham and Cain. Foulke, kneed in stomach by
Nichol, was flat out for five minutes. United's late rally brought one soft goal.

1896/97: FRIENDLIES AND OTHER MATCHES

Mon. 26/10/96   Sheffield *v.* London   1,500   W 7-4
At Olive Grove. Both attacks in superb form.

Sat. 7/11/96   Sheffield *v.* Glasgow   1,500   W 5-1
Foulke occasionally kept busy, but Sheffield attack (containing Needham) domi-
nated. Played at Bramall Lane. 'The lengthy custodian was in great form.' (*Sheffield
Independent*)

Sat. 28/11/96   A   Corinthians   6,000   D 0-0
Foulke nullified much-vaunted threat from the great G.O. Smith.

Mon. 4/1/97   H   Corinthians   1,000   D 2-2
'Some pretty manoeuvring round Foulke gave the visitors an opening, and Gettins
equalised.' (*Sheffield Daily Telegraph*)

Sat. 13/2/97   H   The Wednesday   7,000   D 0-0
Sheffield and Derbyshire League match. Nominally a reserve fixture, but both United
and Wednesday had a free Saturday, so the first teams turned out. William, in saving a
shot, swung on the crossbar, with the inevitable result.

Mon. 15/3/97   Professionals *v.* Amateurs   3,000   W 3-1
Played at Queen's Club, London. Trial match for forthcoming internationals. Foulke
excellent second half.

Mon. 29/3/97   England *v.* Wales   4,900   W 4-0
Foulke's only full international cap. He was virtually a spectator in a very one-sided
game. Played at Bramall Lane.

1897/98: FOOTBALL LEAGUE FIRST DIVISION

Wed. 1/9/97   H   Derby County   2,500   W 2-1
Torrential rain. Derby scored with a penalty. Archie Goodall put another one wide.
'Foulke made several brilliant saves early in the game.' (*Sheffield Independent*)

Sat. 4/9/97   A   Preston North End   4,750   W 3-1
Foulke 'saved some capital shots'. (*Sheffield Independent*). He was uncertain at times,
but United were by far the superior team overall.

Sat. 11/9/97   H   Stoke   12,000   W 4-3
United 0-2 down after six minutes. Shaky performance from Thickett and Cain.
Foulke 'good without being brilliant'. (*Athletic News*)

Sat. 18/9/97   A   Nottingham Forest   8,000   D 1-1
Foulke's 'rare skill' under pressure. 'The Foresters… invariably found Foulke too smart
for them.' (*Sheffield Daily Telegraph*). Cain fisted out – not seen by the ref.!

Sat. 25/9/97   H   Bury   10,000   D 1-1
'Foulke had little to do in comparison with his opposite number.' (*Athletic News*).
United were unable to translate their dominance into goals.

Sat. 2/10/97   A   Wolverhampton Wanderers 9,000   D 1-1
Rough game. 'Foulke, the Goliath among goalkeepers, shone brilliantly in goal.' (*Athletic
News*). He was beaten by a fast low swerving shot that appeared to be going out.

Mon. 4/10/97   H   Blackburn Rovers   8,000   W 5-2
Wilkie scored for Rovers with a close-range shot. Booth netted his team's second
with a deflected free-kick. Two each at half-time. United's massed attack in last twenty minutes brought three goals.

Sat. 9/10/97   A   Bury   8,000   W 5-2
Similar scoring pattern to last game. 'A swinging centre from the right saw Plant tip
the ball past Foulke, who seemed to be nonplussed.' (*Sheffield Daily Telegraph*)

Sat. 16/10/97   A   The Wednesday   26,000   W 1-0
All the Blades defence in superb form. United down to ten men for much of the
game. Spikesley's thunderbolt shots ably held by Foulke, who was illegally charged
into the back of the net by two heavyweight Wednesday forwards.

Sat. 23/10/97   H   Preston North End   11,000   W 2-1
Preston's goal due to an error by Cain, followed by a low shot off the inside of the post by Eccleston.

Sat. 30/10/97   A   Everton   35,000   W 4-1
Bell, Everton's centre forward, scored after four minutes. Enormous early pressure on United, but the Blades carried all before them in the second half. Towards end Foulke saved a shot with a full-length dive, falling on Bell, who had to be carried from the field in some distress. 'The United custodian had a big say in the decisive victory of his team.' (*Sheffield Independent*)

Sat. 13/11/97   A   Derby County   10,000   D 1-1
Foulke executed some spectacular saves, flinging himself to turn shots round the post. He survived a ferocious bombardment from all five County forwards for ten minutes before the interval. 'The manner in which he saved from John Goodall in the last minute beating all comprehension.' (*Derby Daily Telegraph*)

Sat. 20/11/97   A   Blackburn Rovers   12,000   D 1-1
A carping reporter criticised William's habit of clearing a loose ball with a strong kick. The general opinion: 'He played a magnificent game.' (*Sheffield Daily Telegraph*)

Sat. 4/12/97   H   Nottingham Forest   8,000   D 1-1
Forest scored with a penalty after a blatant Thickett trip. 'The Notts. forwards at last broke away, and Richards gave Foulke a scorcher to stop.' (*Sheffield Independent*). United's fourteen successive League games without defeat at start of season (with sixteen teams competing) equalled the record held by Everton.

Sat. 11/12/97   A   Stoke   6,000   L 1-2
Foulke made some excellent saves, and received an ovation from the home crowd at the end. Second goal a 'clearance' immediately returned, as the United 'keeper slipped in the mud.

Mon. 27/12/97   H   The Wednesday   37,389   D 1-1
Record United attendance. William beaten by a Spikesley special.

Wed. 29/12/97   H   Liverpool   4,000   L 1-2
Heavy rain and mud. Thickett scored an own goal. Foulke made a brilliant one-handed diving save from a shot by Hartley. Liverpool the sharper team generally. 'McCowie beat Foulke with a long low fast shot which sent the ball through the corner of the goal.' (*Sheffield Independent*)

Sat. 1/1/98   A   Notts County   11,000   W 3-1
Foulke in outstanding form. Notts scored from penalty.

Sat. 8/1/98   H   Aston Villa   23,587   W 1-0
'Foulke stood firm as a rock.' (*Athletic News*). United had been in special training at Matlock, and dominated throughout.

Sat. 15/1/98   A   Aston Villa   42,000   W 2-1
United 0-1 down until seventy minutes. Cunningham scored winner on eighty-seven minutes. Foulke again in fine form. Villa's first ever defeat on the Lower Aston ground.

Sat. 22/1/98   H   Wolverhampton Wanderers 10,000   W 2-1
Wolves, second in the League, found Foulke unbeatable until the last couple of minutes.

Sat. 5/2/98   A   Liverpool   18,000   W 4-0
'Foulke has a lot to learn in the art of clearing, though he stops the shots right enough, but his former weakness will, I am afraid, go against him when the international honours are being distributed.' (*Athletic News*)

Mon. 7/2/98   H   Bolton Wanderers   6,000   W 4-0
Foulke was rarely called upon. He 'saved a beauty from Wright in very cool fashion.' (*Sheffield Daily Telegraph*)

Sat. 19/2/98   H   Notts County   7,500   L 0-1
The United goalkeeper left his goal to race an opposing forward for the ball. He lost the race, and goal was thus empty, and County scored.

Tue. 22/2/98   H   Everton   9,500   D 0-0
'From fine work by Bell, Foulke was called upon to save, the big 'un running out some distance to clear rather riskily.' (*Sheffield Daily Telegraph*)

Sat. 5/3/98   A   Sunderland   23,500   L 1-3
Crowd constantly encroached onto pitch. United protested to the League that the result should not stand, but were overruled. Sunderland now only 1 point behind United. Howell's two own goals – see text.

Sat. 26/3/98   A   West Bromwich Albion   4,200   L 0-2
Gale-force wind. United outplayed, but Foulke was in good form apart from the two

similar goals: two good saves, but he failed to hold on to the ball, and Garfield then Richards scored from follow-ups.

Sat. 2/4/98   H   Sunderland   23,000   W 1-0
'Foulke never made a mistake.' (*Athletic News*). United forwards in excellent form, but so was Doig in the Sunderland goal – until the seventy-seventh minute. See text for the background machinations.

Fri. 8/4/98   A   Bolton Wanderers   19,395   W 1-0
The game that won the League Championship. Record attendance at Burnden Park (20,000). Needham scored the winner, running in from left-wing position. 'In Foulke the Wanderers encountered an insurmountable barrier.' (*Bolton Evening News*)

Mon. 11/4/98   H   West Bromwich Albion   9,000   W 2-0
Bradshaw in goal.

SHEFFIELD UNITED: FOOTBALL LEAGUE CHAMPIONS 1897/98

1897/98: FA CUP

First Round:
Sat. 29/1/98   H   Burslem Port Vale   12,000   D 1-1
Port Vale were a Midland League team. A McDonald header into the top corner brought them their goal. United equalised with a late penalty.

First Round replay:
Wed. 2/2/98   A   Burslem Port Vale   15,000   L 1-2
Played in a gale. Foulke out of position for winning goal in extra time, scored from a breakaway when United were attacking with eleven men!

1897/98: FRIENDLIES AND OTHER MATCHES.

Sat. 6/11/97   Glasgow v. Sheffield   10,000   D 0-0
'Although the home men shot well, they could not get past Foulke.' (*Sheffield Daily Telegraph*)

Sat. 12/3/98   H   Glasgow Celtic   10,000   W 1-0
Celtic were Scottish Champions. A lively game, with Foulke alert to all attempts on his goal.

Sat. 19/3/98   Sheriff of London Shield, at Crystal Palace
                 Corinthians   19,707   D 0-0
C.B. Fry, Wreford-Brown, and G.O. Smith played for the Corinthians. 'A grand exposition of the game.' (*Sheffield Daily Telegraph*). The United defence was impeccable.

Mon. 4/4/98   Sheriff of London Shield replay, at Crystal Palace
                 Corinthians   8,000   D 1-1
William had little to do. Corinthians scored a late equaliser with a twice-taken freekick of dubious validity. G.O. Smith and C. Wreford-Brown of the Corinthians offered their services for United.

Sat. 9/4/98   Football League *v.* Scottish League 20,000   L 1-2
Easter Saturday, at Villa Park. Controversial winning goal, after clear foul on Thickett. 'Foulke all through played a grand game.' (*Sheffield Daily Telegraph*)

Sat. 16/4/98   A   Glasgow Celtic   12,000   D 1-1
United had won the League the previous week. This match was billed as the Championship of Great Britain.

1898/99: FOOTBALL LEAGUE FIRST DIVISION

Sat. 3/9/98   H   Everton   12,000   D 1-1
Very hot day. Proudfoot scored a simple goal for Everton after some clever approach work.

Sat. 10/9/98   A   Notts County   15,000   D 2-2
William exchanged blows with Hannigan, Notts County's right winger, and was attacked by crowd. He had to be escorted from the pitch at half and full time.

Mon. 12/9/98   H   Wolverhampton Wanderers 4,000   W 1-0
Not much between the two teams, but Foulke in unbeatable mood.

Sat. 17/9/98   H   Stoke   8,000   D 1-1
'Foulke performed admirably.' (*Athletic News*)

Sat. 24/9/98   A   Aston Villa   24,521   D 1-1
'Foulke made mere child's play of many of the long shots.' (*Athletic News*). Devey scored the equaliser for Villa – a well-struck shot – on eighty-five minutes. Foulke injured his hand.

Mon. 26/9/98   H   *Newcastle United*   6,000   D 2-2
Bradshaw in goal.

Sat. 1/10/98   H   Burnley   12,000   D 1-1
'Foulke just touched out a superb long shot from Place when he had three other forwards upon him.' (*Sheffield Daily Telegraph*)

Mon. 3/10/98   A   The Wednesday   16,000   D 1-1
A great shot from Hemmingfield beat the United 'keeper, who had an excellent game.

Sat. 8/10/98   A   Bury   8,000   W 3-1
'Foulke was quite at his best.' (*Athletic News*). United (precariously) top of League.

Sat. 15/10/98   A   Newcastle United   7,000   W 2-1
Foulke 'standing in a sea of mud' beaten by an early 'rocket' from Harvie. Otherwise, a rock of safety especially during fierce late rally from Newcastle.

Sat. 22/10/98   H   Preston North End   9,500   D 1-1
Single Foulke blunder. Generally, a sound game.

Sat. 29/10/98   A   Liverpool   10,000   L 1-2
The famous altercation with Allan. Liverpool equalised with the penalty, then a late own goal gave United their first defeat of the season. See text. 'Foulke appears unable to stop a penalty kick, no matter how simple it looks.' (*Sheffield Independent*)

Sat. 5/11/98   H   Nottingham Forest   8,500   D 2-2
'Foulke is showing international form.' (*Athletic News*)

Sat. 12/11/98   A   Bolton Wanderers   7,500   L 0-3
'Foulke had an off day.' (*Sheffield Daily Telegraph*)

Sat. 19/11/98   H   Derby County   10,000   W 2-1
William won the duel with Bloomer. The Derby forward's goal on five minutes was probably offside. 'It was a treat to watch Foulke. No fewer than four times did Bloomer face him with the ball at his feet, and yet he could not beat him.' (*Sheffield Daily Telegraph*)

Sat. 26/11/98   A   West Bromwich Albion   3,000   L 0-3
A scrappy game. Dunn's 'grovelling battle in the mud' with Foulke, who was 'not at his best.' Thickett scored an own goal. United goalmouth at one point enveloped in smoke!

Sat. 3/12/98   H   Blackburn Rovers   9,000   D 1-1
Moreland scored for Rovers, cleverly slotting ball in as Foulke came out to narrow the angle.

Sat. 17/12/98   H   Sunderland   10,000   W 2-0
Foulke rushed out to intercept ball, missed, and Thickett headed clear from goal line.

Sat. 24/12/98   A   Wolverhampton Wanderers 8,000   L 1-4
'Foulke should not be blamed for any of the shots that beat him.' (*Sheffield Daily Telegraph*)

Mon. 26/12/98   H   The Wednesday   32,500   W 2-1
Foulke gave an impeccable display for most of the match. Hemmingfield scored for Wednesday with a low shot late on.

Sat. 31/12/98   A   Everton   19,000   L 0-1
'Foulke and his backs defended bravely.' (*Manchester Guardian*). Everton scored after five minutes, then United gave a good account of themselves.

Mon. 2/1/99   H   Liverpool   12,000   L 0-2
Foulke made two good saves from consecutive shots by Walker, but was unable to stop the third attempt. He 'could not be blamed for either goal.' (*Sheffield Daily Telegraph*)

Sat. 7/1/99   H   Notts County   7,000   D 2-2
Race between Hannigan and Foulke for a parried, loose ball. Hannigan won, and scored.

Sat. 14/1/99   A   Stoke   10,000   L 1-4
Poor clearances from William, who appeared complacent at times, and 'not seen at his best.' (*Sheffield Independent*). Thickett injured.

Sat. 21/1/99   H   Aston Villa   13,000   L 1-3
Heavy pitch after rains. Villa played well. Foulke had no chance with two of the goals. First from Wilkes after five minutes was a wickedly swerving shot that 'completely deceived' the United 'keeper.

Sat. 4/2/99   H   Bury   9,000   W 4-1
United were 0-1 down at half-time, but 'Foulke very nearly idle in the second half.'
(*Athletic News*)

Sat. 18/2/99   A   Preston North End   7,000   L 0-1
Two days after the cup match – see below. Halsall scored on eleven minutes after a
tricky run from deep. 'Foulke kept goal in fine style.' (*Sheffield Independent*)

Sat. 4/3/99   A   Nottingham Forest   5,000   L 1-2
Foulke carried off with leg sprain. Thickett took over in goal. United with nine men
at the finish (Priest retired).

Sat. 11/3/99   H   Bolton Wanderers   8,500   W 3-1
Bradshaw in goal.

Sat. 25/3/99   H   West Bromwich Albion   3,996   W 5-0
Several Albion men suspended by club for skipping training. 'Foulke all through had
an easy time of it.' (*Sheffield Daily Telegraph*)

Fri. 31/3/99   A   Burnley   7,000   L 0-1
'The Sheffield defence was reliable.' (*Manchester Guardian*)

Sat. 1/4/99   A   Blackburn Rovers   10,000   L 0-1
Third game in as many days! United fielded a weakened team. Foulke in good form.

Sat. 22/4/99   A   Derby County   10,000   L 0-1
The week after the cup final. Bloomer scored.

Sat. 29/4/99   A   Sunderland   3,000   L 0-1
Poor conditions. William played well.

1898/99: FA CUP

First Round:
Sat. 28/1/99   A   Burnley   11,000   D 2-2
United trained at Lytham. Rough game on a frozen pitch. 'Foulke had singularly
very little to do, being at the back of a continually aggressive team.' (*Sheffield Daily
Telegraph*)

First Round replay:

Thu. 2/2/99   H   Burnley   12,000   W 2-1

Burnley scored from penalty after Boyle handball. Apart from this, Foulke had about four shots to save throughout the game. 'His position was almost a sinecure.' (*Sheffield Independent*)

Second Round:

Sat. 11/2/99   A   Preston North End   12,000   D 2-2

'Had it not been for an exhibition of utter nervousness on the part of Foulke, the Sheffielders must have won. As it was, both goals were due to indecision on his part.' (*Sheffield Daily Telegraph*). See text.

Second Round replay:

Thu. 16/2/99   H   Preston North End   18,000   W 2-1

United on top form. Needham missed one penalty but scored with the second. Boyle scooped ball off line with William well beaten. Preston's goal due to an error by Beers.

Third Round:

Sat. 25/2/99   A   Nottingham Forest   33,500   W 1-0

Forest were FA Cup holders. Almond injured. United played all second half with ten men. Foulke's brilliant display, topped off by one stupendous save from Capes. Priest hit the winner on eighty-six minutes.

Semi-final:

Sat. 18/3/99   Liverpool   21,000   D 2-2

At the City Ground, Nottingham. 'Foulke once or twice fisted away when no-one was near.' (*Athletic News*). Two full-back errors led to the Liverpool goals.

Semi-final replay:

Thu 23/3/99   Liverpool   20,000   D 4-4

At Burnden Park, Bolton. Played in strong wind. United were 2-4 down with eight minutes left, so Needham threw nine men into attack!

Semi-final second replay:

Mon 27/3/99   Liverpool   30,000   0-1

At Fallowfield, Manchester. Match abandoned. 'A more complete fiasco could not be imagined.' (*Manchester Guardian*). See text.

Semi-final third replay:

| Thu 30/3/99 | Liverpool | 18,000 | W 1-0 |

At the Baseball Ground, Derby. Beers scored on eighty-seven minutes 'A battle brimful of incident.' (*Athletic News*). 'Foulke's clearances put the Liverpool men well downfield.' (Liverpool Daily Post)

| Final: Sat. 15/4/99 | Derby County | 78,833 | W 4-1 |

At Crystal Palace. United 0-1 down at half-time. Bloomer *v.* Foulke duel, in which the Sheffield man came out clearly ahead. 'Somehow Bloomer cannot appear to beat Foulke, even when he gets to close quarters.' (*Derby Daily Telegraph*)

SHEFFIELD UNITED: FA CUP WINNERS 1899

1898/99: FRIENDLIES AND OTHER MATCHES

| Mon. 24/10/98 | Sheffield *v.* London | | W 3-2 |

Played at Olive Grove. Poor attendance. Sheffield 0-2 down after fifteen minutes Torrential rain turned pitch into a mudbath. Only thirty-five minutes played each way.

| Sat. 10/12/98 | Sheffield *v.* Glasgow | 5,500 | W 2-1 |

Played at Bramall Lane. Foulke had a good game.

| Tue. 27/12/98 | H | Corinthians | 4,000 | W 5-3 |

Needham's benefit match. Foulke bombarded by lively Corinthian forwards, especially G.O. Smith.

1899/1900: FOOTBALL LEAGUE FIRST DIVISION

| Sat. 2/9/99 | A | Everton | 27,000 | W 2-1 |

'United don't seem to mind how much work Foulke is called upon to do, and place the most implicit confidence in him.' (*Athletic News*). Settle scored first for Everton, with a fast low shot which the United 'keeper touched but couldn't stop.

| Sat. 9/9/99 | H | Blackburn Rovers | 14,000 | W 3-0 |

'Foulke… was mostly in silent communion with one of his posts.' (*Athletic News*)

| Sat. 16/9/99 | A | Derby County | 10,000 | W 1-0 |

Once again, William won the mind games with Bloomer playing at centre forward. 'He appeared coolness itself.' (*Sheffield Independent*)

Sat. 23/9/99   H   Bury   9,500   W 4-0
Foulke seldom in trouble.

Sat. 30/9/99   A   Notts County   10,000   W 2-1
Fletcher scored for County with a speedy shot on twenty-five minutes 'Foulke kept
a fine, safe goal, and his ponderous thumps and kicks, half, and sometimes three-
quarters, the length of the field, were a continual source of merriment and wonder.'
(*Sheffield Daily Telegraph*)

Mon. 2/10/99   H   Sunderland   7,636   D 2-2
An open, attacking game. Hogg scored Sunderland's first, a rebound down from the
crossbar. Foulke failed to deal adequately with another Hogg shot, and Becton (ex-
United) hit in the rebound.

Sat. 7/10/99   H   Manchester City   21,600   W 3-0
Foulke had little to do after early City pressure. Meredith excellent on City wing,
gave United goalie most work to do.

Sat. 14/10/99   H   Wolverhampton Wanderers 12,823   W 5-2
A bizarre own goal from Needham. The second Wolves' goal was a deflection.

Sat. 21/10/99   A   Newcastle United   30,000   D 0-0
Newcastle's record attendance. 'Foulke's work was quite faultless.' (*Athletic News*)

Sat. 28/10/99   H   Aston Villa   30,000   W 2-1
Top of the table clash. Villa's goal a lucky ricochet off the crossbar. Foulke equal to all
other shots.

Sat. 4/11/99   A   Liverpool   22,000   D 2-2
Robertson scored a 'clearly offside' goal for Liverpool, who were at their best for the
first ten minutes of the second half. 'Foulke kept out some stinging shots, but was not
at his best.' (*Sheffield Independent*)

Mon. 6/11/99   A   West Bromwich Albion   14,905   W 2-1
'Foulke distinguished himself by getting rid of several long shots fired at his charge.'
(*Sheffield Independent*). Perry opened the scoring for WBA on twenty minutes with a
powerful cross-shot.

Sat. 11/11/99   H   Burnley   6.900   D 0-0
A rough, ragged game played in stormy weather. William had little to do.

Sat. 18/11/99   A   Preston North End   8,000   W 1-0
'Foulke was never in difficulty.' (*Sheffield Independent*). He had just two shots to stop throughout the entire second half.

Sat. 25/11/99   H   Nottingham Forest   13,000   W 3-0
United displayed superior finishing. 'Long shots are not much good against the great William.' (*Athletic News*)

Sat. 2/12/99   A   Glossop North End   5,000   D 2-2
Rough game which finished in semi-darkness. There was a late start and a long half-time interval (because of a brass band recital). Glossop's late equalising goal was scored in the gloom.

Sat. 9/12/99   H   Stoke   14,000   W 1-0
In-form United 'keeper made many smart saves from Stoke attack.

Sat. 16/12/99   A   Sunderland   16,000   D 1-1
Hogg (Sunderland centre forward) made a solo run for goal, looking likely to score, but Foulke ran out and plucked the ball from his feet. 'A wonderful save.' (*Athletic News*)

Sat. 23/12/99   H   West Bromwich Albion   8,000   D 1-1
'On at least two occasions Foulke came out with saves of the highest order.' (*Sheffield Daily Telegraph*)

Mon. 25/12/99   A   Manchester City   28,000   W 2-1
'The Manchester men gave Foulke a lot of work to do, and had not the big goalkeeper been in his best form the result might have been very different.' (*Sheffield Independent*)

Sat. 30/12/99   H   Everton   10,500   W 5-0
Just the one fumble from Foulke, who dropped a soft shot from Everton's Boyle. The referee, after discussion with a linesman, decided the ball hadn't crossed the line.

Sat. 13/1/00   H   Derby County   14,000   D 1-1
Bloomer not playing (suspended), but Foulke well beaten by Boag on six minutes, after some rapid inter-passing from Derby forwards. United equalled Preston's record of twenty-two consecutive games without defeat in a season.

Sat. 20/1/00   A   Bury   15,141   L 1-2
Foulke arguably charged while not in possession of the ball, and thus distracted allowed Wood to chip over him for the winner.

Sat. 3/2/00   H   Notts County   6,000   D 1-1
Bad-tempered game. On forty-seven minutes Foulke saved but only parried into path
of McMain, who, with a hint of handball, bundled in the rebound.

Sat. 3/3/00   A   Aston Villa   50,000   D 1-1
Top-of-the-table clash. Record Villa attendance. United had four key players missing.
William's fisted clearance set up United goal. 'Evidently the cares of the captainship
sat lightly upon his broad shoulders.' (*Sheffield Independent*)

Sat. 10/3/00   H   Liverpool   14,500   L 1-2
Foulke captain again. United weakened by injuries once more. Two fine goals conceded in first twenty minutes: one after a miskick by Boyle, the other a high one out
of 'keeper's reach.

Sat. 24/3/00   H   Preston North End   8,000   W 1-0
United domination not reflected in the scoreline. Late shot from distance by
Henderson caused a moment of palpitation, 'the United custodian only just turning
the ball aside.' (*Sheffield Independent*)

Mon. 26/3/00   H   Newcastle United   4,000   W 3-1
Newcastle outplayed until late rally. Visitors' goal a fast ground shot into far corner.

Sat. 31/3/00   A   Nottingham Forest   7,000   L 0-4
Biggar in goal. William playing for Football League – see below.

Sat. 7/4/00   H   Glossop North End   5,000   W 4-0
'Evans broke away… much amusement being caused by the Glossop lightweight
charging into the burly Foulke from whom he cannoned off without making the
slightest impression.' (*Glossop Chronicle*)

Fri. 13/4/00   A   Blackburn Rovers   10,000   D 3-3
Foulke's error led to Rovers' second goal: he ran out to fist away, but not cleanly
enough. Hulse pounced on the loose ball and scored.

Sat. 14/4/00   A   Stoke   6,000   D 1-1
Stoke's goal deflected in off Morren, to the immobile Foulke's astonishment.

Tue. 17/4/00   A   Wolverhampton Wanderers 6,000   W 2-1
Some controversy about whether Wolves' goal had actually crossed the line.

Mon. 23/4/00   A   Burnley   6,000   L 0-1
The match United had to win 8-0 to overtake Villa for the Championship! More
than a hint of offside to Burnley's goal. 'On several occasions only the dexterity of
Foulke in goal saved his side from disaster.' (*Sheffield Independent*)

SHEFFIELD UNITED: FOOTBALL LEAGUE RUNNERS–UP 1899/1900

1899/1900: FA CUP

First Round: Sat. 27/1/00   H   Leicester Fosse   12,000   W 1-0
'Foulke never really extended.' (*Athletic News*)

Second Round: Sat. 10/2/00   H   The Wednesday   32,381   0-0
Match abandoned. Heavy snow.

Second Round: Sat. 17/2/00   H   The Wednesday   28,374   D 1-1
Rough match. 'Foulke, considering that his weight is now 20st. 7lb., showed extreme
nimbleness. He is a wonder.' (*Athletic News*)

Second Round replay:
Mon. 19/2/00   A   The Wednesday   23,000   W 2-0
Violent game. Played at Wednesday's new Owlerton ground. Two Wednesday players
sent off. 'Superb goalkeeping on the part of Foulke.' (*Sheffield Independent*)

Third Round: Sat. 24/2/00   H   Bury   21,017   D 2-2
Spectacular save: long-range shot, spotted late, was heading for the opposite top corner. Foulke hurled himself across the goal, and fisted clear.

Third Round replay: Thu 1/3/00   A   Bury   20,139   L 0-2
A hobbling Thickett was the weak defensive link, exploited for both Bury goals.
William in great form. Bury were eventual cup winners.

1899/1900: FRIENDLIES AND OTHER MATCHES

Mon. 16/10/99   Sheffield *v.* London   2,500   W 7-0
Played at Olive Grove. Foulke rarely troubled, but did make two good saves.

Mon. 23/10/99   H   Kaffirs   4,500   W 7-2
African touring side. Foulke scored two!

Tue. 26/12/99   H   The Wednesday   13,000   L 0-1
Friendly. Wednesday in Second Division. Foulke beaten by a fast low shot from Wright with 2 minutes left.

Sat. 31/3/00   Football League *v.* Scottish League 7,000   D 2-2
At Crystal Palace. William played well in a quiet game. This was tantamount to a trial for the following week's full international. Again, Robinson was preferred.

Wed. 18/4/00   A   South Wales XI   3,000   W 2-0
Played at Cardiff, first match on Welsh tour. Foulke had to handle the ball only once.

Thu. 19/4/00   A   Aberdare   5,000   L 1-2
United beaten by a spirited village side. 'Foulke played a brilliant game.' (*Sheffield Independent*)

Sat. 28/4/00   A   Glasgow Rangers   10,000   W 1-0
The Glaswegians were impressed by United in general, and Foulke in particular.

1900/01: FOOTBALL LEAGUE FIRST DIVISION

Sat. 1/9/00   H   Bury   18,200   L 0-3
United were 'completely outplayed on all points' (*Athletic News*). Thickett miskicked a clearance to allow McLuckie to send in a fast low shot for Bury's first.

Sat. 8/9/00   A   Nottingham Forest   12,000   L 0-2
Forest's first goal a 'long high shot', then a penalty. 'Foulke and the two backs did very well, and could scarcely be blamed for the defeat.' (*Sheffield Independent*)

Sat. 15/9/00   H   Blackburn Rovers   12,000   W 2-1
Rovers equalised against run of play. Left-winger scored with a 'grand long shot'.

Sat. 22/9/00   A   Stoke   7,000   W 1-0
In the last five minutes Foulke stopped a shot from two yards out 'with his face'. (*Athletic News*)

Sat. 29/9/00   H   West Bromwich Albion   15,000   D 1-1
Rough game. United backs played well. After several fine saves, Foulke beaten by a Simmons header.

Sat. 6/10/00   A   Everton   20,000   L 1-3
Everton, helped by a strong wind, scored two late goals in a drawish game. Settle's
repeated attempts to charge Foulke into the net were looked upon by the crowd with
some amusement.

Sat. 13/10/00   H   Sunderland   15,000   W 2-0
Sunderland's first defeat of the season. United backs in fine form, so Foulke had little
to do.

Sat. 20/10/00   A   Derby County   10,000   L 0-4
For once, Bloomer won the duel, scoring a hat-trick, the first a superb volleyed return
of a Foulke clearance. 'Wombwell caused some amusement by his attempts, needless
to say futile, to charge the Sheffield giant through the goal.' (*Derby Daily Telegraph*)

Sat. 27/10/00   H   Bolton Wanderers   15,000   L 0-2
Constant United attacking came to nought. Bolton scored a fine goal on three minutes, after a cross-field pass and a smart shot from the right wing by Bell. Foulke
shook hands with fellow England goalkeeper Sutcliffe as the teams left the field.

Sat. 3/11/00   A   Notts County   12,000   W 4-2
'Foulke did well as usual.' (*Athletic News*). Morris opened the scoring for County on
seven mins with a close-in header, after which it was United's game.

Sat. 10/11/00   H   Preston North End   12,000   W 2-1
'Foulke had little to do.' (*Athletic News*). Preston North End scored a late goal: Foulke
parried a fierce shot, but was unable to hold it. Becton snapped up the rebound.

Sat. 17/11/00   A   Wolverhampton Wanderers 5,000   L 0-3
Wolves' forwards in rampant form. Despite making some fine saves, Foulke had no
answer to the three high-quality strikes.

Sat. 24/11/00   H   Aston Villa   15,000   D 2-2
Two fast crosses and close-in shots in the first half beat Foulke. United scored twice
in the second half.

Sat. 1/12/00   A   Liverpool   15,000   W 2-1
United had spent the week at Matlock. 'Foulke gave a capital display of custodianship.'
(*Athletic News*). United defence showed great tenacity in the face of enormous pres-
sure. Liverpool went on to win the Championship.

Sat. 8/12/00   H   Newcastle United   15,594   W 2-0
'Foulke never really troubled by Newcastle attack.' (*Athletic News*)

Sat. 15/12/00   H   The Wednesday   25,000   W 1-0
A relatively quiet affair, evenly matched, dominated by the defences, and by a referee determined there shouldn't be a resumption of FA Cup hostilities. William hurt and limping during the game.

Sat. 22/12/00   A   Manchester City   18,000   L 1-2
United netted first, on five minutes. A pin-point centre from Meredith enabled Gillespie to equalise for City, then Meredith scored, gathering a poor clearance from Boyle and hitting in a lightning shot between Foulke's legs.

Tue. 25/12/00   H   Everton   17,000   W 2-1
On fifteen minutes Foulke saved but didn't hold, and Settle netted the rebound. United hit the winner with a minute to go. Everton's vigorous challenges didn't worry the United 'keeper.

Wed. 26/12/00   H   Manchester City   25,500   D 1-1
Biggar in goal. Foulke injured. See text.

Sat. 29/12/00   A   Bury   6,500   D 1-1
Biggar in goal.

Sat. 5/1/01   H   Nottingham Forest   16,610   L 0-1
Biggar in goal

Sat. 12/1/01   A   Blackburn Rovers   8,000   L 0-1
Biggar in goal

Sat. 19/1/01   H   Stoke   3,000   L 0-4
Heavy rain, muddy pitch. A makeshift United team totally outplayed. Foulke's performance reasonable, considering it was his first game back from injury.

Sat. 16/2/01   A   Sunderland   11,841   L 0-3
Constant, ferocious attacks from Sunderland. Foulke kicked out, but ball hit McLatchie and rebounded into the net. Torrential rain in second half.

Sat. 2/3/01   A   Bolton Wanderers   2,000   D 0-0
William won the psychological battle with Bolton forwards. Muddy pitch, high wind.
'Foulke and his clever backs.' (*Bolton Evening News*)

Sat. 9/3/01   H   Notts County   13,634   W 4-2
Both County goals similar: smart centre from the wing and hard shot out of Foulke's
reach. It was 3-2 until the last minute, when Bennett made it safe.

Mon. 11/3/01   H   Derby County   12,500   W 2-1
Bloomer, clear away with only William to beat, shot feebly. At one point the United
'keeper ran out and kicked the ball off Boag's toe. 'Foulke sparkled out into all his old
brilliance.' (*Sheffield Independent*)

Sat. 16/3/01   A   Preston North End   5,000   L 1-3
A weakened United team were outplayed. A couple of soft goals conceded.

Mon. 25/3/01   H   Wolverhampton Wanderers 5,000   D 1-1
Foulke beaten by a lob from far out. He was 'cheered for a grand save from Miller.'
(*Sheffield Independent*)

Sat. 30/3/01   A   Aston Villa   8,000   D 0-0
Scrappy game between two depleted teams. Minds were clearly on the following
Saturday's FA Cup semi-final. Foulke was injured and went off for ten minutes, but
played on.

Sat. 13/4/01   A   Newcastle United   16,000   L 0-3
Biggar in goal

Mon. 22/4/01   H   Liverpool   8,000   L 0-2
This match took place in the week between the cup final and the replay. Foulke could
do nothing about the two splendid Liverpool strikes.

Mon. 29/4/01   A   The Wednesday   11,000   L 0-1
Wednesday had a purple patch just after the interval. Spikesley's fierce shot brought
off a half-save from Foulke, and Wilson netted the ball before it could be cleared.

Tue. 30/4/01   A   West Bromwich Albion   1,050   W 2-0
WBA, already relegated, put up a poor show. William rarely troubled.

1900/01: FA CUP

First Round: Sat. 9/2/01   A   Sunderland   25,787   W 2-1
'Foulke brought off some really fine saves.' (*Athletic News*). He also saved a penalty.

Second Round: Sat. 23/2/01   H   Everton   24,659   W 2-0
'Turner putting in a hot one to Foulke, who saved in his usual style.' (*Liverpool Daily Post*). Very few attacks filtered through the fine United defence.

Third Round:
Sat. 23/3/01   H   Wolverhampton Wanderers   27,000   W 4-0
Foulke – 'amiable and mountainous' (Percy M. Young) – saved a penalty when 1-0. United superior in all departments.

Semi-final: Sat. 6/4/01   Aston Villa   31,000   D 2-2
At the City Ground, Nottingham. A fine attacking game. Foulke had little chance with two superb Villa goals. Garratty cut through and scored with a 'fast, rising shot', and Devey placed a speedy header into the top corner.

Semi-final replay: Thu 11/4/01   Aston Villa   23,000   W 3-0
At the Baseball Ground, Derby. A brilliant save from Templeton's shot from the right, touched over the bar. 'In goal Foulke proved himself as capable as ever.' (*Birmingham Daily Post*)

Final: Sat. 20/4/01   Tottenham Hotspur   110,802   D 2-2
At Crystal Palace. Attendance world record at the time. United scored late disputed equaliser.

Final replay: Sat. 27/4/01   Tottenham Hotspur   20,740   L 1-3
At Burnden Park, Bolton. 'Pie Saturday'. United could have no complaints about losing this one. See text.

SHEFFIELD UNITED: FA CUP FINALISTS 1901

1900/01: FRIENDLIES AND OTHER MATCHES

Mon. 29/10/00   Sheffield v. Glasgow   4,000   W 3-1
Played at Bramall Lane. Glasgow sent one of their strongest sides for years. McPherson scored for visitors on nineteen minutes, thereafter Foulke did well to contain the viperish Scots attack.

1901/02: FOOTBALL LEAGUE FIRST DIVISION

Mon. 2/9/01   A   Sunderland   14,271   L 1-3
Common scored twice in the last fifteen minutes for Sunderland, both goals results of corners.

Sat. 7/9/01   A   Nottingham Forest   12,000   L 1-2
Morris scored for Forest with a short-range shot into corner. Foulke just failed to reach it, despite his full-length dive.

Sat. 14/9/01   H   Bury   18,000   W 3-1
'Foulke several times ran out in a very risky manner.' (*Athletic News*). After one such foray, a long shot on his empty goal hit the post and went out for a goal kick.

Mon. 16/9/01   A   Aston Villa   12,000   W 2-1
Villa scored a late consolation goal, Wilkes hitting a fast high shot into the far corner of the net. William a mobile, dominant presence.

Sat. 21/9/01   A   Blackburn Rovers   8,000   L 1-2
Referee decreed that Foulke carried one collected shot over goal line, giving away a corner from which Rovers scored. Foulke in vehement disagreement.

Sat. 28/9/01   H   Stoke   12,000   D 1-1
Foulke had little to do, but very much against the run of play Stoke scored with a glancing header from Higgins on twenty-two minutes.

Sat. 5/10/01   A   Everton   15,000   L 1-2
Some entertainment as two of the diminutive Everton forwards tried to hustle the United goalkeeper '…endeavouring to paint a living picture of the Stag at Bay.' (*Athletic News*). Some controversy about Everton's first goal: William insisted he had kicked clear without the ball crossing the line.

Sat. 12/10/01   H   Sunderland   14,642   L 0-1
Just the one crucial error in an otherwise quality performance. Foulke fisted out an easy shot, mishit, and Gemmell had a simple 'walk-in' goal.

Sat. 19/10/01   A   Small Heath   15,000   L 1-5
'Foulke had no chance perhaps with some of the shots that beat him, but his judgment was not faultless.' (*Athletic News*)

Sat. 26/10/01   H   Derby County   14,454   W 3-0
Thickett's tackling and Foulke's saves kept the sheet clean.

Sat. 2/11/01   A   The Wednesday   28,000   L 0-1
Alf Common's first game for United. A deflected shot was the only one to beat
Foulke. A brilliant save from Wilson early on was 'loudly cheered.'

Sat. 9/11/01   H   Notts County   10,865   W 3-0
'Foulke never really pressed.' A sprain put him out of action until after Christmas.

Sat. 23/11/01   H   Manchester City   10,527   W 5-0
Biggar in goal.

Sat. 30/11/01   A   Wolverhampton Wanderers   8,000   D 1-1
Biggar in goal.

Sat. 7/12/01   H   Liverpool   13,276   W 2-1
Biggar in goal.

Sat. 14/12/01   A   Newcastle United   18,000   D 1-1
Biggar in goal.

Thu. 26/12/01   A   Stoke   12,000   L 2-3
Biggar in goal.

Sat. 28/12/01   A   Grimsby Town   4,000   W 1-0
'Foulke thrice saved brilliantly.' (*Manchester Guardian*). Terrain was 'greasy and treach-
erous'.

Wed. 1/1/02   H   Aston Villa   27,576   W 6-0
Villa were League leaders at the time. 'Foulke had one slice of luck from a shot by
McLuckie, but otherwise he kept goal right enough, without having a great deal to
do.' (*Sheffield Independent*)

Sat. 4/1/02   H   Nottingham Forest   8,269   D 2-2
An eye-catching one-handed save from Foulke.

Sat. 11/1/02   A   Bury   30,000   W 2-1
'Foulke was in fine form.' (*Manchester Guardian*)

Sat. 18/1/02   H   Blackburn Rovers   18,228   W 4-1
On eight minutes William stopped a shot but was unable to clear. Dewhurst pounced and scored for Rovers. United 'keeper's performance was flawless after that.

Sat. 1/2/02   H   Everton   14,306   D 0-0
A poor game on a soft and slippery pitch. A bitterly cold day. Foulke had virtually nothing to do throughout.

Tue. 11/2/02   H   Grimsby Town   9,493   D 2-2
Boyle tried to dribble across his own area, was dispossessed, and Grimsby scored first goal. A swerving cross deceived Foulke, who came out to collect but couldn't reach it and Grimsby's second was headed past him. He hurt his wrist after a collision with an opposing forward.

Sat. 15/2/02   H   Small Heath   12,280   L 1-4
Biggar in goal.

Sat. 1/3/02   H   The Wednesday   28,426   W 3-0
Wednesday put two shots wide with Foulke well beaten, but overall United were well worth their win.

Sat. 8/3/02   A   Notts County   10,000   L 0-4
'Foulke had not much chance with the shots which scored, and he dealt with many in masterly style.' (*Athletic News*). United in 'apathetic' mood, mind clearly on next week's semi-final v. Derby.

Sat. 22/3/02   A   Manchester City   19,000   L 0-4
Biggar in goal.

Fri. 28/3/02   A   Bolton Wanderers   20,000   L 0-1
'Foulke was in no way to blame for the point.' (*Sheffield Independent*)

Sat. 29/3/02   H   Wolverhampton Wanderers 12,000   D 0-0
High wind. 'Foulke saved three in quick succession.' (*Athletic News*)

Sat. 5/4/02   A   Liverpool   5,000   L 0-1
'Raybould, Fleming and Robertson stuck round the gigantic Foulke like so many leeches.' (*Liverpool Echo*). Bizarre goal: ball was centred, and Raybould, running forward on the greasy pitch, lost his footing and slid at speed into the goal, flukily taking the ball with him.

Mon. 7/4/02   H   Bolton Wanderers   3,000   W 2-0

With William out of goal, Johnson saved the day by hooking the ball out from under the bar.

Sat. 12/4/02   H   *Newcastle United*   *7,873*   *W 1-0*

Biggar in goal.

Mon. 28/4/02   A   Derby County   5,000   L 1-3

Match played during United's return from Crystal Palace to Sheffield, the Monday afternoon after the Cup Final! Boag, in lively form, netted twice.

1901/02: FA CUP

First Round:

Sat. 25/1/02   A   Northampton Town   15,000   W 2-0

Record crowd. Foulke was called upon infrequently, and each time did the required.

Second Round:

Sat. 8/2/02   H   Bolton Wanderers   13,009   W 2-1

United 0-1 down: Foulke, most untypically, stayed goal-bound when advancing to meet attacker might have been preferable. Williams missed a sitter in the second half.

Third Round:

Sat. 22/2/02   A   Newcastle United   20,416   D 1-1

'It was excruciatingly funny to see "wee Orr" challenge the burly custodian for the ball...' (*Athletic News*). On seventy-five minutes Roberts shot hard and low. Foulke dived and parried, but Stewart followed up and equalised. Pitch covered with layers of frost, burnt straw, rain, and sand.

Third Round replay:

Thu. 27/2/02   H   Newcastle United   25,100   W 2-1

McColl scored for the visitors, hitting a fast shot from twenty yards through a crowd of players, with William unsighted. 'Newcastle seemed to play without judgment when near Foulke.' (*Newcastle Evening Chronicle*)

Semi-final: Sat. 15/3/02   Derby County   33,603   D 1-1

At The Hawthorns, WBA. Bloomer on form. Foulke parried one of his hard, low shots, only for Warren to lob back the half-chance for Derby's goal. 'Boyle was useful, and the same may be said of Foulke – but no more.' (*Athletic News*)

Semi-final replay: Thu. 20/3/02   Derby County   13,284   D 1-1
At Molineux, Wolves. Wombwell intended a cross to the left wing, but the strong
wind carried the ball past an affronted Foulke into the net.

Semi-final second replay: Thu. 27/3/02   Derby County   15,000   W 1-0
At the City Ground, Nottingham. Wombwell and Boag both fluffed apparently easy
chances, and Foulke twice saved well from Bloomer.

Final: Sat. 19/4/02   Southampton   76,914   D 1-1
At Crystal Palace. Wood scored a late, famously controversial equaliser for
Southampton.

Final replay: Sat. 26/4/02   Southampton   33,068   W 2-1
At Crystal Palace. Foulke's huge clearance kick on two minutes led to United's first
goal. He was in outstanding form throughout.

SHEFFIELD UNITED: FA CUP WINNERS 1902

1901/02: FRIENDLIES AND OTHER MATCHES

Wed. 11/9/01   Glasgow *v.* Sheffield   3,000   D 1-1
Played at Glasgow. Foulke performed well, despite constant attacking from home side.
'His bulk, coolness and cleverness were all appreciated by the crowd, and the burly
United man was repeatedly cheered.' (*Sheffield Independent*)

Mon. 21/10/01   H   Glasgow Celtic   2,500   D 2-2
Foulke's benefit match. Despite the 'friendly' tag, this was a keenly fought game.
Thickett was dispossessed by Meir for first Celtic goal.

Sat. 21/12/01   H   Glasgow Rangers   2,000   W 1-0
'Foulke safely got rid of Speedie's shot, hard and straight though it was.' (*Sheffield
Independent*). The 'keeper's performance in this friendly went a long way to persuad-
ing the committee that he was ready for first-team reinstatement.

Tue. 1/4/02   A   Tottenham Hotspur   12,000   L 2-3
Friendly. Kirwan hit Spurs' winner.

Sat. 3/5/02   A   The Wednesday   4,000   L 0-3
Charity match in aid of Ibrox disaster fund.

1902/03: FOOTBALL LEAGUE FIRST DIVISION

Mon. 1/9/02   H   The Wednesday   20,113   L 2–3
Spikesley was devastatingly on song. He scored the first for Wednesday, and made the other two. The precise cross and well-directed header was finding Foulke out.

Sat. 6/9/02   H   Bury   14,253   W 1–0
'The United defence made few mistakes.' (*Athletic News*). Recently recovered film footage from this game exists.

Sat. 13/9/02   A   Blackburn Rovers   6,000   L 0–2
An inch-perfect cross barely eluded Foulke, and fell just right for Dewhurst: 1–0. The second goal was a deflection off Boyle's head.

Sat. 20/9/02   H   Sunderland   16,564   W 1–0
'Foulke was never beaten, but truth to tell he was not very highly tried.' (*Athletic News*)

Sat. 27/9/02   A   Stoke   10,000   W 1–0
Stoke enjoyed greater possession, but their attacks were laboured. Lockett had a great chance in front of goal with just Foulke to beat, but he hit it just wide. Thickett and Boyle had a good game.

Sat. 4/10/02   H   Everton   13,998   L 0–2
United's retreating defence strategy allowed Everton forwards too much room. The first goal was a long shot into the far corner of the goal. The second was a penalty, after a handball (deliberate?) by Boyle. 'Foulke can still lay claim to being the greatest goalkeeper.' (*Athletic News*)

Sat. 11/10/02   A   The Wednesday   21,500   W 1–0
'Foulke in brilliant style… had a big share in the success of his side.' (*Athletic News*). 'The consistent magnificence of Foulke.' (Sheffield Daily Telegraph). He showed a calm courage in the face of enormous Wednesday pressure.

Mon. 13/10/02   H   Nottingham Forest   5,144   W 2–0
'Foulke's ability to deal with low shots will soon be acknowledged, for he had many such… and dealt with them all splendidly.' (*Sheffield Daily Telegraph*)

Sat. 18/10/02   H   West Bromwich Albion   13,495   L 1–2
William, out of position, well beaten by precisely placed header for first goal. Second had a hint of offside. Several one-on-one situations resulted in WBA misses.

Sat. 25/10/02   A   Notts County   12,000   D 1–1
United's team, partly composed of young reserves, fought well, leaving Foulke with comparatively little to do.

Sat. 8/11/02   A   Middlesbrough   5,000   W 2–0
'Middlesbrough sent in long shots, but they were lacking in force and thus easily cleared.' (*Athletic News*)

Sat. 15/11/02   H   Newcastle United   14,040   W 2–1
A haphazard game dominated by Sheffield United defence. Rutherford burst through and looked a certain scorer, but Foulke won the race and booted clear.

Sat. 22/11/02   A   Wolverhampton Wanderers 5,000   W 3–1
Foulke strong under pressure from Wolves' forwards – most of it legal. 'Wooldridge and Beats hustled friend Falstaff for the ball and when both sat on top of him referee Howcroft thought it time to blow his whistle.' (*Athletic News*)

Sat. 29/11/02   H   Liverpool   9,152   W 2–0
Lewis in goal. Foulke had a bad cold.

Sat. 6/12/02   A   Derby County   10,000   L 0–1
Lewis in goal.

Sat. 13/12/02   A   Grimsby Town   5,000   W 2–1
'Foulke came out like a giant refreshed.' (*Athletic News*). An oblique cross-shot went in off the far post for Grimsby's goal.

Sat. 20/12/02   H   Aston Villa   17,000   L 2–4
Villa's second goal came after Foulke had failed to collect cleanly, and Templeton netted from close range. The third was a weak shot which went between the goalkeeper's legs. 'The big man… was far from at his best.' (*Sheffield Daily Telegraph*)

Fri. 26/12/02   H   Bolton Wanderers   21,806   W 7–1
Foulke made one or two smart saves from rare Bolton attacks.

Sat. 27/12/02   A   Nottingham Forest   16,000   D 2-2
'Foulke on occasions was far from safe, and displayed a hesitancy that is far from common with him.' (*Sheffield Daily Telegraph*)

Sat. 3/1/03   A   Bury   11,000   L 1-3
William wrenched knee; out for next nine games, including both FA Cup ties.

Sat. 10/1/03   H   Blackburn Rovers   12,000   W 2-1
Lewis in goal.

Sat. 17/1/03   A   Sunderland   12,000   D 0-0
Lewis in goal.

Sat. 24/1/03   H   Stoke   12,000   L 1-3
Lewis in goal.

Sat. 31/1/03   A   Everton   16,000   L 0-1
Lewis in goal.

Sat. 14/2/03   A   West Bromwich Albion   17,122   D 3-3
Lewis in goal.

Sat. 28/2/03   A   Bolton Wanderers   12,000   L 0-1
Lewis in goal.

Sat. 7/3/03   H   Middlesbrough   11,000   L 1-3
Lewis in goal.

Sat. 14/3/03   A   Newcastle United   20,000   D 0-0
Foulke's return. 'The defence of the Blades was invincible.' (*Athletic News*)

Sat. 21/3/03   H   Wolverhampton Wanderers 12,000   W 3-0
Mostly United domination, although one shot hit the post with Foulke beaten.

Sat. 28/3/03   A   Liverpool   15,000   W 4-2
All goals scored in the first half. William was 'the man of the hour and the idol of the crowd.' (*Sheffield Daily Telegraph*). 'The mountainous Foulke was like a conjuror in goal.' (*Liverpool Echo*)

Mon. 30/3/03   H   Derby County   5,000   W 3-2
Match took place in torrential rain, with much 'floundering and sliding' in a 'sea of
mud'. (*Sheffield Daily Telegraph*) See text.

Fri. 10/4/03   H   Notts County   8,000   W 3-0
Foulke's fists did the necessary in defence.

Sat. 11/4/03   H   Grimsby Town   8,000   W 3-0
'Foulke was extended only two or three times during the game.' (*Athletic News*). The
little he did, though, was quality goalkeeping, saving a couple of rasping shots.

Sat. 18/4/03   A   Aston Villa   19,000   L 2-4
United were outclassed by Villa, with McLuckie hitting a hat-trick. Three of Villa's
goals were the result of fast sweeping centres and well-directed headers. United finished fourth, three points behind Champions The Wednesday.

1902/03: FA CUP

First Round: Sat. 7/2/03   A   Woolwich Arsenal   24,000   W 3-1
Lewis in goal. Played at Manor Field, Plumstead.

Second Round: Sat. 21/2/03   H   Bury   24,103   L 0-1
Lewis in goal.

1902/03: FRIENDLIES AND OTHER MATCHES

Mon. 6/4/03   A   West Yorkshire XI   7,500   W 8-5
Played at Manningham (about to become Bradford City) – at the time a rugby league
ground. Spreading the association gospel!

Tue. 14/4/03   A   Bohemians, Dublin 2,000   D 3-3
Foulke saved a penalty.

1903/04: FOOTBALL LEAGUE FIRST DIVISION

Sat. 5/9/03   A   Small Heath   14,000   W 3-1
Lewis in goal.

Sat. 12/9/03   H   Everton   18,592   W 2-1
Lewis in goal.

Sat. 19/9/03   *A*   *Stoke*   *12,000*   *W 4-3*
Lewis in goal.

Sat. 26/9/03   *H*   *Derby County*   *20,000*   *W 3-2*
Lewis in goal.

Sat. 3/10/03   A   Manchester City   28,000   W 1-0
William returned from injury, and 'gave a remarkable display in goal, and certainly
saved his side from defeat.' (*Manchester Guardian*)

Sat. 10/10/03   H   Notts County   18,000   W 3-1
'Foulke was never extended.' (*Athletic News*). Goal conceded was a last-minute penalty.

Sat. 17/10/03   H   Wolverhampton Wanderers 18,000   W 7-2
'Foulke had plenty of work, but did it excellently.' (*Sheffield Daily Telegraph*). A stun-
ning volley from Preston was deftly turned over the bar.

Sat. 24/10/03   A   Newcastle United   29,000   W 1-0
Almost non-stop pressure from Newcastle, but Foulke was equal to it all. United's
eighth consecutive win at start of season was then a record. There were 24 goals
scored at this stage, and only ten conceded.

Sat. 31/10/03   H   Aston Villa   25,000   L 1-2
'Foulke made some excellent saves, and had no chance whatever with the two goals.'
(*Athletic News*). He also injured himself during the match. Villa forwards ran the
United backs ragged, and only supreme form of the goalkeeper kept the score down.

Sat. 7/11/03   A   Middlesbrough   25,000   L 1-4
All goals in the first half, including three for Middlesbrough in five minutes. William
very unlucky with the penalty taken against him. See text.

Sat. 14/11/03   H   Liverpool   13,500   W 2-1
Liverpool were awarded a penalty, which Fleming shot straight into Foulke's arms.
Goddard later netted a penalty for Liverpool's goal.

Sat. 21/11/03   A   Bury   6,000   W 1-0
'Foulke did much that was risky. It seems to come off all right, though…' (*Athletic
News*). Played in a high wind: United 'keeper's powerful fisting and kicking against
the wind was a contributory factor to his team's win.

Sat. 28/11/03   H   Blackburn Rovers   6,401   D 2-2

Foulke ran out to clear, slipped in the mud, and allowed Dewhurst to score. In the second half he was 'limping and lame from an injury'. (*Athletic News*). Blackburn equalised in the last thirty seconds of the game, in gathering darkness.

Sat. 5/12/03   A   Nottingham Forest   12,000   D 1-1

Lewis in goal.

Sat. 12/12/03   H   The Wednesday   34,500   D 1-1

'Match of the season.' United and Wednesday first and second in table. 'Wednesday did not test Foulke too often.' (*Athletic News*). Wilson profited from United's defensive confusion to hit Wednesday's goal.

Sat. 19/12/03   A   Sunderland   15,000   L 1-2

Lewis in goal.

Fri. 25/12/03   H   Newcastle United   20,237   D 2-2

A couple of neat headers beat Foulke in the second half.

Sat. 26/12/03   H   West Bromwich Albion   20,324   W 4-0

'Foulke was very safe and showed fine judgment.' (*Sheffield Daily Telegraph*). Not that he had much to do in this game.

Mon. 28/12/03   H   Manchester City   28,513   W 5-3

Meredith was subdued by a tenacious Boyle, and poor finishing (and good goalkeeping) kept City out of the game until late rally. United 4-0 up in this top-of-the-table clash.

Sat. 2/1/04   H   Small Heath   12,235   D 1-1

Jones scored for Small Heath on eighteen minutes with a fine shot on the volley, giving Foulke no chance. Hartwell hit the post with a penalty.

Sat. 9/1/04   A   Everton   30,000   L 0-2

Everton's Ablott hit the first into the top corner, despite Foulke's valiant leap. Settle walked in the second, while an 'astounded' United goalkeeper looked on. 'Many powerful clearances and good saves' (*Sheffield Daily Telegraph*)

Sat. 16/1/04   H   Stoke   10,734   D 1-1

Gallimore dribbled through and scored a fine individual goal for Stoke. Drake's header equalised for United during time added on for time-wasting by Roose, Stoke's goalkeeper.

Sat. 23/1/04   A   Derby County   12,000   W 5-3
Bloomer headed in a loose ball to make the score 1-1, then scored another after a solo
run. Overall clear United superiority, and William was in good form, though 'given a
lively time'. (*Derby Daily Telegraph*)

Sat. 13/2/04   A   Wolverhampton Wanderers 8,000   L 0-1
Played in a gale. Wolves scored with a penalty, after referee's bizarre interpretation of
the new advantage law. 'I never saw Foulke drop so many shots.' (*Athletic News*)

Sat. 27/2/04   A   Aston Villa   13,000   L 1-6
Foulke made some good saves, despite receiving a kick to the head at one point.
United were without Needham and Johnson. Villa forwards rampant in the second
half, when they scored four goals, helped by a couple of kind rebounds.

Sat. 12/3/04   A   Liverpool   20,000   L 0-3
United had no answer to Liverpool's fast breakaway attacks. Goddard's goal left Foulke
'completely baffled'. (*Liverpool Echo*). United played seven reserves.

Sat. 19/3/04   H   Bury   7,000   D 0-0
Foulke coped with several probing crosses and dangerous shots without too much
concern.

Sat. 26/3/04   A   Blackburn Rovers   5,000   L 0-3
'Foulke not so successful as usual.' (*Athletic News*). For the second goal he was about
to collect the ball when Thickett tried to kick clear. The full-back slipped in kicking,
and the ball skewed into the net.

Mon. 28/3/04   H   Middlesbrough   4,000   W 3-0
Needham returned after injury. William wasn't often troubled, as there was little cohesion in rare Middlesbrough attacks.

Sat. 2/4/04   H   Nottingham Forest   8,500   W 2-0
Foulke had little to do.

Mon. 4/4/04   A   Notts County   13,000   L 1-2
'When barely a yard away from Foulke, Green and Gee missed the easiest of chances.'
(*Sheffield Daily Telegraph*). Two short-range first-half shots brought County their goals.

Sat. 9/4/04   A   The Wednesday   17,000   L 0-3
A cheeky back-heel from Harry Chapman (Herbert's younger brother) outwitted

Foulke in the opening minute. A fast and cleverly disguised shot from the same player on seventy-five minutes made it 2-0. Wednesday went on to be League Champions.

Sat. 16/4/04   H   Sunderland   12,000   L 1-2
Bridgett, Sunderland's inside right, was on form, scoring both goals. Otherwise, Foulke had a good game.

Sat. 23/4/04   A   West Bromwich Albion   4,467   D 2-2
'Foulke proved that he is still a custodian to be reckoned with.' (*Athletic News*). Nippy Albion forwards exploited the slower United backs. Albion equalised with a last-kick penalty.

1903/04: FA CUP

First Round: Sat. 6/2/04   A   Bristol City   17,909   W 3-1
'The Sheffielders were supreme.' (*Athletic News*). Very muddy pitch. One 'magnificent one-handed save' from Foulke.

Second Round: Sat. 20/2/04   A   Bury   23,291   W 2-1
Bury were cup holders. United were without Needham and Johnson. Sagar scored for Bury with a fine half-volley on twenty minutes. In the second half Foulke made a series of fine saves.

Third Round:
Sat. 5/3/04   H   Bolton Wanderers   29,984   L 0-2
Foulke 'not comfortable at any part of the game'. (*Athletic News*). His fumble led to simple tap-in from Yenson for first goal. Marsh scored number two following a scramble in front of goal.

1903/04: FRIENDLIES AND OTHER MATCHES

Mon. 5/10/03   H   The Wednesday   10,158   L 1-3
Inaugural United *v.* Wednesday charity game. The sum of £238 was raised for the university.

Sat. 30/4/04   A   Bradford City   5,500   W 4-0
Bradford had just completed their first ever Football League season, finishing midway up Division Two. One-sided game, in which William had just three shots to stop throughout.

1904/05: FOOTBALL LEAGUE FIRST DIVISION

Sat. 3/9/04   H   Derby County   17,906   W 3-1
On twenty minutes 'Foulke stopped a fast one from Bloomer.' (*Derby Daily Telegraph*).
Warren scored for Derby with a speedy ground-level free-kick.

Mon. 5/9/04   A   Wolverhampton Wanderers 10,000   L 2-4
'Foulke had no chance with the first three shots that beat him, for he had in front of him
two backs neither of whom was up to the required standard.' (*Sheffield Daily Telegraph*)

Sat. 10/9/04   A   Everton   25,000   L 0-2
'Foulke could not be blamed for either of the shots which took effect. The giant 'keep-
er is a great favourite in Liverpool, and his display in goal was worthy of his best days.'
(*Athletic News*). The full-backs weren't covering for the United goalkeeper's forays.

Sat. 17/9/04   H   Small Heath   12,500   W 2-1
Leivesley in goal.

Sat. 24/9/04   A   Manchester City   23,000   D 1-1
Leivesley in goal.

Sat. 1/10/04   H   Notts County   12,500   W 2-1
Leivesley in goal.

Sat. 8/10/04   A   Stoke   7,000   L 1-2
Stoke's first goal was a lucky deflected shot. Then Hall, after a fine run, netted their
second from six yards.

Sat. 15/10/04   A   Newcastle United   23,263   D 1-1
'Excellent work by Foulke' (*Sheffield Daily Telegraph*). Although he was lucky once
when, having riskily run out of goal, he allowed Veitch an open goal, which was inexplicably missed.

Sat. 22/10/04   H   Preston North End   17,500   W 1-0
Foulke had little to do in a United-dominated game.

Sat. 29/10/04   A   Middlesbrough   15,000   W 1-0
United goal under great second-half pressure. 'The unbeatable Foulke.' (*Athletic News*)

Sat. 5/11/04   H   Wolverhampton Wanderers 11,000   W 4-2
Some of Wolves' shots were dangerous, but fortunately 'cannoned back off defenders'.

Sat. 12/11/04   A   Bury   9,000   L 1-7
The score was 1-1 after twelve minutes, and 2-1 at half-time. 'Foulke's weakness is his
ability to capture low shots.' (*Athletic News*). Sagar played out of his skin for Bury, netting four goals in quick succession.

Sat. 19/11/04   H   Aston Villa   16,000   L 0-3
William Foulke's last League game for United. One goal possibly offside, one hit
through his legs, one from a penalty after Annan had held back Garratty.

Leivesley kept goal until the end of the season.

1904/05: FRIENDLIES AND OTHER MATCHES

Mon. 3/10/04   A   The Wednesday   7,991   W 2-0
Charity match, used by Foulke to stake his claim on his first-team place, recently
usurped by Joe Leivesley.

Thu. 29/12/04   H   The Corinthians   3,213   L 1-2
Walter Bennett's benefit match. Mellin dribbled through entire United defence, then
shot feebly at Foulke. Corinthians scored two fine second-half goals.

Sat. 18/2/05   A   Leeds City   3,000   D 2-2
Friendly. City were a new club. They specifically requested Foulke!

Sat. 4/3/05   A   West Ham United   5,000   W 3-1
Friendly. Played at Boleyn Castle. Foulke beaten by quick centre and strike.

Sat. 15/4/05   A   Hull City   10,000   L 1-3
Friendly. Foulke's last ever appearance in Sheffield United colours. Within a month
he had signed for Chelsea.

(B) CHELSEA

1905/06: FOOTBALL LEAGUE SECOND DIVISION

Sat. 2/9/05   A   Stockport County   7,000   L 0-1
High wind. Foulke saved a penalty, but only pushed it out as far as Dodd, who forced it, along with a Chelsea defender, into the net.

Sat. 9/9/05   A   Blackpool   4,000   W 1-0
'Bennett should have scored but the Chelsea custodian met the ball in grand style.' (*News of the World*). Pitch was covered with muddy pools of water, in which William floundered and splashed, appearing to enjoy himself immensely. 'To see him run, scattering the mud and water to right and left, was a sight for the gods.' (*Blackpool Gazette*)

Mon. 11/9/05   H   Hull City   6,000   W 5-1
'Foulke skipped about like a two-year-old, and saved a penalty in the opening half.' (*Hull Daily Mail*) He sprinted round the track on a 'lap of honour' at the end of the game!

Sat. 16/9/05   A   Bradford City   17,000   D 1-1
'Foulke and his backs presented a stubborn defence.' (*News of the World*). Bradford's second-half attacks were especially forceful.

Sat. 23/9/05   H   West Bromwich Albion   10,123   W 1-0
Fierce late onslaught from WBA beaten off by Foulke. See text.

Sat. 30/9/05   A   Leicester Fosse   7,000   W 1-0
Leicester's clever inter-passing was repelled by no-nonsense Chelsea defence.

Sat. 14/10/05   A   Lincoln City   3,000   W 4-1
Lincoln had a lively first half, but Foulke was in form. Second half was all Chelsea's.

Sat. 21/10/05   H   Chesterfield   10,000   L 0-1
Foulke injured leg (twisted knee) midway through first half, was limping throughout the game, but played well.

Mon. 30/10/05   A   Burslem Port Vale   6,000   L 2-3
'Ashworth shot accurately, and just as the ball seemed to be curling into the net Foulke rushed across and caught it as he would a cricket ball, his smart clearance being greeted with cheers.' (*Staffordshire Sentinel*). Capes headed first goal, reaching a cross before United 'keeper. The game became very rough in the second half.

Sat. 4/11/05   H   Barnsley   8,000   W 6-0

Foulke mostly idle, after he had easily contained the early Barnsley fizz.

Sat. 11/11/05   A   Clapton Orient   8,000   W 3-0

Foulke showed 'wonderful agility' (*News of the World*). He dealt equally well with high and low shots.

Sat. 18/11/05   H   Burnley   8,000   W 1-0

'Foulke was an interested spectator.' (*News of the World*)

Sat. 25/11/05   A   Leeds City   20,000   D 0-0

'... one warm effort from Parnell... Foulke only saved by going down full length... An intensely exciting game.' (*Athletic News*)

Sat. 2/12/05   H   Burton United   7,000   W 3-0

A mighty clearance from Foulke set up the third goal.

Sat. 9/12/05   H   Grimsby Town   7,000   W 2-0

Chelsea did virtually all the attacking. Foulke had little to do.

Sat. 16/12/05   A   Gainsborough Trinity   8,000   W 2-0

Foulke rarely troubled.

Sat. 23/12/05   H   Bristol City   25,000   D 0-0

Cracking game of constant attacks. 'Foulke was prominent.' (*Sunday Times*). City forward Gilligan burst through for one-to-one on 'keeper, but declined to shoot, passing out to Hilton, who was tackled by Mackie.

Mon. 25/12/05   A   Manchester United   35,000   D 0-0

This was William's ninth consecutive clean sheet in the League. 'A glorious and memorable struggle... an almost deafening tumult of incitement.' (*Manchester Guardian*). Manchester United missed a penalty with a couple of minutes left.

Tue. 26/12/05   A   Glossop North End   2,500   W 4-2

'Foulke gave a mighty fist out, the clearance of the massive custodian evoking both amusement and applause.' (*Glossop Chronicle*). The first goal scored against the United 'keeper in ten games was the result of a speculative high shot, his view obscured by players in front of him.

Sat. 30/12/05   H   Stockport County   12,000   W 4-2
One controversial goal: Waters of Stockport hit a free-kick against the bar, and Foulke cleared. The referee (forty yards away) insisted it had dropped behind the line before the clearance.

Sat. 6/1/06   H   Blackpool   6,000   W 6-0
'Foulke, who must have perished in the cold, was only once seriously troubled.' (*Athletic News*). High wind blowing across the field.

Sat. 20/1/06   H   Bradford City   14,000   W 4-2
Chelsea 4-0 up at one point. 'Foulke did his work well, his sledgehammer fist and great foot never failing him.' (*News of the World*)

Sat. 27/1/06   A   West Bromwich Albion   25,000   D 1-1
The usual WBA bombardment brought out the best in Foulke.

Mon. 5/2/06   H   Leicester Fosse   6,000   D 3-3
An enthralling end-to-end tussle, with all goals scored in the first half. Foulke well beaten by three superbly worked approaches and shots.

Sat. 10/2/06   A   Hull City   7,000   L 3-4
Foulke absent through 'indisposition'. Byrne in goal.

Sat. 17/2/06   H   Lincoln City   3,000   W 4-2
Pitch an 'ocean of sludge'. 'The huge bulk of Foulke seemed to intimidate [the Lincoln forwards].' (*News of the World*). Two powerful well-placed shots beat him.

Sat. 24/2/06   A   Chesterfield   7,000   W 2-0
An easy job for Foulke – he didn't have to handle once throughout the entire second half.

Sat. 3/3/06   H   Burslem Port Vale   10,000   W 7-0
Foulke had little to do apart from two penalty saves in quick succession. Both saves were comfortable – 'as if he were playing at catch-ball.' (*Athletic News*)

Sat. 10/3/06   A   Barnsley   7,900   W 2-1
Crowd was ground record. Barnsley's goal debatable: defender headed out from under bar before Foulke's clearance.

Sat. 17/3/06   H   Clapton Orient   15,000   W 6-1
Byrne in goal.

Sat. 24/3/06   A   Burnley   8,000   L 0-2

First goal followed a scuffle in front of the net; second was a fine centre and shot out of Foulke's reach.

Sat. 31/3/06   H   Leeds City   9,000   W 4-0

'Lavery slipped when he only had Foulke to beat.' (*News of the World*)

Sat. 7/4/06   A   Burton United   10,000   W 4-2

'Foulke brought off several smart saves, but he had no chance with Bradshaw's low shot.' (*Athletic News*). Burton scored from breakaways, as Chelsea dominated.

Fri. 13/4/06   H   Manchester United   67,000   D 1-1

Smart goal from Sagar for Manchester United. His quick trap and shot gave Foulke no chance.

Sat. 14/4/06   A   Grimsby Town   6,000   D 1-1

'Baker next showed up, and Foulke had to execute a long hop to get the ball away in time.' (*News of the World*)

Mon. 16/4/06   H   Glossop North End   30,000   D 0-0

Foulke had little to do. 'The burly Chelsea defender was on his best behaviour.' (*Glossop Chronicle*)

April 1906: Foulke transferred to Bradford City – see below. Byrne in goal for Chelsea until end of season.

1905/06: FA CUP

First Qualifying Round:
Sat. 7/10/05   H   1st Grenadiers   6,000   W 6-1

One-sided game *v.* Grenadier Guards amateurs. Foulke rarely called upon.

Second Qualifying Round:
Sat. 28/10/05   A   Southend United   7,000   W 1-0

Foulke injured from previous game. Mackie in goal.

Third Qualifying Round:
Sat. 18/11/05   A   Crystal Palace   3,000   L 1-7

Chelsea fielded a reserve side for this match. See text.

(C) BRADFORD CITY

1905/06: FOOTBALL LEAGUE SECOND DIVISION

Sat. 28/4/06   H   Barnsley   11,000   D 0-0
Foulke's debut for Bradford City, last game of season. He was given 'a grand reception'
by the crowd, which was 3,000 up on the previous home game. City did most of the
attacking, bringing out the best from the Barnsley 'keeper.

1906/07: FOOTBALL LEAGUE SECOND DIVISION

Sat. 1/9/06   A   Leeds City   16,400   D 1-1
Blazing hot day. Foulke beaten by a fast low shot on eighty-five minutes. Bradford
had ninety per cent of the play, and William spent most of the game as a spectator.

Mon. 3/9/06   A   Burnley   5,000   W 1-0
'McFarlane was well placed, and he shot with great force, but Foulke saved beauti-
fully.' (*Bradford Daily Argus*). A forceful and agile display in goal from William – 'he
came out and scattered the defenders like chaff.'

Sat. 8/9/06   H   Barnsley   13,000   W 2-0
William showed cool and capable domination of Barnsley forwards, and his huge
kicks started many a City attack.

Sat. 15/9/06   A   Chelsea   10,000   L 1-5
Chelsea forwards were on song, following deliberate policy of hitting hard low shots
at their former colleague.

Sat. 22/9/06   H   Wolverhampton Wanderers 14,000   L 2-3
'Foulke took a flying kick and missing the ball it rolled into the net.' (*Athletic News*)

Sat. 29/9/06   A   Clapton Orient   9,000   D 1-1
Orient's goal dubious; ball rebounded from inside of post back into play.

Sat. 6/10/06   H   Gainsborough Trinity   10,000   D 1-1
Farren tried to head clear a ball which he should have left to Foulke. Northey pounced
on the ball and scored for Gainsborough.

Sat. 13/10/06   A   Stockport County   6,000   L 1-2
Stockport forward Bardsley collided with Foulke, who fell on top of him. Bardsley

had to be taken to Stockport Infirmary with a suspected broken leg. 'Foulke had lots of work and he did it creditably, although he ran a risk by arguing with the home forwards in front of goal with the ball under his arm.' (*Bradford Argus*)

| Sat. 20/10/06 | H | Hull City | 16,000 | W 1-0 |

Bradford full-backs Farren and Campbell were in excellent form, leaving their goal-keeper with little to do.

| Sat. 27/10/06 | A | Glossop North End | 2,000 | W 2-1 |

McMillan shot over bar with only Foulke to beat. 'Rowbotham scored with a low shot, the 'keeper being too slow in dropping across goal to save.' (*Glossop Chronicle*)

| Sat. 3/11/06 | H | Blackpool | 7,000 | W 3-0 |

Foulke had no shot to deal with throughout the first half. A demoralised Blackpool had only Collier who displayed any spirit up front, but the Bradford goalkeeper had his measure, once beating him in a sprint for a loose ball.

| Sat. 10/11/06 | H | Chesterfield | 12,000 | W 1-0 |

Chesterfield forwards were lively and dangerous, but Foulke was in form.

| Sat. 17/11/06 | A | West Bromwich Albion | 9,000 | L 0-3 |

Bradford conceded two late goals. 'Foulke showed remarkable agility for a man of his bulk.' (*Athletic News*). 'Some of his saves were astonishing.' (Bradford Argus)

| Sat. 24/11/06 | H | Leicester Fosse | 17,000 | W 3-1 |

The goal that Bradford conceded was a low shot that shaved the inside of the far post.

| Sat. 1/12/06 | A | Nottingham Forest | 8,000 | L 0-3 |

Forest were Second Division leaders. One remarkable save from Foulke.

| Sat. 8/12/06 | H | Lincoln City | 9,000 | W 3-0 |

'Foulke not only kept goal, but he also acted as assistant referee in matters of offside by the visitors.' (*Bradford Argus*). An easy game for him, in which he was 'largely a spectator'.

| Sat. 15/12/06 | A | Burton United | 3,000 | L 0-1 |

A close-in ground shot led to Burton's goal.

| Sat. 22/12/06 | H | Grimsby Town | 8,000 | W 1-0 |

Rough game. Foggy. 'Several times Bradford had to thank Foulke, who with his lofty kicks repulsed the Grimsby attack.' (*Athletic News*)

Tue. 25/12/06   A   Burslem Port Vale   8,000   W 3-2
Bradford led 2-1 at half-time. Vale equalised 'Foulke fumbling a shot from Carter'.
(*Staffordshire Sentinel*)

Sat. 29/12/06   H   Leeds City   17,000   D 2-2
Played on an icy pitch. 'It was only a few minutes off time, when the ball was taken
across to the home goal and bungled by Foulke, who let in Wilson.' (*Athletic News*)

Tue. 1/1/07)   H   *Burnley*   *13,000*   *W 3-1*
Wise in goal.

Sat. 5/1/07   A   *Barnsley*   *4,000*   *L 1-3*
Wise in goal.

Sat. 26/1/07   A   *Wolverhampton Wanderers*   *6,000*   *D 1-1*
Wise in goal.

Sat. 9/2/07   A   Gainsborough Trinity   1,500   L 1-4
William Foulke's last competitive match. Wise was goalkeeper until end of season. All
goals scored in the first thirty minutes.

1906/07: FA CUP

First Round: Sat. 12/1/07   H   Reading   18,000   W 2-0
'Foulke played a splendid game in goal, and though he got several hot shots to deal
with he met them all coolly and safely.' (*Bradford Daily Telegraph*)

Second Round:
Sat. 2/2/07   H   Accrington Stanley   16,000   W 1-0
'Foulke saves the day.' (*Athletic News*)

Third Round:
Sat. 23/2/07   A   *Liverpool*   *18,000*   *L 0-1*
Wise in goal.

Summary of all Football League and FA Cup matches

FOOTBALL LEAGUE

(A) SHEFFIELD UNITED

Season	P	W	D	L	F	A
1894/95	29	14	4	11	57	53
1895/96	28	10	6	12	40	44
1896/97	30	13	10	7	42	29
1897/98	29	16	8	5	54	31
1898/99	32	8	10	14	40	48
1899/1900	33	18	12	3	63	29
1900/01	29	12	5	12	33	45
1901/02	26	10	5	11	40	34
1902/03	25	15	3	7	49	31
1903/04	27	11	6	10	46	45
1904/05	10	4	1	5	14	22
TOTAL	299	132	70	97	478	406

(B) CHELSEA

	P	W	D	L	F	A
1905/06	34	21	9	4	79	27

(C) BRADFORD CITY

	P	W	D	L	F	A
1905/06	1	0	1	0	0	0
1906/07	21	10	4	7	30	30
TOTAL	22	10	5	7	30	30

	P	W	D	L	F	A
GRAND TOTAL	355	163	84	108	587	463

FA CUP (NOT INCLUDING ABANDONED GAMES)

(A) SHEFFIELD UNITED

Season	P	W	D	L	F	A
1894/95	3	1	1	1	5	4
1895/96	2	1	0	1	1	3
1896/97	1	0	0	1	1	2
1897/98	2	0	1	1	2	3
1898/99	9	5	4	0	20	13
1899/1900	5	2	2	1	6	5
1900/01	7	4	2	1	16	8
1901/02	9	5	4	0	13	6
1902/03	–	–	–	–	–	–
1903/04	3	2	0	1	5	4
TOTAL	41	20	14	7	69	48

(B) CHELSEA

	P	W	D	L	F	A
1905/06	1	1	0	0	6	1

(C) BRADFORD CITY

	P	W	D	L	F	A
1906/07	2	2	0	0	3	0
GRAND TOTAL	44	23	14	7	78	49

CAREER TOTAL OF ALL FOOTBALL
LEAGUE AND FA CUP GAMES:

399	186	98	115	665	512

NUMBER OF CLEAN SHEETS IN ALL LEAGUE AND FA CUP GAMES: 116

CAREER AVERAGE OF GOALS PER GAME CONCEDED: 1.28

Football League Tables 1894-1907, showing records of Willie Foulke's clubs

FIRST DIVISION 1894/95

	P	W	D	L	F	A	Pts
Sunderland	30	21	5	4	80	37	47
Everton	30	18	6	6	82	50	42
Aston Villa	30	17	5	8	82	43	39
Preston North End	30	15	5	10	62	46	35
Blackburn Rovers	30	11	10	9	59	49	32
Sheffield United	**30**	**14**	**4**	**12**	**57**	**55**	**32**
Nottingham Forest	30	13	5	12	50	56	31
The Wednesday	30	12	4	14	50	55	28
Burnley	30	11	4	15	44	56	26
Bolton Wanderers	30	9	7	14	61	62	25
Wolverhampton Wanderers	30	9	7	14	43	63	25
Small Heath	30	9	7	14	50	74	25
West Bromwich Albion	30	10	4	16	51	66	24
Stoke	30	9	6	15	50	67	24
Derby County	30	7	9	14	45	68	23
Liverpool	30	7	8	15	51	70	22

FIRST DIVISION 1895/96

	P	W	D	L	F	A	Pts
Aston Villa	30	21	5	4	73	38	47
Derby County	30	17	7	6	68	35	41
Everton	30	16	7	7	66	43	39
Bolton Wanderers	30	16	5	9	49	37	37
Sunderland	30	15	7	8	52	41	37
Stoke	30	15	0	15	56	47	30
The Wednesday	30	12	5	13	44	53	29
Blackburn Rovers	30	12	5	13	40	50	29

	P	W	D	L	F	A	Pts
Preston North End	30	11	6	13	44	48	28
Burnley	30	10	7	13	48	44	27
Bury	30	12	3	15	50	56	27
Sheffield United	**30**	**10**	**6**	**14**	**40**	**50**	**26**
Nottingham Forest	30	11	3	16	42	57	25
Wolverhampton Wanderers	30	10	1	19	51	65	21
Small Heath	30	8	4	18	39	79	20
West Bromwich Albion	30	6	7	17	30	59	19

FIRST DIVISION 1896/97

	P	W	D	L	F	A	Pts
Aston Villa	30	21	5	4	73	38	47
Sheffield United	**30**	**13**	**10**	**7**	**42**	**29**	**36**
Derby County	30	16	4	10	70	50	36
Preston North End	30	11	12	7	55	40	34
Liverpool	30	12	9	9	46	38	33
The Wednesday	30	10	11	9	42	37	31
Everton	30	14	3	13	62	57	31
Bolton Wanderers	30	12	6	12	40	43	30
Bury	30	10	10	10	39	44	30
Wolverhampton Wanderers	30	11	6	13	45	41	28
Nottingham Forest	30	9	8	13	44	49	26
West Bromwich Albion	30	10	6	14	33	56	26
Stoke	30	11	3	16	48	59	25
Blackburn Rovers	30	11	3	16	35	62	25
Sunderland	30	7	9	14	34	47	23
Burnley	30	6	7	17	43	61	19

FIRST DIVISION 1897/98

	P	W	D	L	F	A	Pts
Sheffield United	**30**	**17**	**8**	**5**	**56**	**31**	**42**
Sunderland	30	16	5	9	43	30	37
Wolverhampton Wanderers	30	14	7	9	57	41	35
Everton	30	13	9	8	48	39	35
The Wednesday	30	15	3	12	51	42	33
Aston Villa	30	14	5	11	61	51	33
West Bromwich Albion	30	11	10	9	44	45	32
Nottingham Forest	30	11	9	10	47	49	31

Liverpool	30	11	6	13	48	45	28
Derby County	30	11	6	13	57	61	28
Bolton Wanderers	30	11	4	15	28	41	26
Preston North End	30	8	8	14	35	43	24
Notts County	30	8	8	14	36	46	24
Bury	30	8	8	14	39	51	24
Blackburn Rovers	30	7	10	13	39	54	24
Stoke	30	8	8	14	35	55	24

FIRST DIVISION 1898/99

	P	W	D	L	F	A	Pts
Aston Villa	34	19	7	8	76	40	45
Liverpool	34	19	5	10	49	33	43
Burnley	34	15	9	10	45	47	39
Everton	34	15	8	11	48	41	38
Notts County	34	12	13	9	47	51	37
Blackburn Rovers	34	14	8	12	60	52	36
Sunderland	34	15	6	13	41	41	36
Wolverhampton Wanderers	34	14	7	13	54	48	35
Derby County	34	12	11	11	62	57	35
Bury	34	14	7	13	48	49	35
Nottingham Forest	34	11	11	12	42	42	33
Stoke	34	13	7	14	47	52	33
Newcastle United	34	11	8	15	49	48	30
West Bromwich Albion	34	12	6	16	42	57	30
Preston North End	34	10	9	15	44	47	29
Sheffield United	**34**	**9**	**11**	**14**	**45**	**51**	**29**
Bolton Wanderers	34	9	7	18	37	51	25
The Wednesday	34	8	8	18	32	61	24

FIRST DIVISION 1899/1900

	P	W	D	L	F	A	Pts
Aston Villa	34	22	6	6	77	35	50
Sheffield United	**34**	**18**	**12**	**4**	**63**	**33**	**48**
Sunderland	34	19	3	12	50	35	41
Wolverhampton Wanderers	34	15	9	10	48	37	39
Newcastle United	34	13	10	11	53	43	36
Derby County	34	14	8	12	45	43	36

Manchester City	34	13	8	13	50	44	34
Nottingham Forest	34	13	8	13	56	55	34
Stoke	34	10	14	10	37	45	34
Liverpool	34	14	5	15	49	45	33
Everton	34	13	7	14	47	49	33
Bury	34	13	6	15	40	44	32
West Bromwich Albion	34	11	8	15	43	51	30
Blackburn Rovers	34	13	4	17	49	61	30
Notts County	34	9	11	14	46	60	29
Preston North End	34	12	4	18	38	48	28
Burnley	34	11	5	18	34	54	27
Glossop North End	34	4	10	20	31	74	18

FIRST DIVISION 1900/01

	P	W	D	L	F	A	Pts
Liverpool	34	19	7	8	59	35	45
Sunderland	34	15	13	6	57	26	43
Notts County	34	18	4	12	54	46	40
Nottingham Forest	34	16	7	11	53	36	39
Bury	34	16	7	11	53	36	39
Newcastle United	34	14	10	10	42	37	38
Everton	34	16	5	13	55	42	37
The Wednesday	34	13	10	11	52	42	36
Blackburn Rovers	34	12	9	13	39	47	33
Bolton Wanderers	34	13	7	14	39	55	33
Manchester City	34	13	6	15	48	58	32
Derby County	34	12	7	15	55	42	31
Wolverhampton Wanderers	34	9	13	12	39	55	31
Sheffield United	**34**	**12**	**7**	**15**	**35**	**52**	**31**
Aston Villa	34	10	10	14	45	51	30
Stoke	34	11	5	18	46	57	27
Preston North End	34	9	7	18	49	75	25
West Bromwich Albion	34	7	8	19	35	62	22

FIRST DIVISION 1901/02

	P	W	D	L	F	A	Pts
Sunderland	34	19	6	9	50	35	44
Everton	34	17	7	10	53	35	41

Newcastle United	34	14	9	11	48	34	37
Blackburn Rovers	34	15	6	13	52	48	36
Nottingham Forest	34	13	9	12	43	43	35
Derby County	34	13	9	12	39	41	35
Bury	34	13	8	13	44	38	34
Aston Villa	34	13	8	13	42	40	34
The Wednesday	34	13	8	13	48	52	34
Sheffield United	**34**	**13**	**7**	**14**	**53**	**48**	**33**
Liverpool	34	10	12	12	42	38	32
Bolton Wanderers	34	12	8	14	51	56	32
Notts County	34	14	4	16	51	57	32
Wolverhampton Wanderers	34	13	6	15	46	57	32
Grimsby Town	34	13	6	15	44	60	32
Stoke	34	11	9	14	45	55	31
Small Heath	34	11	8	15	47	45	30
Manchester City	34	11	6	17	42	58	28

FIRST DIVISION 1902/03

	P	W	D	L	F	A	Pts
The Wednesday	34	19	4	11	54	36	42
Aston Villa	34	19	3	12	61	40	41
Sunderland	34	16	9	9	51	36	41
Sheffield United	**34**	**17**	**5**	**12**	**58**	**44**	**39**
Liverpool	34	17	4	13	68	49	38
Stoke	34	15	7	12	46	38	37
West Bromwich Albion	34	16	4	14	54	53	36
Bury	34	16	3	15	54	43	35
Derby County	34	16	3	15	50	47	35
Nottingham Forest	34	14	7	13	49	47	35
Wolverhampton Wanderers	34	14	5	15	48	57	33
Everton	34	13	6	15	45	47	32
Middlesbrough	34	14	4	16	41	50	32
Newcastle United	34	14	4	16	41	51	32
Notts County	34	12	7	15	41	49	31
Blackburn Rovers	34	12	5	17	44	63	29
Grimsby Town	34	8	9	17	43	62	25
Bolton Wanderers	34	8	3	23	37	73	19

FIRST DIVISION 1903/04

	P	W	D	L	F	A	Pts
The Wednesday	34	20	7	7	48	28	47
Manchester City	34	19	6	9	71	45	44
Everton	34	19	5	10	59	32	43
Newcastle United	34	18	6	10	58	45	42
Aston Villa	34	17	7	10	70	48	41
Sunderland	34	17	5	12	63	49	39
Sheffield United	**34**	**15**	**8**	**11**	**62**	**57**	**38**
Wolverhampton Wanderers	34	14	8	12	44	66	36
Nottingham Forest	34	11	9	14	57	57	31
Middlesbrough	34	9	12	13	46	47	30
Small Heath	34	11	8	15	39	52	30
Bury	34	7	15	12	40	33	29
Notts County	34	12	5	17	37	61	29
Derby County	34	9	10	15	58	60	28
Blackburn Rovers	34	11	6	17	48	60	28
Stoke	34	10	7	17	54	57	27
Liverpool	34	9	8	17	49	62	26
West Bromwich Albion	34	7	10	17	36	60	24

FIRST DIVISION 1904/05

	P	W	D	L	F	A	Pts
Newcastle United	34	23	2	9	72	33	48
Everton	34	21	5	8	63	36	47
Manchester City	34	20	6	8	66	37	46
Aston Villa	34	19	4	11	63	43	42
Sunderland	34	16	8	10	60	44	40
Sheffield United	**34**	**19**	**2**	**13**	**64**	**56**	**40**
Small Heath	34	17	5	12	54	38	39
Preston North End	34	13	10	11	42	37	36
The Wednesday	34	14	5	15	61	57	33
Woolwich Arsenal	34	12	9	13	36	40	33
Derby County	34	12	8	14	37	48	32
Stoke	34	13	4	17	40	58	30
Blackburn Rovers	34	11	5	18	40	51	27
Wolverhampton Wanderers	34	11	4	19	47	73	26
Middlesbrough	34	9	8	17	36	56	26
Nottingham Forest	34	9	7	18	40	61	25

	P	W	D	L	F	A	Pts
Bury	34	10	4	20	47	67	24
Notts County	34	5	8	21	36	69	18

SECOND DIVISION 1905/06

	P	W	D	L	F	A	Pts
Bristol City	38	30	6	2	83	28	66
Manchester United	38	28	6	4	90	28	62
Chelsea	**38**	**22**	**9**	**7**	**90**	**37**	**53**
West Bromwich Albion	38	22	8	8	79	36	52
Hull City	38	19	6	13	67	54	44
Leeds City	38	17	9	12	59	47	43
Leicester Fosse	38	15	12	11	53	48	42
Grimsby Town	38	15	10	13	46	46	40
Burnley	38	15	8	15	42	53	38
Stockport County	38	13	9	16	44	56	35
Bradford City	38	13	8	17	46	60	34
Barnsley	38	12	9	17	60	62	33
Lincoln City	38	12	6	20	69	72	30
Blackpool	38	10	9	19	37	62	29
Gainsborough Trinity	38	12	4	22	44	57	28
Glossop North End	38	10	8	20	49	71	28
Burslem Port Vale	38	12	4	22	49	82	28
Chesterfield	38	10	8	20	40	72	28
Burton United	38	10	6	22	34	67	26
Clapton Orient	38	7	7	24	35	78	21

Foulke played the last game of the season for Bradford City, 30 April, in the 0-0 home draw with Barnsley.

Sheffield United's record in the First Division 1905/06: P 38, W 15, D 6, L 17, F 57, A 62, Pts 36; 13th

SECOND DIVISION 1906/07

	P	W	D	L	F	A	Pts
Nottingham Forest	38	28	4	6	74	36	60
Chelsea	**38**	**26**	**5**	**7**	**80**	**34**	**57**
Leicester Fosse	38	20	8	10	62	39	48
West Bromwich Albion	38	21	5	12	83	45	47
Bradford City	38	21	5	12	70	53	47

Wolverhampton Wanderers	38	17	7	14	66	53	41
Burnley	38	17	6	15	62	47	40
Barnsley	38	15	8	15	73	55	38
Hull City	38	15	7	16	65	57	37
Leeds City	38	13	10	15	55	63	36
Grimsby Town	38	16	3	19	57	62	35
Stockport County	38	12	11	15	42	52	35
Blackpool	38	11	11	16	33	51	33
Gainsborough Trinity	38	14	5	19	45	72	33
Glossop North End	38	13	6	19	53	79	32
Burslem Port Vale	38	12	7	19	60	83	31
Clapton Orient	38	11	8	19	45	67	30
Chesterfield	38	11	7	20	50	66	29
Lincoln City	38	12	4	22	46	73	28
Burton United	38	8	7	23	34	68	23

Foulke played his last Football League game against Gainsborough Trinity on 9 February 1907 (A). L 1–4. He did not appear on Bradford City's books for 1907/08.

Foulke's Inter-Association and Representative Matches: A Summary

1) FULL INTERNATIONAL

29/3/97	England v. Wales	W 4-0	At Bramall Lane

2) SHEFFIELD v. GLASGOW

7/12/95	Glasgow	L 1-3
7/11/96	Bramall Lane	W 5-1
6/11/97	Glasgow	D 0-0
10/12/98	Bramall Lane	W 2-1
29/10/00	Bramall Lane	W 3-1
11/9/01	Glasgow	D 1-1

3) SHEFFIELD v. LONDON

24/11/94	Bramall Lane	W 10-0
20/11/95	Leyton, Essex	W 2-0
26/10/96	Olive Grove	W 7-4
24/10/98	Olive Grove	W 3-2
16/11/99	Bramall Lane	W 7-0

4) FOOTBALL LEAGUE SELECT XI

18/2/95	v. Scottish League	Bramall Lane	W 3-1

(William Hendry's benefit match, not officially included in this list)

9/4/98	v. Scottish League	Villa Park	L 1-2
31/3/00	v. Scottish League	Crystal Palace	D 2-2

5) OTHERS

15/3/97	Professionals v. Amateurs	W 3-1

At Queen's Club, London

SUMMARY OF FOULKE'S MATCHES *V.* THE CORINTHIANS

(All for Sheffield United)

27/12/94	Bramall Lane	L 3-7
23/3/95	Leyton, Essex	W 2-1
27/12/95	Bramall Lane	W 1-0
21/3/96	Queen's Club	W 4-0
28/11/96	Queen's Club	D 0-0
4/1/97	Bramall Lane	D 2-2
6/11/97	Bramall Lane	D 2-2
27/11/97	Queen's Club	L 0-2
19/3/98	Crystal Palace (Dewar Trophy)	D 0-0
4/4/98	Crystal Palace (Dewar Trophy replay)	D 1-1
27/12/98	Bramall Lane (Needham's benefit)	W 5-3
16/4/00	Crystal Palace	W 4-0
29/12/04	Bramall Lane (Bennett's benefit)	L 1-2

P	W	D	L	F	A
13	5	5	3	25	20

SUMMARY OF SHEFFIELD UNITED *V.* WEDNESDAY GAMES IN WHICH FOULKE TOOK PART:

27/10/94	Football League	Olive Grove	W 3-2
12/1/95	Football League	Bramall Lane	W 1-0
8/4/95	United Counties League	Bramall Lane	D 0-0
20/4/95	United Counties League	Olive Grove	D 1-1
7/9/95	Football League	Olive Grove	L 0-1
26/12/95	Football League	Bramall Lane	D 1-1
2/3/96	Benefit match	Olive Grove	W 5-0
26/12/96	Football League	Bramall Lane	W 2-0
13/2/97	Sheffield and Derbys. League	Bramall Lane	D 0-0
2/3/97	Football League	Olive Grove	D 1-1
19/4/97	Sheffield and Derbys. League	Olive Grove	L 1-2
16/10/97	Football League	Olive Grove	W 1-0
27/12/97	Football League	Bramall Lane	D 1-1
3/10/98	Football League	Olive Grove	D 1-1
26/12/98	Football League	Bramall Lane	W 2-1
26/12/99	Friendly	Bramall Lane	L 0-1

17/2/00	FA Cup Second Round	Bramall Lane	D 1–1
19/2/00	FA Cup Second Round replay	Owlerton	W 2–0
15/12/00	Football League	Bramall Lane	W 1–0
29/4/01	Football League	Owlerton	L 0–1
2/11/01	Football League	Owlerton	L 0–1
1/3/02	Football League	Bramall Lane	W 3–0
3/5/02	Charity match	Owlerton	L 0–3
1/9/02	Football League	Bramall Lane	L 2–3
11/10/02	Football League	Owlerton	W 1–0
5/10/03	Charity match	Bramall Lane	L 1–3
12/12/03	Football League	Bramall Lane	D 1–1
9/4/04	Football League	Owlerton	L 0–3
3/10/04	Charity match	Owlerton	W 2–0

P	W	D	L	F	A
29	11	9	9	34	28

Willie Foulke's County Cricketing Statistics

William Henry Foulke played cricket four times for Derbyshire during the summer of 1900.

1. v. ESSEX, AT THE COUNTY GROUND, LEYTON. 28–30 JUNE 1900

Derbyshire, 1st innings:

L.G. Wright	c Young	b Kortright	170
H. Bagshaw	c Kortright	b Mead	55
W. Storer	c Russell	b Buckenham	176
W. Chatterton	b Buckenham		4
W. Sugg	c Russell	b Kortright	17
J.J. Hulme	c & b Kortright		0
W.H. Foulke	**st Russell**	**b Mead**	**53**
J.H. Young	c Carpenter	b Reeves	2
W.B. Delacombe	c & b Reeves		4
J. Humphries	c Russell	b Buckenham	11
W. Bestwick	not out		0
Extras	(b 8, lb 7, nb 1)		16
Total	(all out, 150.2 overs)		508

Essex, 1st innings: 368 all out, 141.2 overs

Derbyshire, 2nd innings: 0 for 1 declared, 0.2 overs

Essex, 2nd innings: 35 for 2, 21.2 overs

MATCH DRAWN

2. v. WARWICKSHIRE, AT EDGBASTON, 23–25 JULY 1900

Warwickshire, 1st innings: 635 all out, 152.1 overs

Bowling	O	M	R	W
Foulke	**4**	**0**	**34**	**0**

Derbyshire, 1st innings:

L.G. Wright	b Field		40
H. Bagshaw	c Lilley	b W.G. Quaife	61
W. Storer	c & b W. G. Quaife		10
W. Chatterton	c & b Field		64
E.M. Ashcroft	b Hargreave		21
W.H. Foulke	**c & b Kinneir**		**1**
S.H. Wood	run out		66
A.E. Lawton	c Fishwick	b Field	0
J.J. Hulme	b Lilley		53
J. Humphries	c Devey	b Hargreave	4
W. Bestwick	not out		8
Extras	(b 8, lb 6, nb 2)		16
Total	(all out, 121.2 overs)		344

Derbyshire, 2nd innings (following on):

L.G. Wright	c Bainbridge	b Hargreave	79
H. Bagshaw	c Fishwick	b Field	23
W. Storer	b Charlesworth		27
W. Chatterton	not out		35
E.M. Ashcroft	c & b Bainbridge		17
W.H. Foulke	**not out**		**1**
Extras	(b 4, lb 9, w 3, nb 4)		20
Total	(4 wickets, 64 overs)		202

MATCH DRAWN

3. v. LANCASHIRE, AT GLOSSOP, 30 JULY–1 AUGUST 1900

Lancashire, 1st innings: 168 all out, 47.5 overs
Derbyshire, 1st innings:

H. Bagshaw	c Webb	b Cuttell	14
L.G. Wright	lbw	b Briggs	25
W. Storer	b Cuttell		48
W. Chatterton	lbw	b Briggs	52
E.M. Ashcroft	c Webb	b Cuttell	4
W.H. Foulke	**run out**		**0**
A.E. Lawton	c Hartley	b Briggs	11
S.H. Wood	b Cuttell		3
J.A. Berwick	not out		8
J. Humphries	c Hartley	b Bridge	3
W. Bestwick	b Cuttell		4
Extras	(b 6, lb 3)		9
Total	(all out, 83.3 overs) 1		81

Lancashire, 2nd innings: 362 for 9 dec., 93.4 overs

Bowling	O	M	R	W
Foulke	**4**	**0**	**22**	**0**

Derbyshire, 2nd innings:

H. Bagshaw	b Briggs		54
L.G. Wright	c Sharp	b Cuttell	34
W. Storer	b Briggs		7
W. Chatterton	b Cuttell		1
E.M. Ashcroft	lbw	b Briggs	7
W.H. Foulke	**c Ward**	**b Cuttell**	**5**
A.E. Lawton	c MacLaren	b Briggs	2
S.H. Wood	run out		4
J.A. Berwick	c Sharp	b Cuttell	3
J. Humphries	c Cuttell	b Briggs	0
W. Bestwick	not out		0
Extras	(b 2, lb 4, nb 2)		8
Total	(all out, 93.5 overs)		125

LANCASHIRE WON BY 224 RUNS

4. v. NOTTINGHAMSHIRE, AT CHESTERFIELD, 20–22 AUGUST 1900

Notts, 1st innings: 249 all out, 76.3 overs

This innings included:

P. Mason	**b Foulke**		**16**
J. Atkinson	**c Humphries**	**b Foulke**	**0**

Bowling	O	M	R	W
Foulke	**4**	**1**	**15**	**2**

Derbyshire, 1st innings:

H. Bagshaw	c Dench	b Wass	0
L.G. Wright	b Atkinson		1
W. Storer	c Mason	b Wass	41
W. Chatterton	b Dench		48
E.M. Ashcroft	c Dench	b Wass	1
A.E. Lawton	b Wass		5
J.J. Hulme	b Wass		3
W.H. Foulke	**c & b Dench**		**4**
J.W. Hancock	run out		5
J. Humphries	not out		1
Extras	(b 2, lb 5)		7
Total	(all out, 44.4 overs) 1		20

Notts, 2nd innings: 198 all out, 73 overs

This innings included:

J. Carlin	**c Foulke**	**b Bagshaw**	**4**

Bowling	O	M	R	W
Foulke	**7**	**1**	**21**	**0**

Derbyshire, 2nd innings:

H. Bagshaw	c Shrewsbury	b Wass	63
L.G. Wright	c Dench	b J. R. Gunn	22
W. Storer	c & b J.R. Gunn		0
W. Chatterton	b Atkinson		50

E.M. Ashcroft	b Atkinson		5
W.H. Foulke	**b Wass**		**1**
A.E. Lawton	not out		5
J.J. Hulme	c J.R. Gunn	b Atkinson	0
J.W. Hancock	c Carlin	b Wass	0
J. Humphries	lbw	b Wass	4
W. Bestwick	c W. Gunn	b Atkinson	1
Extras	(b 4, lb 4, nb 3)		11
Total	(all out, 61.1 overs)		162

NOTTINGHAMSHIRE WON BY 165 RUNS

WILLIAM HENRY FOULKE'S CAREER STATISTICS (FIRST CLASS ONLY):

Batting and fielding:

M	I	NO	Runs	HS	Ave	100s	50s	Ct	St
4	7	1	65	53	10.83	0	1	2	0

Bowling:

Balls	M	R	W	Ave	BBI	5	10	SR
114	2	92	2	46.00	2-15	0	0	57.0

Extracts from match reports of Foulke's debut for Sheffield United, 1 September 1894

... Play was soon raging round the United goal, where after a bit of scuffling Taggart got an opening, and scored West Bromwich their first goal with a rattling shot after ten minutes' play since the interval. The game after this became more exciting, and the play faster, but the combination was not so good on either side as at the opening.

... After a corner to the United a similar advantage was conceded to the visitors. This was well dropped, and Foulke rushing out, cleared the ball cleverly, but to the surprise of everybody the referee allowed a penalty kick. That Foulke handled the ball was certain, and clearly apparent to all, but the referee held that in the scrimmage some other player had done so also. The penalty kick was taken by McLeod, but to the intense relief of the spectators the ball went outside, Foulke just touching it.

Sheffield Independent (3/9/94)

In goal Foulke, who was perhaps as much watched by the crowd as any other two men in the team, did his work well and performed his part with considerable credit. He might, perhaps, have got back to his place before Taggart scored the goal for Albion, but inasmuch as he had just saved grandly, his rashness is to be excused. He was by no means lightly tried, and came off with undoubted honours.

Sheffield Daily Telegraph (3/9/94)

From Foulke's Benefit Match Programme 21/10/01

LITTLE WILLIE!

This afternoon we give a benefit to one of our most popular players in William Foulke, our stalwart goalkeeper, who is known under the soubriquet given above.

He is one of those men whom we delight to honour, has been in the forefront of all our great success – perhaps in view of his position on the field, it would be more exact to say in the background, and has drawn to himself in the course of his association with our club much notice from the powers. He has had several honours given him, though the greatest honour of all, the cap for England against Scotland, has been denied him. We are rather inclined to think that in this he has hardly had fair treatment for of the general quality of his work between the sticks there can hardly be a difference of opinion. It has often been said that he is poor at low shots yet those who say so find it hard to substantiate this argument, and to our mind he stops all sorts, and has done splendidly even against the fastest shots on the ground. He has been faced by the finest sharpshooters in both this country and Scotland, has had pick of the forwards in both Leagues to face, and yet has always done well.

Of course, a man of his build – he is not called 'Little Willie' for nothing – is always prone to accident on hard ground and more than once this coupled with the pleasant pastime, which some forwards have of administering a skilfully concealed parting hack when the referee's back is the other way, has led to his leg in real bodily pain at times when doing duty. For all that he has never flinched, and we have seen him when actually unfit for work virtually standing on one leg, and yet fisting out shots of every description and keeping his citadel intact. To our mind Foulke is the personification of pluck and courage.

Born at Dawley in Shropshire, on April 12th 26 (*sic*) years ago, Foulke has lived most of his life at Blackwell, in Derbyshire, where all is being done that is possible in so small a place to make to the general success of his benefit. For the past two-and-a-half years, however, he has lived in Sheffield close to the ground. He is a man of but few clubs as the only one for which he played prior to joining ours was that of Blackwell for which he kept goal for three seasons, and he is now in his eighth year of excellent service with us.

We only got him by the skin of our teeth, so to speak. Our representatives only saw him once, but once was quite enough, and our old friend Mr Swaine (now of Hathersage) who acted as referee in the Blackwell match against Staveley was so impressed by what he saw that he forthwith reported him to us as a likely recruit. The consequence was that we signed him the following Friday evening at Blackwell. As we came out of the room the representatives of Derby County came in, but they were just too late, while Nottingham Forest's representatives turned up the next Monday, only to hear to their cha-grin, after sending for Foulke from the pit, that he had signed for us, and that he was no longer available for the Forresters! So tight a duel was it between the three of us.

As we have already hinted, our opinion is that Foulke has hardly received full official recognition of his prowess as a custodian, and the list of his hon-ours is not a long one. It embraces one international cap against Wales at Bramall Lane, two appearances for the English League against Scotland at Birmingham and the Crystal Palace, and one in the final match at Queen's Club, when Campbell of the Corinthians was his vis-à-vis. In all these he did good work, and yet has never yet represented his country against the Thistle! His League record is a particularly good one, and he refers with pride to the fact that in three successive seasons of League football he only lost 31, 33 and 29 goals respectively. He can very well pride himself on such figures.

A man of vast ability, he commands full attention and admiration on the field from the spectators, and also obtains a measure of unfair attention from visiting players which he hardly appreciates. That he deserves a handsome benefit is certain, and we trust he may have one. Good luck to 'Wee Willie'!

Author's notes: (1) I give a slightly different account of the race to acquire Foulke from Blackwell in chapter two. (Source: *Derby Daily Telegraph*). The match preceding the Charity Cup final was the semi against Matlock, and not against Staveley as given above.

(2) the 'final match at Queen's Club' referred to was the Professionals *v.* Amateurs match in March 1897.

Text of the 1913 *London Evening News* 'Life's Story'
(as given as part of Foulke's obituary in the 'Green 'Un' Sports Special Saturday 6 May 1916)

THE TRUE ALLAN STORY

As the biggest man who ever played football, I have naturally had a few stories told about me, and I should just like to say that some of them ARE stories. You may have heard that there was a very great rivalry between the old Liverpool centre forward Allan and myself; that prior to one match we breathed fire and slaughter at each other, that at last he made a rush at me as I was saving a shot, and that I dropped the ball, caught him by the middle, turned him clean over in a twinkling, and stood him on his head, giving him such a shock that he never played again.

Well, the story is one which might be described as a 'bit of each'. In reality, Allan and I were quite good friends off the field. On it we were opponents, of course, and there's no doubt he was ready to give chaff for chaff with me. What actually happened on the occasion referred to was that Allan (a big strong chap, mind you) once bore down on me with all his weight when I was saving.

I bent forward to protect myself, and Allan, striking my shoulder, flew right over me and fell heavily. He had a shaking up, I admit, but quite the worst thing about the whole business was that the referee gave a penalty against us and it cost Sheffield United the match.

WHAT HAPPENED TO BELL

There is another story about an Everton forward, Bell, who had threatened me. They will tell you how I got the best of him by bowling him over, then rubbing his nose in the mud, and picking him up with one hand to give him to his trainer to be cared for.

It was really all an accident. Just as I was reaching for a high ball Bell came at me, and the result of the collision was that we both tumbled down, but it was his bad luck to be underneath, and I could not prevent myself from falling with both knees in his back.

At that time I weighed about twenty-two-and-a-half stone, and I knew I must have hurt him, but when I saw his face I got about the worst shock I ever have had on the football field. He looked as if he was dead. I picked him up in my arms as tenderly as a baby, and all I could say was 'Oh dear! Oh dear!' But I am happy to say the affair was not so serious as it looked, and the Everton man came round all right.

FOND OF A JOKE

Nobody is fonder of fun or 'divvlemint' than I am, but nobody who knows me would suggest that I would try to hurt an opponent – though a few of them have hurt me in my time! Talking of fun, I don't mind admitting that I think I had as much as most men during my football career. To my mind almost the best time for a joke is after the team has lost.

When we'd won I was as ready to go to sleep in the railway carriage as anybody. All was peace and comfort then! But when we'd lost I made it my business to be a clown. Once when we were very disappointed I begged some black stuff from the engine driver and rubbed it over my face. There I was sitting on the table and playing some silly game, with all the team round me, laughing like kiddies at a Punch and Judy show, when some grumpy committeeman looked in. Ask the old team, the boys who won the League Championship once and the Cup twice, if a bit of 'Little Willie's' foolery didn't help to chirp 'em up before a tough match.

ON KEEPING YOUR TEMPER

I sometimes had a hard job to keep my temper on the field, though. You might have thought that forwards would steer clear of such a big chap. Some did, but others seemed to get wild when they couldn't get the ball into goal, and I suffered a lot through kicks administered when the referee wasn't looking.

Although it is more than five years since I gave up playing football, I can still show patches of bruising six inches long on my legs. There is one scar across the shin which looks as if it will never fairly heal up.

'A MARVELLOUS LINE OF MIDGETS'

I would rather be excused from saying too much about my share in what was accomplished. It is a bit late in the day for me to begin to talk about myself. There were times when the papers used to say a fair amount about Foulke saving his side – when we'd won! And I was often recommended for international caps, though it was my luck to get only one. But I do not wish to claim more credit than as a member of a great side, for United were wonderfully warm in my day.

We had backs like Bob Cain, Mick Whitham, Thickett and Boyle, and some of the finest halves I ever saw. When I hear the talk nowadays of the need for big halves, and look back on that marvellous line of midgets that we had, with Howell on the right, Tom Morren in the middle, and Ernest Needham on the left, I think I remember some little 'uns that would give the best of the big 'uns a start and a beating!

'SH! I'LL BUST THE BALL.'

One of the matches I remember the best was our first at Stockport. There were a whole lot of supporters on the ground, for Chelsea folks were keen on helping you along, and there was great disappointment because we lost. I remember the ball coming in as if it were yesterday. I said 'Right O,' and could have had it safe as a bank, but Miller [Chelsea full-back] said, 'Sh! I'll bust the ball!' and he made a terrific kick which half missed, and sent the ball flying in wide of me.

I have never been one to blame anybody for a mistake, but that was cruel luck, and perhaps I said something which wasn't very soothing to poor Miller. He was a wonderful player, that chap.

THE 'MYSTERIOUS FASCINATION'

Just one other word, in reply to the question which has often been asked me privately, and that was what the 'mysterious fascination' I was supposed to exert over forwards who came in to shoot. There's no doubt a lot of 'em hit me when they ought to have scored, but in all fairness I must say it wasn't a case of pure good luck for me.

I stand 6ft 2.5in. in my bare feet, and my greatest weight when playing was 25 stones. When I joined Sheffield United as a lad of twenty I weighed 12st. 10lb.

AS A COUNTY CRICKETER

Writing in the *Yorkshire Telegraph and Star*, 'J.H.S.' says:

Incidentally it was my good fortune to introduce Foulke to the notice of the Derbyshire County Cricket Committee as a potential fast bowler and a fine natural hitter. He played some very useful innings for the club, notably one very fine bit of forcing cricket at Leyton, but he never gave of his best in county cricket, otherwise, he must have made a name for himself there as well. And incidentally Bill Foulke has played golf. Once, long years ago when the United team was training at Lytham, I happened to have my clubs there, and one morning after breakfast the players sauntered out, and Foulke picked up a driver, had a ball teed up, and then hit it. It was the first stroke he ever played at golf, but we, the whole party of us, solemnly paced that drive out until we came to where we knew the ball had pitched, and we stopped there at 230 paces – dead straight.

A DRINK FOR SIR HOWARD!
Very quaint was he in many ways. Sir Howard Vincent, then MP for our Central Division, on one occasion when the United players were in town in quest of the Cup, took them over the House, and after showing them everything he could, was shaking hands with them when Foulke turned to his colleagues and in a loud aside declared that they would be a mean lot if they didn't stand that fellow a drink!

NEVER AT COLLEGE
Speaking of colleagues recalls another saying. It occurred on the Derby platform when the United men were waiting for a connection, and one of the officials seeing their train come in walked up to Foulke and said, 'Have you seen your colleagues?' And Foulke turned to him with a stare, 'Th'art a bit of a leear, I niver were at college in my life.'

WHAT THE SCALES TOLD
Once again, on the Ambergate platform, when the players were on their way home after special training at Matlock, Foulke got on to an automatic weighing machine and it registered eighteen-and-a-half stones. He was horrified, for that meant he had put on a stone in training. So the railway officials proposed to put him on one of their own scales to make sure, and after all the weights available had been put into the balance against him, Foulke mounted, but drew the weights up with ease.

Obituary in *The Sporting Chronicle*, 3 May 1916

I have just seen that William Foulke, the giant goalkeeper, has died in a nursing home at Sheffield. Born at Dawley, in Shropshire, forty-two years ago, he was in his day at once the most wonderful and the most popular player in England...

For such a huge man his quickness was phenomenal, and only equalled by his strength, for he could punch the ball to the halfway line. His celerity of movement, coupled with his reach, and his immense expanse, made him a difficult man to beat.

Found at Blackwell, a Derbyshire colliery village, he was associated with the triumphs of Sheffield United, as he was a member of their team who won the English Cup in 1899 and 1902. He assisted in gaining the League Championship for his club in 1897/98, he kept goal for England against Wales in 1897, and he twice played for the English League against the Scottish League. Thus only one of the great honours of the game was denied him – his cap against Scotland. Later in his career he was identified with Chelsea, and he had the honour, like Ernest Needham, of playing cricket for Derbyshire.

Foulke was a thoroughly good-tempered man, who had the spirit of a true sportsman. He had a real love for football, and watched matches for years after he gave over playing his part. He took a real interest in Simmons, his nephew, now a Sheffield United forward. He was the Daniel Lambert of the game, and will never be forgotten by those who had the peculiar pleasure of seeing this Leviathan handle a football with greater ease than if it were a pill.
'C.J.'

Author's note: Comparing Willie Foulke to the 'prodigy in nature' Daniel Lambert seems to me to be facetious and unhelpful, not to mention discourteous to the goalkeeper. Leicestershire man Lambert (1770-1809), these days a familiar figure from The Guinness Book of Records, grew to a freakish 52st 11lb, and though a fairly adept weightlifter, had little of the top-class athletic ability of Foulke.

Olden Goalie

William H. 'Fatty' Foulke,
A truly gargantuan bloke,
Played for Sheffield's red and white,
Keeping goal with all his might.

At twenty stone and six foot three,
A defender of enormity,
He weighed in with England's team
When Victoria was our Queen.

There was nowt that Fatty feared,
He had the goalmouth commandeered,
Stout in resolve and with redoubt
Fatty Foulke would keep 'em out.

Ever larger Fatty grew,
Until the final whistle blew,
It was full-time for one so brave,
But legends live beyond the grave.

Rest in Peace goalie bold,
Safely in the Keeper's fold,
A man of men from days of yore,
They don't make 'em like that any more.

Llew Beaton (11/12/2003)

Historical Perspective

What happened in the world at large during Willie Foulke's lifetime (1874-1916)

1874:
Formal rules for tennis set down.
First Boots' the Chemist opens in Nottingham.
Ten-hour day in factories.
Birth of Eric Weiss, *aka* Houdini.
Birth of Winston Churchill.
Birth of G.K. Chesterton.
William Henry Foulke born, 12 April, Dawley, Shropshire.
William and elder brother Tommy move to Blackwell, Derbyshire.

1875:
Captain Webb (b. in Dawley, Shropshire 1848) swims the Channel.
Crossbar replaces tape.

1876:
Blackwell Colliery School founded.
Invention of the telephone.
Queen Victoria appointed Empress of India.
Custer's Last Stand at the Little Big Horn.

1877:
First Wimbledon tennis final.

1878:
First Australian cricket tour of England.
Referee's whistle first used.
Bramall Lane stages first ever floodlit football match.

1879:
Zulu War; Rorke's Drift.
Tay Bridge disaster.

Electric street lighting introduced.

First telephone exchange opens in London.

2-3-5 team deployment begins to make its appearance.

1880:

W.G. Grace scores 152 against Australia at The Oval.

1881:

Opening of Savoy Theatre, London.

Birth of Picasso.

Barnum and Bailey's Circus formed.

1882:

Australia defeat England at cricket: the 'Ashes' saga begins.

Two-handed throw-in introduced (Sept.).

Formation of Corinthians football team.

1883:

Death of Karl Marx.

Treasure Island published.

Blackburn Olympic win the FA Cup, the first team from the provinces to do so.

Home International Championship introduced.

1884:

Reform Act: electorate increased to five million.

Alfred Tennyson, Poet Laureate, becomes a Lord.

First Ladies' Tennis Championship at Wimbledon.

Preston North End disqualified from FA Cup for illegal payment to players.

Corinthians defeat Cup-winners Blackburn Rovers 8-1.

1885:

Birth of D.H. Lawrence.

Death of General Gordon at Khartoum.

Introduction of 'safety bicycle'.

The Mikado at the Savoy Theatre.

Professionalism in football made legal.

1886:

Blackburn Rovers complete hat-trick of FA Cup wins.

1887:
Queen Victoria's Golden Jubilee.
First Sherlock Holmes story published.
Preston North End's record 26-0 FA Cup victory.

1888:
Jack the Ripper's reign of terror.
Football League begins.

1889:
Birth of Adolf Hitler.
Eiffel Tower completed.
Sheffield United formed.
Preston North End win double of League and FA Cup.

1890:
Completion of Forth Bridge.
London Underground becomes all-electric.

1891:
London-Paris telephone link.
Goal nets and penalty kick introduced; first appearance of internal pitch markings; penalty area is denoted by two arcs of 6 yards (5.5 metres) radius.
Linesmen replace umpires.
September: Foulke plays for Blackwell Colliery FC.

1892:
Keir Hardie first Labour MP.
'Gentleman' Jim Corbett defeats John L. Sullivan to gain World Heavyweight Boxing crown.
Goalkeeper may be charged only when in possession of the ball.

1893:
Sheffield attains status of City.
Independent Labour Party founded.
First Ladies' Golf Championship, at Royal Lytham.
C.B. Fry equals world long jump record.
Professional football legalised in Scotland.
First short-lived attempt at forming a footballers' union.
Blackwell Colliery FC are Derbyshire League Champions – William and

Tommy Foulke are on the team.
Sheffield United gain promotion to old First Division.

1894:
Opening of Manchester Ship Canal.
Tower Bridge and Blackpool Tower completed.
Alfred Dreyfus imprisoned.
Rudyard Kipling's *The Jungle Book* published.
England team v. Wales contains eleven Corinthians.
Foulke's League debut for Sheffield United, 1 September.

1895:
Blackwell Colliery mine disaster.
Formation of Rugby League.
National Trust founded.
The Big Wheel at Earl's Court, London, completed.
H.G. Wells' *The Time Machine* published.
Blackwell Colliery Cricket Club win Derbyshire League.
FA Cup stolen from a Birmingham shop window (11/9).

1896:
First cinemas open in Britain.
First medical use of X-rays.
First electric tram in Sheffield.
Daily Mail launched.
Red Flag Act (motoring) repealed.
First Olympic Games of the modern era, held in Athens.
The Mears brothers acquire freehold of Stamford Bridge stadium.
The Wednesday win the FA Cup.
Foulke marries Beatrice on 22 June.

1897:
Queen Victoria's Diamond Jubilee.
Bram Stoker's Dracula published.
Bob Fitzsimmons is World Heavyweight Boxing Champion.
Association Footballers' Union formed – lasts less than a year.
Sheffield United League runners-up to Aston Villa, who also win the FA Cup.
Birth of Foulke's first child, John Robert, in Blackwell.
Foulke gains England cap.

1898:
Kitchener victorious in the Sudan.
Sheffield United win Football League Championship.

1899:
Outbreak of Boer War
Elgar's *Enigma Variations.*
The Wednesday relegated. They leave Olive Grove for Owlerton (Hillsborough).
Sheffield United buy Bramall Lane from the Duke of Norfolk for £10,134.
Sheffield United win FA Cup, beating Derby 4-1.
The Foulkes move to Belgrave Square, Sheffield.

1900:
Relief of Mafeking.
Boxer Rebellion.
First flight of the Zeppelin.
Daily Express launched.
Olympic Games held in Paris.
Sheffield United League Runners-up to Aston Villa.
Foulke plays four games for Derbyshire County Cricket Club.
Birth of Foulke's second son, William Redvers.

1901:
Death of Queen Victoria.
Marconi pioneers wireless telegraphy across the Atlantic.
Ernest Needham publishes *Association Football.*
Professional footballers' maximum wage £4 a week.
Sheffield United lose in FA Cup Final to Spurs (2-2, 1-3).
Record crowd of 110,820 in first match at Crystal Palace.
Rule change for September: if goalkeeper passes outside the six-yard line, he may be charged whether or not he is in possession of the ball.
Foulke's benefit in October.

1902:
Edward VII crowned King.
Ibrox Park disaster.
April: Sheffield United win FA Cup, beating Southampton (1-1, 2-1).
September: penalty area becomes rectangle of 18 yards by 44 yards.

1903:

Wright brothers' first flight.

Suffragettes formed.

The Curies receive Nobel Prize for Physics.

The *Daily Mirror* launched.

Buffalo Bill's Wild West Show in Bradford.

The Wednesday League Champions 1902/03.

Sheffield United win first eight League games 1903/04 – a record at the time.

Direct free-kicks and advantage rule introduced.

Bradford City formed.

Birth of Foulkes' daughter, Selina.

The Foulkes buy their first shop, on Asline Road, Sheffield.

1904:

Rolls-Royce company formed.

Olympic Games held in St Louis.

Formation of FIFA in Paris.

The Wednesday League Champions again.

1905:

First £1,000 transfer fee: Alf Common moves from Sunderland to Middlesbrough. He had been transferred from Sheffield United to Sunderland the previous year for a then record £520.

New rule: goalkeeper must remain on his line for penalty until ball is kicked.

Chelsea formed and admitted to the Second Division.

Foulke leaves Sheffield United for Chelsea.

1906:

British Empire covers one-fifth of the globe.

Liberal landslide victory in General Election.

Motor buses first appear in London.

Chelsea just fail to achieve promotion from Second Division.

April: Foulke joins Bradford City.

1907:

First Scout troops formed.

Re-formation of footballers' Players' Union.

Birth of 'Dixie' Dean.

Chelsea promoted.

February: Foulke plays last League and cup games.

June: birth of James Rigby Foulke.
November: Foulke retires from football.
The Foulkes at 363 Bramall Lane.

1908:
Olympic Games held in London.
April: death of Walter Bennett in mining accident, Denaby Main Colliery.
Bradford City promoted to First Division.
The Foulkes take up ownership of beerhouse The Duke, 11 Matilda Street, Sheffield.

1909:
Old age pensions introduced for people over seventy.
Louis Blériot flies across the Channel.
Colour films are screened for the first time in Britain.
Henry Ford starts his 'assembly line' car production.
Robert Peary reaches North Pole.
Goalkeeper has to wear shirt of different colour from that of his teammates.
February: birth of Stanley Foulke.

1910:
Death of Edward VII.
Charles Chaplin and Stan Laurel at the Hippodrome, Sheffield.
Girl Guides formed.
Police raid on illegal gambling in The Duke.
Foulkes move to corner shop, 10 Matilda Street.
October: death of Stanley Foulke.

1911:
George V crowned King.
Winston Churchill made First Lord of the Admiralty.
Amundsen reaches South Pole.
Goalkeeper's use of hands restricted to penalty area.

1912:
Titanic disaster.
The socialist newspaper, the *Daily Herald*, launched.
Olympic Games held in Stockholm.
Miners' strike in UK.

1913:
Shaw's *Pygmalion* opens.
D.H. Lawrence's *Sons and Lovers* published.
First motor bus in Sheffield.
January: death of James Rigby Foulke.

1914:
George V first reigning British monarch to attend an FA Cup final.
Owlerton renamed Hillsborough.
Panama Canal opened.
Outbreak of First World War.
Defence of the Realm Act introduced.

1915:
Einstein publishes *General Theory of Relativity.*
Chaplin's *The Tramp* released in cinemas.
Death of W.G. Grace, aged sixty-seven.
*Sheffield United win FA Cup in 'Khaki Final'; Foulke's nephew, Jimmy Simmons,
scores opening goal.*

1916:
Conscription introduced.
Zeppelin raids on Attercliffe and Burngreave, Sheffield.
Dublin Easter Rising.
Death of Willie Foulke, 1 May, in a Sheffield nursing home.

Bibliography

(1) SPORT

Sheffield United CC and AFC Committee Logbooks (SUFC 1897-1905)

Association Football, Ernest Needham (Skeffington, London 1901)

Football Who's Who, (C. Arthur Pearson Ltd, London 1900-03)

Men Famous in Football, E.C. Price (London 1904)

Association Football and the Men Who Made It, Alfred Gibson and William Pickford (Caxton 1906)

The Book of Football, Ed. Clive Leatherdale (Desert Island Books 1997 – original magazine 1905-06)

Famous Football Clubs: Sheffield United, Richard A. Sparling (Newservice 1949)

Soccer, the World Game: A Popular History, Geoffrey Green (Pan 1956)

The Wolves: The First Eighty Years, Percy M. Young (Stanley Paul 1959)

A History of Bolton Wanderers, Percy M. Young (Stanley Paul 1961)

Football in Sheffield, Percy M. Young (Stanley Paul 1962)

Tokyo 1964: A Diary of the XVIIIth Olympiad, Christopher Brasher (Stanley Paul 1964)

A Century of English International Football 1872-1972, Morley Farror and Douglas Lamming (Robert Hale and Company 1972)

Purnell's Encyclopedia of Association Football, Ed. Norman S. Barrett MA (Purnell 1972)

The Giant Killers, Bryon Butler (Pelham Books 1982)

Great Sporting Eccentrics, David Randall (W.H. Allen 1985)

League Football and the Men Who Made It, Simon Inglis (Collins Willow 1988)

Bradford City: A Complete Record, Terry Frost (Breedon Books 1988)

A Game That Would Pay: A Business History of Professional Football in Bradford, A.J. Arnold (Duckworth 1988)

Sheffield United FC: The First 100 Years, Denis Clarebrough (SUFC 1989)

History of Derbyshire County Cricket Club, J. Shawcroft (Helm 1989)

Sport and the British: A Modern History, Richard Holt (OUP 1990)

Fever Pitch, Nick Hornby (Victor Gollancz 1992)

The Guinness Record of the FA Cup, Mike Collett (Guinness Publishing 1993)

The Football League: The Official Illustrated History, Bryon Butler (Blitz Bookmart 1993)

The People's Game, James Walvin (Mainstream 1994)

Sheffield Football: A History, Vol. I 1857-1961, Keith Farnsworth (Hallamshire Press 1995)

The Cassell Soccer Companion, David Pickering (Cassell 1995)

The Official Illustrated History of the FA Cup, Bryon Butler (Headline 1996)

Tottenham Hotspur: The Official Illustrated History 1882-1996, Phil Soar (Hastings Hilton 1996)

Football and the English, Dave Russell (Carnegie 1997)

Olympic FC: The Forgotten Giant-Killers, Graham Phythian (New Millennium 1998)★

Images of England: Sheffield United Football Club, comp. Denis Clarebrough (Tempus 1998)

The First Black Footballer: Arthur Wharton 1865-1930, Phil Vasili (Frank Cass 1998)

Football Wizard: The Billy Meredith Story, John Harding (Robson Books 1998)

City Memories: An Illustrated History of Bradford City AFC, John Dewhirst (True North Books 1998)

A Complete Record of Sheffield United Football Club 1889-1999, Denis Clarebrough and Andrew Kirkham (SUFC 1999)

Steve Bloomer: The Story of Football's First Superstar, Peter Seddon (Breedon Books 1999)

Schmeichel: The Autobiography, Peter Schmeichel (Virgin 1999)

The FA Cup Complete Results, Tony Brown (Soccer Data 1999)

Proud Preston, Ian Rigby and Mike Payne (Carnegie 1999)

Blue Tomorrow: The Football, Finance and Future of Chelsea Football Club, Mark Meehan (Empire Publications 2000)

England's Number Ones, Dean Hayes (Aureus 2000)

Claret and Amber in Black and White, Ian Beesley (Darkroom Press 2000)

100 Greats: Sheffield United Football Club, Denis Clarebrough (Tempus 2001)

C.B. Fry: King of Sport, Iain Wilton (Metro 2002)

Bloomer and Before, Edward Giles (Hallamshire Press 2002)

The Legends of Chelsea, Scott Cheshire (Breedon Books 2003)

Banksy: The Autobiography, Gordon Banks (Penguin 2003)

Bob Wilson: My Autobiography (Hodder & Stoughton 2003)

The Official Encyclopædia of Sheffield United, Matthews, Clarebrough, Kirkham (Britespot 2003)

(★available from the author)

(2) GENERAL

Blackwell Colliery Infants/Mixed School Logbooks 1879–88

Kelly's Directory: Derbyshire 1881/1891 (Kelly and Co.)

Sheffield Trade Directories 1898–1916 (Pawson and Brailsford)

Sheffield at the Opening of the Twentieth Century, Addy and Pike (Pike's New Century Series 1901)

The Making of Sheffield, J.H. Stainton (E. Weston and Sons 1924)

The Derbyshire Miners, J.E. Williams (Allen and Unwin 1962)

My Autobiography, Charles Chaplin (Penguin 1966)

The Northern Music Hall, G.J. Mellor (Frank Graham 1970)

The Parish of Blackwell, Eddie Storer (Higham Press 1994)

A Pub on Every Corner, Douglas Lamb (Hallamshire 1996)
A History of Sheffield, David Hey (Carnegie 1998)
Blackwell, Parish of Old, Eddie Storer (Acorn 2002)

(3) NEWSPAPERS AND PERIODICALS

Sheffield Daily Telegraph, 1894–1916
Sheffield Telegraph Sports Special – the 'Green 'Un', 1912–13, 1916
Sheffield Independent, 1894–1916
Football World – Independent Special Supplement, 1895–96
Sheffield United FC Match Programmes 1897–1905
Yorkshire Telegraph and Star, 1899, 1916
Athletic News, 1896–1916
Derby Daily Telegraph, 1889–1906
Derby Daily Express, 1889–1895, 1900
Manchester Guardian, 1894–1907
Scottish Sport, January 1895
Bolton Evening News, 1895–1902
Glasgow Herald, April 1900
Western Mail (Cardiff) April 1900
Birmingham Daily Post, 1901
Liverpool Daily Post, 1894–1901
Liverpool Echo, 1898–04
London Evening News, 1899–1902, 1905–06, 1913
Glossop Chronicle, 1899–1900, 1905–06
Newcastle Evening Chronicle, February 1902
Southern Echo, April 1902
Staffordshire Sentinel, 1904–06
Chelsea Chronicle, (match programme) 1905–06
Hull Daily Mail, September 1905
Leicester Mercury, February 1906
Daily Express, 1905–06
Sunday Times, 1905–06
Cheshire Daily Echo, 1905–07
Blackpool Gazette, 1905–06
News of the World, 1905–06
Bradford Daily Telegraph, 1906–07
Bradford Daily Argus, 1906–07
The Sporting Chronicle, 1901-2, May 1916
Article in *The Star* (Sheffield) 19/10/1998

Acknowledgements

My sincere thanks are due to the following:

John Garrett of the Sheffield United Academy, for invaluable information and liaison, and permission to use many original archive photographs;

Dave Hunt, of the Bramall Lane Hall of Fame – well worth a visit!;

Eric Youle, for co-ordination of information on the Duke Inn;

Alan Damms of 'Supporting Strokes' (0114 – 239430) – Limited Edition Sporting Prints – for permission to use 'Dream Team' portrait;

Dr Bob Mihajlovic, for elucidation of medical matters;

John Moakes, for a guided tour of Blackwell and Primrose Hill;

Llew Beaton, for permission to use his poem 'Olden Goalie';

Sarah Phythian, for Hall of Fame photography;

Nick and Janine for transport and computer services.

The staff of:

Sheffield Local History Library

Sheffield Archives

British Library, London

British Library Newspaper Archives

National Film and TV Archives, London

Manchester Central Library

The Office of National Statistics, Southport

The National (Census) Archives

Derby Local Studies Centre

Derbyshire Records Office, Matlock

Bradford Local History Library

Bolton Local Studies and Archives Library

Liverpool Local Studies Library

Stockport Library

Blackpool Local Studies Library

Buxton Local History Library

Southampton City Library Archives

Glossop Local Studies Library

Hull Local Studies Library

Nottinghamshire Archives

Barnsley Local Studies Library

Leicestershire Record Office
Cardiff Central Library Local Studies

And of course, James Howarth, Holly Bennion and the team at Tempus Publishing

A NOTE ON SOURCES

In general I have gone straight to the primary source (usually contemporary news-paper reports) for basis of the narrative. Where there has been a contradiction among these reports, I have generally given preference to the majority verdict. Secondary sources (usually given in the text) have mostly been used simply as a means to dig out the original version.

There are two incidents that I have omitted: (1) the alleged throwing of stones at Foulke by Wednesday supporters during the derby match of March 1897, and the 'keeper's subsequent reaction, and (2) the charge at Foulke by the young Harry Hampton (November 1904) which was said to have ended with the Villa forward entangled upside down in the net. I have been unable to find any primary evidence for either of these, but would of course be pleased to be proven wrong.

The only change I have made to any of the quotations used is, where necessary, to correct the spelling of the subject's name. The main variations, with explanations, are given in chapter 1.

Incidentally I have opted for 'Leivesley' as the correct spelling of the name of Foulke's understudy and successor, this being the man's preferred version.

I welcome comments, additions, disagreements, and so on. My e-mail address is gphyth@btinternet.com. It would be helpful if you could quote your own source as and when necessary.

Every reasonable effort has been made, where applicable, to trace copyright owners of visual material used herein. Any omissions or oversights should be notified in writing to the author, c/o the publishers.

Index

Note: references to some major clubs in the match-by-match section are not given entries here. Please refer to relevant season pp.117-170

Other titles published by Tempus

Sheffield United Football Club
DENIS CLAREBROUGH

Sheffield United have a long and proud history, and this book captures something of the heritage that belongs to the club and its loyal supporters. Over 200 photographs illustrate moments from the Blades' glorious past, and Denis Clarebrough's text contains a wealth of fact, anecdote and opinion, providing a clear picture of the character of the club and some of its heroes over the generations.
0 7524 1059 8

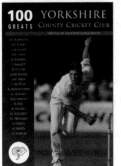

Yorkshire County Cricket Club 100 Greats
MICK POPE & PAUL DYSON

Yorkshire County Cricket Club has been massively successful over the years, and this book celebrates some of the men who have brought this success. Including batsmen like Geoffrey Boycott and Len Hutton, and bowlers like Fred Trueman and Darren Gough, it features 100 of the cricketers who have shaped the club. Compiled by two of Yorkshire cricket's most prominent researchers, it includes career histories, photographs and statistical information and is sure to stimulate lively debate among Tykes of all ages.
0 7524 2179 4

Forever England A History of the National Side
MARK SHAOUL & TONY WILLIAMSON

The definitive history of the English national side. From the days of the amateur gentlemen of the 1870s to the present day, *Forever England* is an insightful and fascinating illustrated account of the history of the national football team which covers the careers of England's all-time greats and is an essential read for anyone interested in the history of the Three Lions.
0 7524 2939 6

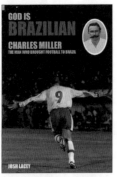

God is Brazilian Charles Miller, the Man Who Brought Football to Brazil
JOSH LACEY

In 1894 Charles Miller carried a football from Southampton to São Paulo. When he arrived he was shocked to discover that no one knew how to play, so he marked out a pitch, gathered twenty young men and divided them into two teams… Today, Brazil is the greatest football-playing nation in the world and Miller has been forgotten. This is his story – a gripping narrative of one man's love of football and the clash between two very different cultures.
0 7524 3414 4

If you are interested in purchasing other books published by Tempus, or in case you have difficulty finding any Tempus books in your local bookshop, you can also place orders directly through our website

www.tempus-publishing.com